AF781063

LEGAL KNOWLEDGE AND INFORMATION SYSTEMS

Frontiers in Artificial Intelligence and Applications

Series Editors: J. Breuker, R. López de Mántaras, M. Mohammadian, S. Ohsuga and W. Swartout

Volume 70

Previously published in this series:

Vol. 69, N. Baba et al. (Eds.), Knowledge-Based Intelligent Information Engineering Systems & Allied Technologies
Vol. 68, J.D. Moore et al. (Eds.), Artificial Intelligence in Education
Vol. 67, H. Jaakkola et al. (Eds.), Information Modelling and Knowledge Bases XII
Vol. 66, H.H. Lund et al. (Eds.), Seventh Scandinavian Conference on Artificial Intelligence
Vol. 65, In production
Vol. 64, J. Breuker et al. (Eds.), Legal Knowledge and Information Systems
Vol. 63, I. Gent et al. (Eds.), SAT2000
Vol. 62, T. Hruška and M. Hashimoto (Eds.), Knowledge-Based Software Engineering
Vol. 61, E. Kawaguchi et al. (Eds.), Information Modelling and Knowledge Bases XI
Vol. 60, P. Hoffman and D. Lemke (Eds.), Teaching and Learning in a Network World
Vol. 59, M. Mohammadian (Ed.), Advances in Intelligent Systems: Theory and Applications
Vol. 58, R. Dieng et al. (Eds.), Designing Cooperative Systems
Vol. 57, M. Mohammadian (Ed.), New Frontiers in Computational Intelligence and its Applications
Vol. 56, M.I. Torres and A. Sanfeliu (Eds.), Pattern Recognition and Applications
Vol. 55, G. Cumming et al. (Eds.), Advanced Research in Computers and Communications in Education
Vol. 54, W. Horn (Ed.), ECAI 2000
Vol. 53, E. Motta, Reusable Components for Knowledge Modelling
Vol. 52, In production
Vol. 51, H. Jaakkola et al. (Eds.), Information Modelling and Knowledge Bases X
Vol. 50, S.P. Lajoie and M. Vivet (Eds.), Artificial Intelligence in Education
Vol. 49, P. McNamara and H. Prakken (Eds.), Norms, Logics and Information Systems
Vol. 48, P. Návrat and H. Ueno (Eds.), Knowledge-Based Software Engineering
Vol. 47, M.T. Escrig and F. Toledo, Qualitative Spatial Reasoning: Theory and Practice
Vol. 46, N. Guarino (Ed.), Formal Ontology in Information Systems
Vol. 45, P.-J. Charrel et al. (Eds.), Information Modelling and Knowledge Bases IX
Vol. 44, K. de Koning, Model-Based Reasoning about Learner Behaviour
Vol. 43, M. Gams et al. (Eds.), Mind Versus Computer
Vol. 41, F.C. Morabito (Ed.), Advances in Intelligent Systems
Vol. 40, G. Grahne (Ed.), Sixth Scandinavian Conference on Artificial Intelligence
Vol. 39, B. du Boulay and R. Mizoguchi (Eds.), Artificial Intelligence in Education
Vol. 38, H. Kangassalo et al. (Eds.), Information Modelling and Knowledge Bases VIII
Vol. 37, F.L. Silva et al. (Eds.), Spatiotemporal Models in Biological and Artificial Systems
Vol. 36, S. Albayrak (Ed.), Intelligent Agents for Telecommunications Applications

ISSN: 0922-6389

Legal Knowledge and Information Systems

JURIX 2001: The Fourteenth Annual Conference

Edited by

Bart Verheij

Department of Metajuridica, Universiteit Maastricht, Maastricht, The Netherlands

Arno R. Lodder

Computer/Law Institute, Vrije Universiteit, Amsterdam, The Netherlands

Ronald P. Loui

Department of Computer Science, Washington University of St. Louis, St. Louis, Missouri, USA

and

Antoinette J. Muntjewerff

Department of Computer Science & Law, University of Amsterdam, Amsterdam, The Netherlands

IOS Press

Ohmsha

Amsterdam • Berlin • Oxford • Tokyo • Washington, DC

© 2001, The authors mentioned in the Table of Contents

All rights reserved. No part of this book may be reproduced, stored in a retrieval system, or transmitted, in any form or by any means, without the prior written permission from the publisher.

ISBN 1 58603 201 1 (IOS Press)
ISBN 4 274 90488 1 C3000 (Ohmsha)
Library of Congress Control Number: 2001098034

Publisher
IOS Press
Nieuwe Hemweg 6B
1013 BG Amsterdam
The Netherlands
fax: +31 20 620 3419
e-mail: order@iospress.nl

Distributor in the UK and Ireland
IOS Press/Lavis Marketing
73 Lime Walk
Headington
Oxford OX3 7AD
England
fax: +44 1865 75 0079

Distributor in the USA and Canada
IOS Press, Inc.
5795-G Burke Centre Parkway
Burke, VA 22015
USA
fax: +1 703 323 3668
e-mail: iosbooks@iospress.com

Distributor in Germany, Austria and Switzerland
IOS Press/LSL.de
Gerichtsweg 28
D-04103 Leipzig
Germany
fax: +49 341 995 4255

Distributor in Japan
Ohmsha, Ltd.
3-1 Kanda Nishiki-cho
Chiyoda-ku, Tokyo 101
Japan
fax: +81 3 3233 2426

LEGAL NOTICE
The publisher is not responsible for the use which might be made of the following information.

PRINTED IN THE NETHERLANDS

Contents

Preface

This volume contains the proceedings of the fourteenth JURIX conference, held on December 13 and 14, 2001, at the Universiteit van Amsterdam, The Netherlands. In accordance with the tradition set by the uninterrupted series of annual conferences, the research presented at JURIX 2001 illustrates the forefront of academic research in the field of legal information technology, and in particular on the development and application of artificial intelligence in the legal domain.

Invited Speakers

Two speakers were invited to address the conference. The Dutch Minister for Urban Policy and Integration of Ethnic minorities Roger van Boxtel was a natural choice because of his continuing efforts to stimulate the application of information technology by the government (cf. his web site at http://www.ministervanboxtel.nl/). Anne Gardner's acceptance of the invitation to speak at JURIX 2001 is also a privilege. Her book 'An Artificial Intelligence Approach to Legal Reasoning' has become a classic in the field and continues to influence researchers with an interest in artificial intelligence and law.

The Contributions

This year's papers cover a wide range of topics, including knowledge systems, case-based reasoning, hybrid approaches, logic and foundations, and argumentation.

With respect to legal knowledge systems, Spreeuwenberg, Van Engers and Gerrits address the problems of verification and validation. Apistola and Oskamp argue for the improvement of existing methods of legal knowledge management.

The continuing interest in case based reasoning is exemplified by two papers. Roth presents case-based reasoning as a kind of dialectical argumentation, and Bench-Capon and Rissland revitalize the topic of case dimensions.

In their paper on theory coherence, Bench-Capon and Sartor try to connect qualitative and quantitative approaches to legal justification. Governatori and Stranieri also discuss a hybrid approach, when they show how knowledge discovery techniques can be used to identify defeasible rules.

Three papers are about logic and foundations. Hage claims in his first paper that legal logic should take the law itself as its starting point, and illustrates this point in a second paper by arguing that some problems of deontic logic are the result of a wrong conception of obligations. Maranhao deals with normative systems, and shows a way to deal with normative gaps in terms of revision by refinement.

Two papers deal with argumentation. Lodder and Huygen present a system for online dispute resolution, and Prakken and Renooij discuss reasoning about evidence, from the viewpoints of defeasible argumentation and abduction.

Workshops and Demonstrations

In conjunction with JURIX 2001 two workshops took place, namely the Second International Workshop on Legal Ontologies and the First International Workshop on Law & Educational Technologies. The former was organized by Radboud Winkels, Tom van Engers and Trevor Bench-Capon, the latter by Antoinette Muntjewerff, Vincent Aleven, Paul Maharg, Irvette van Hunen and Jeroen Leijen. There was also a session dedicated to the demonstration of working systems.

Acknowledgments

Of the sixteen submitted papers, eleven have been accepted. The selection was made with the help of the review reports of the following people:

Kevin Ashley	Anja Oskamp
Trevor Bench-Capon	Henry Prakken
Bob Brouwer	Giovanni Sartor
Thomas F. Gordon	Andrew Stranieri
Jaap van den Herik	Kees de Vey Mestdagh
Ronald Leenes	Radboud Winkels
Marie-Francine Moens	John Zeleznikow

The organization committee consisted of Radboud Winkels (chair), Yolanda Carasco, Rinke Hoekstra and Antoinette Muntjewerff. The committee was assisted by Abdullatif Elhag.

The conference would not have been possible without the help of these people and the program committee owes all of them special thanks for their efforts.

The program committee

Bart Verheij (chair)
Arno R. Lodder
Ronald P. Loui
Antoinette J. Muntjewerff

The Role of Verification in Improving the Quality of Legal Decision-Making

Silvie Spreeuwenberg
LibRT B.V.
Amsterdam
The Netherlands
silvie@librt.com

Tom van Engers
Belastingdienst
Utrecht
The Netherlands
t.m.van.engers@acm.org

Rik Gerrits
LibRT B.V.
Amsterdam
The Netherlands
rik@librt.com

Abstract. Many Public Administrations (PA's) use knowledge-based systems to support their legal decision making processes. The quality of the decisions made depends on the quality of the underlying knowledge. In the POWER research program (Program for an Ontology-based Working Environment for Rules and regulations) conducted by the Dutch Tax and Customs Administration (DTCA in Dutch: Belastingdienst) verification techniques are used to improve legal decision making. This paper describes a state-of-the art verification and validation technique for legal knowledge systems: VALENS. Within the POWER-program VALENS is used to verify legal knowledge. We will furthermore describe the experiences with VALENS in a recently finished project. The POWER-program in which VALENS has been used aims at improving law enforcement. In POWER methods and tools have been developed that help legislation drafters to improve the quality of (new) legislation. Legislation is transformed to formal legal specifications that can be used in knowledge-based systems. These formal legal specifications can also be subjected to further inquiries aimed especially at discovering anomalies. One of the aims of POWER is to improve legislation quality by communicating detected defects to the legal sources. We will give an example to show that communicating anomalies to a domain expert in an intuitive way is a non-trivial task. VALENS makes use of the fact that POWER-models support tractability (i.e. the formal specifications contain references to the original knowledge-sources they are based upon). This allows VALENS to communicate the verification results to domain experts, e.g. legislation drafters. They may consequently adjust the legal sources and solve the defects. Currently we are further improving the representations of anomalies to make them easier to understand for legislation drafters and domain experts.

Keywords. Verification, Validation, Legal knowledge systems, legal knowledge representation, Methodologies for the development of legal systems.

1 Introduction

Drafting and implementing new legislation is a rather time, energy and money consuming process. The many inter-connected processes and the large number of people involved make

Silvie Spreeuwenberg, Tom van Engers and Rik Gerrits, 'The Role of Verification in Improving the Quality of Legal Decision-Making' in Bart Verheij, Arno R. Lodder, Ronald P. Loui and Antoinette J. Muntjewerff (eds.), *Legal Knowledge and Information Systems. Jurix 2001: The Fourteenth Annual Conference*. Amsterdam: IOS Press, 2001, pp. 1-15.

it very vulnerable to errors. Varying interests have to be aligned and communication difficulties due to differences in technical jargon have to be overcome in both drafting and implementing changes to legislation or even completely new legislation. The knowledge and experience needed to create new laws, specify, design and implement procedures and systems in legislative domains is very scarce. However, getting the right knowledge at the right place at the right time is a critical success factor for the ability to effectuate the legislative power to regulate and control.

The Dutch Tax and Customs Administration (DTCA) has started the research program POWER (Program for an Ontology-based Working Environment for Rules and regulations), that aims to develop a method and supporting tools for the whole chain of processes from legislation drafting to executing the law by government employees. The goal of the POWER-program is to improve legislation quality by the use of formal methods and verification techniques. Integration of the VALENS tool in the POWER tool-suite supports the verification of legal models.

In this article we will describe the role and implementation of verification techniques in the POWER-program. The final goal is to improve the quality of law-enforcement and optimally support legal experts when drafting legislation. Therefore we are developing a knowledge representation in which anomalies found in the formal models of legislation can be easily understood and resolved by legal experts.

2 Verification of Legal Knowledge Systems

Public administrations like the Dutch Tax and Customs Administration (DTCA or Belastingdienst in Dutch) have the institutional task to enforce the law. To be able to fulfill this task a fine-tuned series of processes have to be executed. These processes have to be connected to the series of forth bringing processes of new legislation. These processes of drafting and implementing new legislation are rather time, energy and money consuming. In these processes a large number of people are involved and the inter-connectedness of these processes makes the overall process vulnerable to errors. To make the situation even more complex; varying interests have to be aligned and communication difficulties due to differences in technical jargon have to be overcome in both drafting and implementing changes to legislation or even completely new legislation. The knowledge and experience needed to create new laws, specify, design and implement procedures and systems in legislative domains is very scarce. The problem public administrations have to cope with is how to make available the right knowledge at the right place at the right time. For public administration knowledge is a critical success factor in the effectuation of the legislative power to regulate and control society.

To support this task the DTCA uses many supporting information systems including knowledge-based systems. These knowledge-based systems are used in diagnosing and selecting cases for specific handling processes and in the handling processes themselves. From a legal view point it may be argued that knowledge based systems are not suited for the scrutineous judgement of cases (including the context of the case) as could be done by people. However the need to achieve equality before the law and the massiveness of the administrative processes make the use of knowledge-based systems in this kind of processes quite acceptable if precautions to prevent injustice are taken.

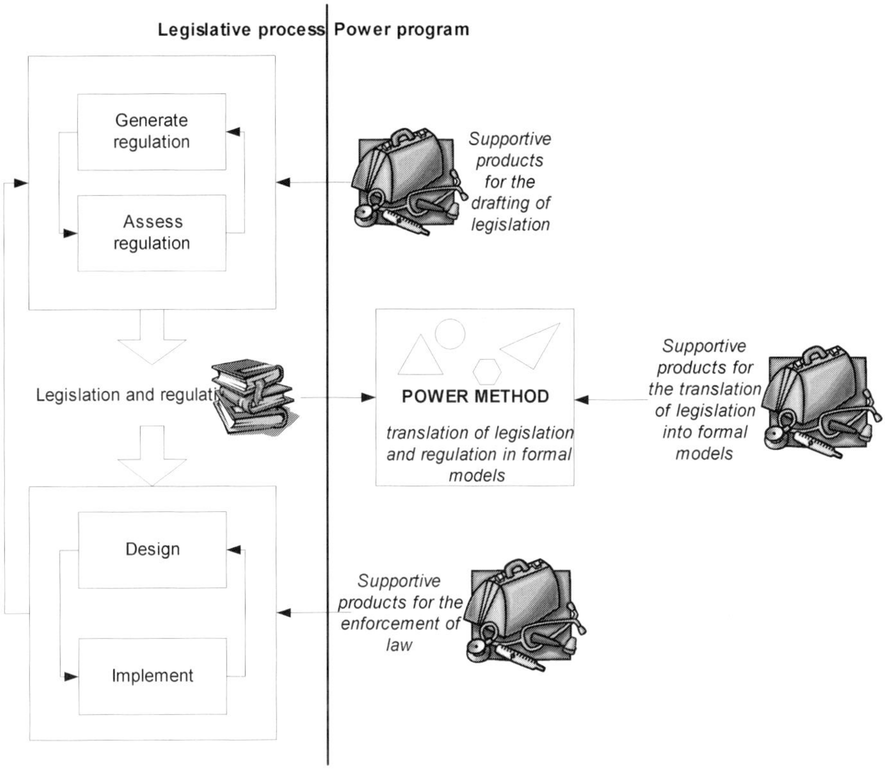

Figure 1: The POWER Program

The quality of the law enforcement depends on the quality of the legislation itself and on the quality of the knowledge-based systems that are actually used in the client handling processes as well. Many approaches have been described that aim at improving the quality of legislation (see e.g. Voermans [1]) or improving the quality of knowledge bases used in knowledge-based systems (see e.g. Preece [2] and Vanthienen[3]). The verification process as applied in the POWER-approach serves both perspectives.

The POWER-program (Van Engers et al [4], Van Engers, Kordelaar [5], Van Engers et al. [6]) has its background in the DTCA's earlier experiences with knowledge-based systems. The DTCA has built knowledge-based systems for many purposes, especially supporting compliance risk assessment, tax-payer case diagnosis and selection, since 1989. These knowledge-based systems proved to be useful systems, but the side effects caused when creating them were perhaps even more important. We found that the specification process in which experts from different disciplines and backgrounds were involved, helped to make knowledge explicit that would otherwise have remained implicit. The knowledge could furthermore be specified in a way that made it easier to establish its validity.

Based on the insight mentioned above the DTCA started the POWER-program that aims at achieving the following main goals:

- Improve legislation quality[1]
- Streamline legislative drafting effort
- Improve quality of law enforcement
- Reduce law enforcement implementation time
- Reduce law enforcement implementation effort

In POWER we focus on the knowledge specification but the program aims to support the whole chain of processes from legislation drafting to implementing law enforcement. In figure 1 the relations between the processes that are part of the POWER-program are visualized. The POWER-method is a central process in this program. This method has been developed to translate legal knowledge sources into formal models. These formal models are used for several purposes. Two of these purposes are:

1 Improving the quality of the legislation
2 Providing a basis for (knowledge-based) systems design.

Both purposes can benefit from a verification process that helps to detect anomalies. In the next section a description of the POWER-method developed thus far is given. This description focuses on the elements of the method that are important for the implementation of a verification process in the POWER-program.

3 The POWER Method

The POWER-method is based on conceptual modeling of legislation and regulations into formal legal specifications. The product of applying the POWER modeling process is, however, not only a conceptual model. We want to produce representations of legislation that computers can reason with. A set of coherent specifications can be delivered as a *knowledge component* [2]. The conceptual model is therefore used in a verification process and, together with a task model, used to generate a knowledge component. In the next paragraphs this process is described in more detail.

3.1 The POWER Modeling Process

Overviewing the POWER process it consists of a number of iterative sub-processes (see figure 2):

1 Translation of legislation and regulations into conceptual models, including completion of the models by expert knowledge elicitation
2 Re-factoring of conceptual models into coherent conceptual models

[1]Legislation quality is defined as absence of anomalies, law enforceability, and effectiveness in obtaining intended effects.

[2]A component is defined as a coherent package of software artifacts that can be independently developed and delivered as a unit and that defines interfaces by which it can be composed with other components to provide and use services (D'Souza [7]).

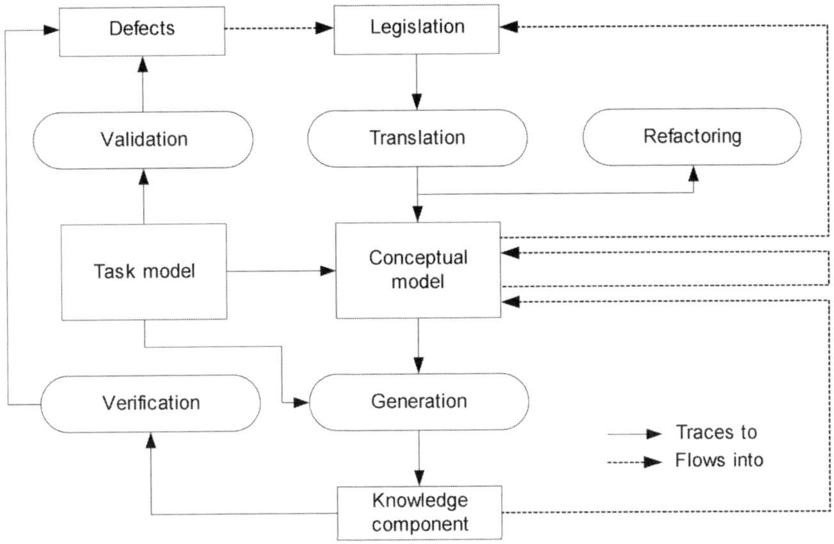

Figure 2: The POWER Modelling Process

3 Verification of conceptual models, including the detection of incompleteness and identification of missing legislation and regulations
4 Generating knowledge-based components for application frameworks, creating knowledge-based systems that can be delivered for implementing law enforcement
5 Testing and validating knowledge components, including the involvement of experts for certification of the knowledge components

The order of the sub-processes may depend on the route chosen by specific legal drafting or law enforcement implementation projects. Eventually, whatever route is chosen, the legislation, conceptual models and knowledge components will establish traceable refinement relationships.

The modeling language used is a proper extension of the ICT-industry standard Unified Modeling Language (UML), largely based on version 1.3, but including some proposed features of the upcoming version 2.0 that are particular to Catalysis (D'Souza [7]). Part of UML 1.3 is the Object Constraint Language (OCL), which is used to express constraints that apply to the model.

3.2 Translation of Legislation into a Conceptual Model

In POWER, we use a translation process that is a somewhat adapted and more rigidly described form of Catalysis business modeling. The difference is due to:

- the deliberate absence of business process information in legislation, which is more often than not left for the law enforcement agencies to set up as effectively as possible, albeit compliant with the legislation;
- the enhanced uniformity of conceptual models, delivered and required by the automated tool support of the POWER method;
- the particular features of the legislative domain, mainly the explicit references whereby a structure block in legislation (e.g. a chapter, article) refers to related structure blocks, combined with the need to create an independent model of each structure block for tractability purposes.

The structuring concept of the UML is the package. Packages are the container concepts that delimit a part of a model and have a hierarchical containment structure. In the translation step, each structure block of the legislation[3] (e.g. law, chapter, section, article, sub, part, sentence) is translated into a package. The hierarchical relationship of legislation structure blocks is reflected in the hierarchical nesting of packages.

Typically modelers have no legal background. Hence, they must often check with legal experts, who are familiar with the legislative culture, to validate the formal interpretation of legal structure blocks in the model. During this in-translation validation, the modelers attempt to detect standard interpretations in the legislative culture, identifiable by a typical legal phrasing. These standard interpretations and typical legal phrasings, are then described with the corresponding formal models, and are called translation patterns.

The in-translation validation with legal experts will also uncover semantic anomalies in the legislation (Kordelaar [8]). Semantic anomalies can occur if the rules used in the legislation or regulations lack clarity. In the POWER-translation processes detected anomalies are reported to legislators. They can repair the anomalies in the legislation before the law is enforced. Thus not only the quality of the legislation is improved but also its enforcement is also facilitated.

Tractability is an important feature in the POWER-method because in legal domains we need to be able to point at the sources of our knowledge on execution time (to be able to motivate our decisions). If we preserve the refinement between the original legal sources (e.g. a specific article in a specific law or a part of case law) we are also able to make impact analyses when we have to make changes in existing legislation. We use the same references in the communication process with legislation drafters who are likely to understand legal texts better than formal representations (e.g. when validating models or reporting anomalies).

3.3 Generation of Knowledge Components

The conceptual model containing the formal specifications of a specific legal domain can be generated into a knowledge component for a modeled task, that is executable by computers. In the context of the POWER project, a knowledge-based component is defined as *a rule based system that supports interfaces to an application framework to perform automated*

[3]The names and kinds of structure blocks depend on legislative culture: they are related to the authoring legislative body or country in a certain time period. Since conceptual models and the translation process have to be applied regardless of legislative culture, both the conceptual model formalism and the translation process description have to remain culture-free.

knowledge intensive tasks. These knowledge components form the basis for a test against syntactic requirements, i.e. the verification process (see e.g. Den Haan [9] and Kordelaar [8]) and the knowledge components can also be used to simulate the effects of legislation and regulations for a certain population (see e.g. Svensson [10]).

To execute the integrated models we need an executing environment that supports:

- Object Orientation (OO).
- An inference engine.
- Component based development (CBD).

An inference engine prevents us from having to restructure the knowledge into a procedural model that has to be evaluated in a particular (task dependent) order. The OCL invariants must be mapped on a one-to-one basis on concepts of the target language. These concepts are usually called (business) rules.

If we want to deliver executable components that can be plugged into an application framework, the component has to be 'framework-aware', which means that the component has to be designed in a way that it is aware of other components that use it. In this paper we will not elaborate on CBD principles.

A tool called FORCE (Factory for Object-oriented, Rule-based and Component-based engineering) generates these components. This tool takes an integrated model (UML/OCL and Process model) as input and generates a knowledge base by conducting the following steps:

1 Transition to a general programming system
Since the POWER-method wants to be (programming) language independent, we have to come up with an approach that helps us to set up a (automated) software factory that can operate in any programming environment that supports the three requirements mentioned above.
To preserve maximum independency the POWER-team has developed a conceptual system that supports the three basic requirements with no specific (industry) language features. This general programming system (GPS) consists of all concepts needed to fulfill the requirements of the knowledgebase generation. The idea is to map all elements of the UML/OCL and Process models on general concepts, to be supported by the target language. An extract of this mapping is shown below.

Paradigm	Model Concept	GPS Concept	Concept in C++
OO	Type	Class	Class
OO	Object	Instance	Object
RB	Invariant	Rule	Method
RB	Task	Inference task	Method
CBD	Interface	Interface	Abstract class
Process	Task	Task	Method

2 Parse and translate invariants
The OCL invariants need to be parsed into a parse tree. If the OCL statement is valid we use this tree to generate the target language. We generate the language of a commercial development environment, but the parse tree will also be used to generate Java.

3 Generate code
Based on the mapping between the concepts in the GPS and the target language (C++, Java or any other language or programming environment that supports the three basic requirements), all the constructs are generated in top-down order.
When all parts of the source are generated, the component is ready to be tested and deployed. It is up to the user of the FORCE-tool how the source code is compiled, based on the deployment models that are supported by the target-programming environment. These components can be subjected to a verification process (Preece et al. [2], den Hartog [6]).

4 Implementation of Verification in POWER

In the beginning of the '90s, universities devoted much attention to verification and validation of rule based systems. Some tools were developed to verify rule bases of which Preece [11] has given an overview and comparison. An even more extensive overview comes from Plant [12] who lists 35 verification tools built in the period 1985 – 1995. The verification[4] tools can be compared using a number of criteria. We have compared some of the widely known systems using the following criteria:

1 Anomalies detected by the tool
2 Language supported by the tool
3 Focus and behavior of the tool in the analysis or development phase of a system

The first criterion is formed by the anomalies that are detected by the tool. Some tools do not detect anomalies in a chain of logic, for example the Rule Checker Program (RCP) [13] and CHECK [14]. Others like RCP, CHECK and EVA [15] do not detect missing rules and unused literals. VALENS is complete with respect to the anomalies defined by Preece [2].

Another criterion is the language that is supported by the tool. Most verification and validation systems, which verify a knowledge base, cope with a restricted language, for example first order predicate logic [17][18] or formal specification language [16] as opposed to the rich language of a (fourth generation) programming environment. There are also tools which have their own internal language defined and which, manually or automatically, translate diverse languages into the internal language. EVA is an example of a system with its own internal language and provides a set of translation programs that translate the rule languages of some expert system tools (for example, ART, OPS5 and LES) to an internal canonical form, based on predicate calculus. PROLOGA works the other way around, it allows a user to create and verify decision trees and then generates code in diverse programming languages (for example, Aion, Delphi and C++). COVER and VALENS work in the programming language they where developed with, which is respectively Prolog and Aion[5]. VALENS is a verification component with a clearly defined interface description. At this moment the interface is implemented for knowledge bases developed with Aion.

The last criterion for comparison of verification tools is their respective behavior in the analysis and development phase of a system. The work of Nouira and Fouet [17] concentrates on the analysis phase of a system but results in a valid and executable knowledge base. The

[4]Tools that focus on validation or testing, like KVAT [22], are excluded from this definition.

[5]Aion is a widely used commercial development environment for rule based systems and a product and trademark from Computer Associates. Aion is a new version of AionDS.

work of van Harmelen [16] also concentrates on the analysis phase and validates formal specification language. The idea is that the formal specification has to be translated to a programming language to obtain an executable program. VALENS can be used by a developer after or during construction of a KB or can be integrated in a tool that allows users to write their own business rules. The output of the tool is a document in which all invalid rules (combinations) detected are reported.

The flexible nature of the VALENS verification component, the completeness and accuracy of the verification algorithms, and the possibilities for integration of VALENS in a modeling workbench have resulted in the decision to integrate VALENS in the POWER-program.

In the next section a description of the VALENS developed so far is given. This description focuses on the aspects of the tool that are important for the integration in the in the POWER-program.

4.1 Verification Algorithm

The verification algorithm that VALENS uses performs three main steps:

1. Construction of meta model
   In this step all rule constructs, necessary to reason with the rules in the KB are instantiated. This step is performed on a "when needed" basis to reduce performance overhead.
2. Select potential anomalies
   Potential anomalies are selected with the use of heuristics. These heuristics have been designed as meta rules but are implemented as procedures due to performance considerations.
3. Proof anomalies
   The theses (potentially invalid rules) are proved by running the rules to be tested in a forward chaining mode, while providing them with the right truth-values (input). We call this process proof-by-processing. The proof-by-processing algorithm resembles the "saturation" process used by Nouira and Fouet [17]. Nouira and Fouet generate the largest possible number of properties for an object that would certainly appear during a real execution and then start forward chaining during which it tries to fire constraints. In VALENS the heuristics defined in the meta rules search for the smallest number of properties for an object of which the potential anomaly can be proved. VALENS does not use explicit constraints. The knowledge contained in the constraints of Nouira and Fouet are integrated in the meta rules of VALENS. In contrast to the meta rules of VALENS, the constraints of Nouira and Fouet contain semantic knowledge. Semantic meta rules are foreseen but not yet implemented in VALENS.

For a more detailed description of the proof-by-processing algorithm used in VALENS to detect anomalies the user is referred to Gerrits and Spreeuwenberg [18].

4.2 Benefits of Proof-by-processing

The proof-by-processing algorithm has some benefits in comparison with the algorithms based on formal logic. The most important benefit is that proof-by-processing allows us to deal with predicate logic (i.e. functions are allowed to be used in rules). The functions that are used in the rules may contain procedural algorithms.

A second important benefit of the proof-by-processing algorithm is that we can work in an object-oriented (OO) environment. The rules work on attributes of the current instance. These attributes can be inherited.

A third and very important benefit of proof-by-processing is that there can be no discrepancy between the run time logic and the logic used in the validation process if the inference engine used in the verification process is the same as the inference engine used to evaluate and fire the knowledge rules in the application.

4.3 Integration of VALENS in the POWER Methodology

VALENS verifies knowledge rules in an executable environment because the proof by processing algorithm is based on the fact that the knowledge can be executed and the inference engine that executes the knowledge can be traced (i.e. the inference engine is able to supply information about the events that have taken place during the inferencing process).

Therefore VALENS is integrated in the FORCE tool that takes an integrated model as input, generates a knowledge base and verifies that knowledge base.

The user selects the tasks within the knowledge base that need to be verified. Invalid rules are reported in a HTML document. An anomaly is defined in [19] as a minimal set of rules, eventually associated to an input fact set that is a sufficient condition to prove an 'anomaly'. In the HTML document we show, beside this information, the rule chain that caused the anomaly to be detected.

Groups of knowledge rules and the status of faults found during verification can be stored in a database to allow regression testing

4.4 Experience with VALENS in the POWER Methodology

The methods and infrastructure that have been designed in the POWER-program support the continuous improvement of knowledge productivity. In POWER we present an architecture that facilitates the processes mentioned and we have created a platform (and communication vehicle) for different stakeholders in the implementation processes.

We had the opportunity to model the (concept version of the) new Dutch Income Tax Law (an ambitious piece of legislation and the first major law revision in years). Since almost nothing of the old law on Income Tax was to remain intact, we were asked to look for anomalies (and to create a basis for further implementation and supporting infrastructure). We modeled the Income Tax working closely together with members of the knowledge groups that have to deal with income tax problems.

Figure 3 shows an example taken from the POWER-model of the new Dutch Income Tax Law. The two articles specify the income tax deduction.

The first article specifies the deduction type based on the tariff group, a tax payer is assigned to. The second article specifies how a tariff group is assigned to a tax payer. The translation of the bold phrases: if the tax payer is assigned to tariff group 1, he may deduct an amount identified by "bovenbasisaftrek". If a tax payer may not deduct an amount identified

LB Art. 20
Lid 2. De belastingvrije som bedraagt:
a. ten aanzien van de in tariefgroep 0 ingedeelde werknemer: nihil;
b. ten aanzien van de in tariefgroep 1 ingedeelde werknemer: de bovenbasisaftrek;
c. ten aanzien van de in tariefgroep 2 ingedeelde werknemer: eenmaal de basisaftrek, vermeerderd met de bovenbasisaftrek;
d. ten aanzien van de in tariefgroep 3 ingedeelde werknemer: tweemaal de basisaftrek, vermeerderd met de bovenbasisaftrek;
e. ten aanzien van de in tariefgroep 4 ingedeelde werknemer: de basisaftrek, vermeerderd met de bovenbasisaftrek en de alleenstaande-ouderaftrek;
f. ten aanzien van de in tariefgroep 5 ingedeelde werknemer: de basisaftrek, vermeerderd met de bovenbasisaftrek, de alleenstaande-ouderaftrek en de aanvullende alleenstaande-ouderaftrek;
De belastingvrije som, bedoeld in de vorige volzin wordt verhoogd met de ouderenaftrek, dan wel met de ouderenaftrek en de aanvullende ouderenaftrek ten aanzien van de in tariefgroep 1, 2, 3, 4 of 5 ingedeelde werknemer die de ouderenaftrek, onderscheidenlijk de ouderenaftrek en de aanvullende ouderenaftrek geniet.

LB Art. 21
Lid 1. Ingedeeld wordt:
a. in tariefgroep 0: de werknemer die geen basisaftrek en geen bovenbasisaftrek geniet;
b. in tariefgroep 1: de werknemer die niet de basisaftrek maar wel de bovenbasisaftrek geniet;
c. in tariefgroep 2: de werknemer die de basisaftrek en maar niet de basisaftrek van een ander of de alleenstaande-ouderaftrek geniet;
d. in tariefgroep 3: de werknemer die mede de basisaftrek van een ander geniet;
e. in tariefgroep 4: de werknemer die alleenstaande-ouderaftrek maar niet de aanvullende aleenstaande-ouderaftrek geniet;
f. in tariefgroep 5: de werknemer die de aanvullende alleenstaande-ouderaftrek geniet.

Figure 3: New Dutch Income Tax Law

by "basisaftrek", but may deduct an amount identified by "bovenbasisaftrek", he is assigned to tariff group 1. These two phrases are modeled in UML/OCL as shown in figure 4.

They are generated as follows into a rule-based environment:

```
rule deductionType
ifrule current._tariffGroup.GroupNr = 1
then
    current._deduction.type = "BovenBasisAftrek"
end
rule tariffGroup
ifrule current._deduction.type ¡¿ "BasisAftrek"
and current._deduction.type = "BovenBasisAftrek"
then
    current._tariffGroup.GroupNr = 1
end
```

When FORCE generates a knowledge base from this model VALENS will detect circularity and present this in an HTML report from which an extract is shown in Figure 5.

We found more then 150 anomalies that were not detected by knowledge groups before. The anomalies were reported to the drafters and repaired. The effectiveness of the feedback process depends of course on representation. Therefore we have conducted some research on law-representations that promote the communication between legislative- and IT-experts (by means of a cognitive ergonomic study).

4.5 Exploitation of the Results of Verification in POWER

The objective of the verification of the POWER models is not only to acquire a certificate of consistency and completeness for the knowledge components which are used to support decision making but mainly to improve the quality of the legal sources.

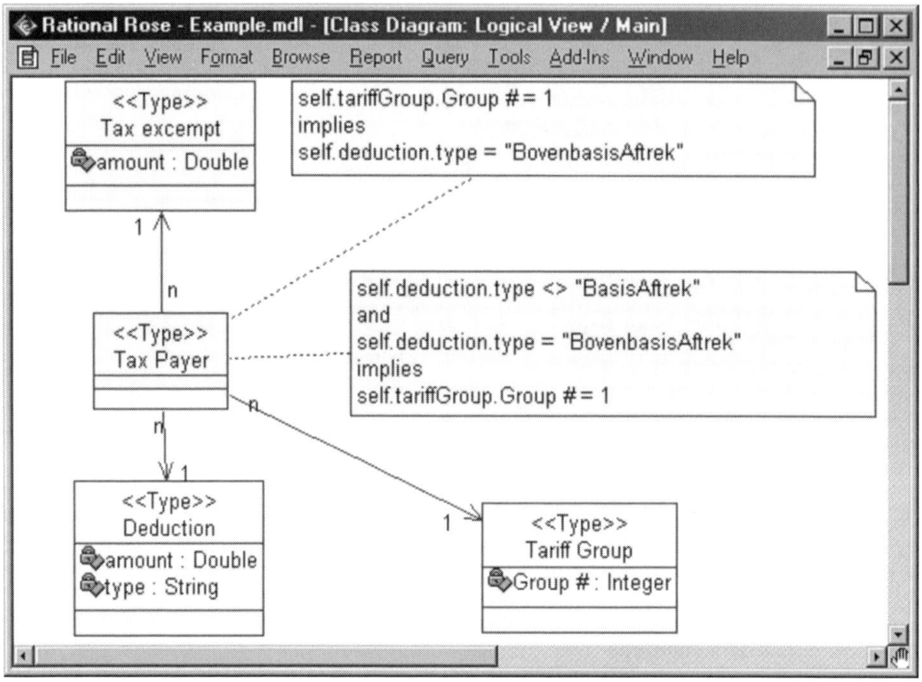

Figure 4: POWER Model

Circular reasoning analysis Look for circular references in rules

Circular reasoning will result in a deadlock in a backward chaining infer block; in a forward chaining infer block, circular reasoning may result in an infinite loop when using ifmatch-rules, or unintended overruling when using production rules

deductionType (rules [TaxPayer]) and tariffGroup (rules [TaxPayer])

Circular reasoning detected for if-rule deductionType (rules [TaxPayer]) and if-rule tariffGroup (rules [TaxPayer])

Circular reasoning is detected when an attribute is both sourced and derived in a reasoning chain. The following table shows the attributes, the truthvalues and the reasoning chain for which circularity is detected

Attribute	TruthValue	Reasoning chain
Type [Deduction] (r)	None	tariffGroup (rules [TaxPayer]) deductionType (rules [TaxPayer])

Figure 5: VALENS Report

Exploitation of the verification results therefore requires effective communication with the legislation experts, since they have to be able to adapt the legislation on the basis of the reported anomalies. Due to the fact that not the legal source, nor the conceptual model, but the knowledge component, is verified, the results of the verification process might be non-intuitive or, at least, difficult to understand by the legislation drafter.

5 The Challenge of Communication

Perhaps even more complex than the verification process itself is the communication of the verification results with domain experts. In the legal context of the POWER-program these experts are often people with a legal background and these people are not familiar with the (formal) representations used by knowledge engineers and information scientists. Furthermore people with a legal background are used to focus on individual cases while knowledge engineers and information scientists focus on the invariance between sets of cases.

The representations of the verification process' results need serious attention. Domain experts (including legislation drafters) have to decide what the impact of these results is in terms of redesign of legislation or chance of legal interpretation. It is obvious that the domain experts can only do this task properly if the representations used are fully understood.

In an attempt to get a better understanding of what representation formats are adequate in communicating anomalies in legal sources to domain experts we set up a small empirical study.

We tested the understandability of five different representation formalisms:

1 Horn clauses
2 Decision trees
3 Production rules
4 Grammar
5 Decision tables

In the experiment the subjects had to find the right representation (formal model) that reflected a legal text and they had to select a legal text that reflected a given representation.

In the experiment 15 legal experts had to answer 10 multiple-choice questions. Five (one for each representation format) considered the selection of the right representation for a given legal source and five related to finding the right legal source for a given representation. Both the results of these tests and the subjects' preferred representation were scored.

The legislation drafters scored higher on both tests:

Legislation drafters	
Find legal text with representation	97%
Find representation with legal text	100%
Other domain experts	
Find legal text with representation	80%
Find representation with legal text	89%

We also found that some representation formats were easier to understand than others:

Representation format	Average	Legislation drafters (n=6)	Other experts (n=9)
Horn clauses	94%	100%	89%
Decision trees	94%	100%	89%
Production rules	94%	100%	89%
Grammars	92%	100%	83%
Decision table	82%	92	72%

A surprising result was that subjects preferred decision tables as representation format although this was the worst understood representation.

The results of this study indicate the importance of designing adequate representation formalism if we want to communicate anomalies in legal sources. Since referring to the original legal sources (i.e. linking the formal representation formalism as used in the POWER-method to the legal source, e.g. a section of the law) is included in the POWER-method, presenting the relevant legal source text is relatively easy.

6 Discussion and Conclusion

The POWER-method (in its current state) aims at improving both the quality of the legal sources and legal decision making at the operational level in PA's. Verification of the formal representations of the legal sources supports these quality improvement efforts. Verification is not a new phenomenon, but structurally applying verification in a juridical context is. VALENS was originally designed to support knowledge engineers but the verification process implemented in VALENS proved very useful in a legal context as well. We experienced that the use of VALENS in the POWER-projects improves the quality of the legal knowledge bases and helps to communicate anomalies in the legal sources to domain experts (members of the knowledge groups and legislation drafters).

Further research is still needed. In the near future we aim at further improving the representation of the verification process results. Another extension will be the inclusion of validation support in the POWER-suite. At this moment we are researching the possibilities to adopt the validation framework from Rainer Knauf [20] whose ideas are attractive because of the very pragmatic approach to knowledge validation. We expect that the research on how to present anomalies (deficits) in an intuitive way to a legislation drafter can be re-used for the presentation of validation results. Validation or testing the results of the reasoning processes that are reflected in the knowledge bases against the aims of the legislation drafters and policy makers cannot be done fully automated. We will therefore incorporate testing facilities and simulation functionality (that is needed to check if the law has the intended effects).

Many people depend on the PA's legal decisions. Information science and knowledge engineering provide the means to improve the quality of legal decision-making and therefore need serious attention. The application of insights from these disciplines in the processes of legislation drafting and law enforcement will consequently lead to a more effective government.

References

[1] Voermans, Computer-assisted legislative drafting in the Netherlands: the LEDA-system, A National Conference on Legislative Drafting in the Global Village 2000

[2] Preece, Shingal, 1994, Foundation and Application of Knowledge Base Verification, International Journal of Intelligent Systems, 9, 683 – 701

[3] J. Vanthienen, C. Mues, G. Wets, 1997, Inter-Tabular Verification in an Interactive Environment, Proceedings Eurovav 97, 155 – 165

[4] Van Engers, T.M., Glassée, E., 2001, Facilitating the Legislation Process using a shared Conceptual Model. In: IEEE Intelligent Systems January 2001, p. 50- 57.

[5] Van Engers, T.M., Kordelaar, P., 1998, POWER: Programme for an Ontology based Working Environment for modeling and use of Regulations and legislation, Proceedings of the ISMICK'99.ISBN 2-913-923-02-X.

[6] Van Engers, T.M., Kordelaar, P.J.M., Den Hartog, J., Glassée,E., 2000, POWER: Programme for an Ontology based Working Environment for modeling and use of Regulations and legislation. In Proceeding of the 11th workshop on Databases and Expert Systems Applications (IEEE) eds. Tjoa, Wagner and Al-Zobaidie, Greenwich London, ISBN 0-7695-0680-1, pp. 327-334.

[7] Souza D.F. and Wills A.C., 1999, Objects, components and frameworks with UML; the Catalysis approach, Addison - Wesley, ISBN 0-201-31012-0

[8] Kordelaar, P.J.M., Betere wetten met kennissystemen, Universiteit Twente, Enschede 1996 (diss).

[9] den Haan, N, Automated Legal Reasoning, University of Amsterdam, Amsterdam, 1996 (diss)

[10] Svensson, J.S., Kennisgebaseerde micro simulatie, Universiteit Twente, Enschede, 1993 (diss.)

[11] A. Preece, 1991, Methods for Verifying Expert System Knowledge Bases.

[12] Robert T. Plant, 1995, Tools for Validation & Verification of Knowledge-Based Systems 1985 – 1995 References, *Internet Source*

[13] M. Suwa, A.C. Scott, E.H. Shortliffe, 1982, An Approach to Verifying Completeness and Consistency in a Rule-Based Expert System, AI Magazine, Vol. 3, Nr. 4

[14] W.A. Perkins, T.J. Laffey, D. Pecora, T.Nguyen, 1989, Knowledge Base Verification, Topics in Expert System Design, 353 – 376

[15] C.L. Chang, J.B. Combs, R.A. Stacowits, 1990, A Report on the Expert Systems Validation Associate (EVA), Expert Systems with Applications, Vol. 1, Nr. 3, 217 – 230

[16] F.V.Harmelen, 1995, Structure Preserving Specification Languages for Knowledge Based Systems, International Journal of Human Computer Studies, Vol. 44, 187-212

[17] Rym Nouira, Jean-Marc Fouet, 1996, A Knowledge Based Tool for the Incremental Construction, Validation and Refinement of Large Knowledge Bases, Workshop Proceedings ECAI96

[18] R. Gerrits, S. Spreeuwenberg 1999, A Knowledge Based Tool to Validate and Verify an Aion Knowledge Base, Validation and Verification of Knowledge Based Systems, Theory, Tools and Practice, 67 – 78, ISBN 0-7923-8645 0

[19] F. Bouali, S. Loiseau, M.C. Rousset, 1997, Revision of Rule Bases, Proceedings Eurovav 97, 193 – 203

[20] Rainer Knauf, Generation of a minimal set of test cases that is functionally equivalent to an exhaustive set, for use in knowledge based system verification, Proceedings of the Florida Artificial Intelligence Research Symposium (FLAIRS-96), pp 280 - 284

Preparing Knowledge Management for Law Practice

Martin Apistola Anja Oskamp
Computer/Law Institute
Vrije Universiteit Amsterdam
The Netherlands
{m.apistola, a.oskamp}@rechten.vu.nl

Abstract. Law practice is paying more and more attention to the deployment of knowledge management (KM). However, the deployment of knowledge management is often based on an ad hoc decision. We claim that the application of KM in law practice needs a good preparation, which is important, but often no part of KM methods. There is still no specific KM method for law practice and most methods approach knowledge management only as a support of the entire organisation. Such an approach of knowledge management is in our view too limited. Knowledge management for an entire organisation may for instance not be fully appropriate to support management of specific legal tasks using specific knowledge. For the development of a KM method for law practice, AI and Law research should be useful.

1 Introduction[1]

Law practice is paying more and more attention to the deployment of knowledge management (KM).[2] A cause of the increasingly popularity is the use of information technology (IT), which makes more and more knowledge, information and data available [25]. Knowledge is even being considered as the most important asset of legal organisations [12], [18]. When knowledge is so important, it should be handled with care. This should also apply to the methods and tools (e.g. knowledge management and IT) which support working with knowledge. But in law practice not much use is made of methods and techniques to support knowledge management nor of IT support [7], [23], [24]. A reason for this may be that there still is no method for knowledge management available for law practice. Risks of not using a method, and thus making decisions on an ad hoc basis, are for example that users do not want to use (new) information technologies and knowledge is not shared in the right way

[1]This paper is based on the first ideas of a PhD. research which started March this year. This paper is meant to explore some of these ideas and to start a discussion on how KM is, or should be, developed and deployed for law practice and how AI and Law research can contribute. Such a discussion could contribute to the way (future research on) KM for law practice is developed and deployed.

[2]Some publications on knowledge management: [35], [9], [20], [6]. We also see the creation of new functions like knowledge manager and knowledge management departments [1].

Martin Apistola and Anja Oskamp, 'Preparing Knowledge Management for Law Practice' in Bart Verheij, Arno R. Lodder, Ronald P. Loui and Antoinette J. Muntjewerff (eds.), *Legal Knowledge and Information Systems. Jurix 2001: The Fourteenth Annual Conference.* Amsterdam: IOS Press, 2001, pp. 17-28.

across the organisation because employees are not stimulated to do this. A solution we suggest is to develop a method for knowledge management in law practice which supports the execution of legal tasks.We believe thatArtificial Intelligence and Law (AI&Law) research, which is aimed at the application of legal knowledge and legal IT, can offer support to the development of such a method [25]. Examples of IT results from AI&Law research are legal databases and legal knowledge based systems [25]. AI&Law research also provided insight in legal reasoning.

In section two of this paper we describe views on how knowledge management is and could be approached. In section three we describe a way to prepare KM projects. Finally, in section four, we describe our conclusions and the future of our research. This is an explorative paper explaining our first ideas on KM and law practice.

2 Views on Knowledge Management

Knowledge management can be looked at from many different points of view. Points of view are for example KM for organisations and KM support for the execution of legal tasks. The most popular, and usually the only, point of view for KM is its deployment to support an entire organisation. See for example [35], [38], [9]. In this view, KM is mainly approached top-down. This approach is, in our view and at least in the legal domain, presently too complex and too limited. The complexity becomes clear when we look at current literature on KM in which vague and global notions of KM are used to describe knowledge management. To be able to apply KM to an entire organisation, we need to reduce the complexity of the organisation as a whole and look at smaller parts of the organisation. With smaller parts we mean divisions of organisations and employees performing legal tasks. We call this approach a bottom-up approach. With the help of KM for small parts of the organisation, it should become easier to develop a knowledge management method for the entire organisation and apply it. In our research and as part of this paper we take a look at KM for the execution of legal tasks. Characteristic for these tasks are that their fundament is found in law and for the deployment of such tasks a basic level of legal knowledge and experience is necessary [21]. Legal tasks are in general aimed at adapting the law to the needs of a specific case and the adaptation (the description) of the case itself to the result wished for [22], [14]. Different kinds of legal tasks exist. Giving legal advice or actually going to court are only two examples.

We see that organisations exist of different levels and groups. It is questionable whether each group can be supported by KM as applied to entire organisations. We believe that each group has, or needs own ways of KM because each group has its own specific characteristics.[3]

We classify four levels cq groups for dealing with legal tasks: legal organisations, legal divisions and legal employees (e.g. legal experts). Legal organisations are groups of people who have chosen to strive after realising joint goals [35], [28]. For example dealing with one or more legal tasks in one or more legal domain. For this they need knowledge on the performance of legal tasks in legal domains and the support of the performance of these tasks by information technology (IT), techniques, methods and knowledge sources. Legal organisations can consist of one or more legal divisions. Legal divisions deal with one or more legal tasks in relation to one or more legal domains as dealt with by the legal organisation.

[3]Parts and characteristics of organisations are a.o. discussed in [19], [28].

Legal employees like legal experts deal with one or more legal tasks in relation to one or more legal domains. Legal experts can perform legal tasks for legal organisations or operate independent from legal organisations.

To illustrate the differences between groups which should be taken into account for KM, we briefly discuss some characteristics of an organisation as a whole and the organisation's operational level, as well as the implications of these characteristics for the application of knowledge management.

2.1 *Two Points of View*

Imagine the following situation. Bert got into a car accident and got physically hurt. The opposite party (Ernie) claimed that Bert caused the accident. Bert claims that Ernie is responsible and decides to seek legal advice. Bert read in the paper that a certain law firm deals with liability cases. When Bert goes to the law firm he wants to know whether he can sue Ernie for the damages. Bert arrives at the law firm. The receptionist asks him what she can do for him. Bert briefly explains the situation. The receptionist sends Bert to a division most capable to deal with the case. When Bert goes to that division, he has to explain his case more detailed so that it is possible for the division's secretary to direct Bert to a legal expert specialised in the field of liability law. Bert has to explain his situation as detailed as possible to the legal expert. The expert decides whether he is capable of giving legal advice to Bert. He makes this decision on basis of his knowledge, experience and the availability of knowledge sources, IT, techniques and methods. When the decision is made, the expert continues his task of giving legal advice.

We see that legal organisations like a law firm and the legal tasks performed within that organisation (e.g. giving legal advice) deal with different elements. Elements are structure, culture, techniques, methods, knowledge sources, tasks and information technology [28]. Such elements help to recognise a specific legal organisation. Although elements like these are important for the way KM is applied, we only take a brief look at the elements people, tasks and IT.[4]

The example shows that within legal organisations employees perform (legal) tasks. Receptionists and secretaries for example may do the first intake and provide administrative support and legal experts give legal advice. Different legal tasks can be assigned to the organisation as a whole or directly to a legal expert. We saw that Bert first came with a task assigned to the law firm as a whole. Later on this assignment was passed through to a legal expert. In other cases, Bert might have known a certain legal expert and could have gone to him straight away.

The employees within a legal organisation can be seen as sources of knowledge. They posses knowledge about the organisation as a whole (e.g. the receptionist) or about a specific legal domain (e.g. the legal expert). Other knowledge sources are paper sources and IT sources. The legal expert for example makes use of legal literature and legal databases. Each knowledge source has different characteristics and might be used for the performance of one or more (different) legal tasks. A legal expert may give advice, but may also go to court. For

[4]This is a limited view on the levels for KM approaches and characteristics of legal organisations. In a forthcoming paper we elaborate on these subjects.

both tasks he uses the same legal literature. With the help of IT, and especially legal decision support systems or expert systems, less experienced employees might perform the same tasks. Most lawyers in the law firm have a high level of knowledge and consequently will mainly use simple technologies like text editors or databases. While less experienced employees have little legal background and therefore are supported by 'high tech' technologies like legal knowledge systems.[5]

For an entire organisation it is important to know which knowledge sources are available within the organisation. Thus a legal task in first instance can be assigned to and performed by a certain knowledge source (e.g. a legal expert). In the example we saw that Bert explained his situation briefly to the receptionist. The receptionist was able to interpret Bert's case correctly and with her knowledge of the organisation as a whole was able to send Bert to the division most likely to deal with his case.

2.2 Consequences for Knowledge Management

From the example we can see that knowledge management should be approached in different ways because we have to deal with different people, tasks, knowledge, techniques and IT. We saw employees like the receptionist or the legal expert who both have the same task of giving advice. The difference in these tasks is that the receptionist gives advice which assigns Bert to the right legal division of the organisation and the legal expert actually gives specific (legal) advice. Both employees have different backgrounds and use a different kind of IT. The receptionist does not necessarily have a legal background while the legal expert is specialised in a legal domain. For the deployment of knowledge management it should be taken into account that receptionists should be provided with knowledge to assign tasks in first instance to the right division. Therefore they apply knowledge which is usually global. The legal expert on the other hand performs (complex) tasks like giving legal advice and consequently needs knowledge which is more complex and specific. KM should also take into account that the amount and kind of techniques used to execute tasks can be different. The receptionist uses non structured interview techniques while the legal expert uses for example structured interview techniques and decision tables. For legal tasks, (different) IT can be used in different ways. The receptionist might use a database to search for a specific division while the legal expert might use legal knowledge based systems and legal databases to give legal advice. When for instance it appears that an expert cannot make use of IT, the management of knowledge within the organisation should be able to give guidelines to the expert on where he can find relevant IT and how this IT should be used.

We saw that legal tasks and employees performing these tasks can be different. This is also true for legal organisations. Bert could also have approached a legal organisation which consists of legal volunteers with only a little legal background. These volunteers need a different kind of knowledge management. While law firms usually can afford to spend a lot of money on developing and applying knowledge management, voluntary organisations often do not have much money and need cheap means to perform their legal tasks. Moreover, the

[5]With the present state of automation the 'expertness' of 'high technologies' is still limited. They don't offer much support to highly trained professionals. More simple techniques, like databases provide the necessary information.

law firm has many legal experts and the voluntary organisation only has employees with little legal background. To perform the same legal task they need for example to be supported by cheap IT which can support them to act partly like the legal expert in the law firm.

Another difference between legal organisations is that some organisations act more open than others and are less afraid of competitors. This should also be taken into account when deploying KM. Knowledge which is freely available within one legal organisation is not necessarily freely available within the other legal organisation.

3 Preparing Knowledge Management

As we showed in section two, we should be aware of differences in the way KM could be deployed for an entire organisation or a smaller part of an organisation. Just one general approach of KM is not enough. On the basis of this idea we can make a first distinction between developing and applying KM. During development we decide whether knowledge management is really necessary. In this phase of availability of KM methods it seems wise not to interfere in either organisations or tasks when there are no problems performing the task. Most KM methods do not even look at the necessity of KM. They presuppose that KM is necessary and will start by applying the method. They often start by telling that the knowledge used in the organisation needs to be analysed. However they are vague about how and when this analysis has to take place and how to carry it out. This may be caused by the fact that it is too difficult to apply KM to an organisation as a whole (see section 2).

So first of all an agreement should be reached on if and how KM will be deployed and which groups and levels will be researched. This could result in a *project plan* based on the selection of a specific group and level. In this paper we maintain two points of view, namely that of an entire organisation and that of the employees performing legal tasks. In general the project plan contains amongst others starting points with conditions, the purpose of the project with results wished for, planning with milestones, project time, capacity and costs, project members involved and responsibilities. When we look at a KM project for the entire organisation, we see that not all of these points play a (similar) role as when deployed for a KM project for the support of a legal task.

Refraining from a project plan enhances the chance of failure of the project [2]. By knowing elements like the goal of the KM project, equipment to be used, planning and costs, agreement can be reached between the person giving the assignment and the person executing the assignment on whether to deploy the project or not. The project plan can also be reused in similar situations in the future.

In the next section we describe what a project plan for KM may look like for both the entire organisation and for the support of a legal task.

3.1 An Example of a Project Plan for KM

To illustrate a project plan for KM, we use the project plan as described in SDM [8] as guideline.[6] This project plan is meant for system development projects but we think it could also be used for knowledge management projects. The project plan describes elements (e.g.

[6]Aspects of project planning and control are also described in [10].

goals of the project, costs, etc.) which at least should be agreed up on before starting the 'real' KM project. There is no particular order in which the project plan is developed. According to us some of the elements are relevant for both a KM project plan for the entire organisation and for a KM project for the support of a legal task. The different levels of these project plans may cause different views of the various elements.

Background

In this part of the plan a brief first introduction is given to the current situation of the organisation. Such an introduction is both relevant to a KM project for the support of a legal task as to a KM project for the entire organisation to know whether the same idea exists about the organisation and about problems. Problems occurring at the level where legal tasks are performed may influence the entire organisation and vice versa.

In case of the law firm we could see that the firm has just started and has legal experts in the area of liability law. A major problem within the firm is that these legal experts are often out of the office. It is important however that, when such a situation occurs, other employees (non legal experts) still can give advice to clients like Bert.

Goal of the lawfirm

The goals of the organisation are relevant to know as that they must be in line with the goals of KM solutions to be developed and applied. This is both relevant to a KM project for the support of a legal task and to a KM project for the entire organisation. When both seem to have very different thoughts about the goal of the organisation, it is questionable whether KM can be deployed in the right manner. The goal of the law firm could be to offer high quality legal support for reasonable prices in such a way that the firm can establish a strong position in the market.

Goals of the KM project

The goals of a KM project for the entire organisation and for the support of a legal task should be in line with the goals of the organisation. To increase the success of the KM project, both the organisation and of the project group should have the same understanding of the goals of the KM project. The goal of the KM project is for example to find a KM solution for the way legal knowledge is managed within the law firm.

Surroundings of the project

There should be agreement on the scale the KM project aims for. This is both relevant to a KM project for the support of a legal task and to a KM project for the entire organisation. Researching large and complex area's may for example need much effort and ask for many legal experts and may therefore cost much more than a smaller area to be researched. For a KM project for the entire organisation it may be relevant to have a global understanding of who was involved in a specific KM project for the support of a legal task and how much such a project costs. Such knowledge may be useful for similar future projects. The KM solution could be developed for the execution of one legal expert task within the firm. Later on a KM solution will be developed for the entire firm.

Starting points / conditions

Organisations can have several demands and restrictions related to their problems. To increase the success of the KM project, the results should meet these demands. When looking at a KM project for the entire organisation, guidelines for demands may exist while a KM project for the support of a legal task asks for different, detailed demands. The most relevant starting point of a KM project for the entire organisation is for example that knowledge of legal experts is kept within the firm and can only be used by non-legal experts within the firm to give legal advice. Conditions are for example that the law firm in The Hague is used as a 'pilot', and KM solutions are applicable to other area's of the firm.

Risks

Every project has risks. Before the project is started, these risks should be identified and analysed. Risks should be weighed and solutions need to be found for risks [15]. The relevance of a risk may be different for a KM project for the entire organisation and for a KM project for the support of a legal task. Risks of a KM project for the support of a legal task are important to the entire organisation in that risks of such a KM project may influence the entire organisation. A great risk for example is insufficient availability and commitment of management, legal experts and supporting staff.

Project organisation

Before the projects starts it is necessary to know who will be involved. This is necessary because not everyone is qualified to perform (parts) of KM projects and it should be clear whom to turn to when problems occur. For a KM project for the entire organisation, global knowledge on who is involved may be relevant, while for a KM project for the support of a legal task, it is relevant to know specific details on the persons involved. The activities of the KM project for the support of a legal task are for example executed by a project group consisting of the following persons: Chris (knowledge engineer), Charlotte (legal expert), John (director of the law firm).

The knowledge engineer acts as an intermediary between parties and systems during the project [21]. The knowledge engineer has several tasks; helping the expert expressing his knowledge and way of working, point at mistakes if necessary, representing knowledge and make sure that the final result meets the demands of the end user(s) [21]. The knowledge engineer should therefore be well qualified. This means for example that he has at least basic knowledge of the domain, knowledge acquisition, representation and analysis techniques [3], [21]. But he should also have good social skills, like tact, diplomacy, patience and cooperation skills. See for example [5], [29]. Because the knowledge engineer will deal with (parts of) the legal domain, he needs to have at least a basic legal background. Someone without legal knowledge will have a lot of trouble identifying relevant legal knowledge. See for example [21], [37], [16]. Chris the knowledge engineer was asked for this project, because he is considered an expert within the field of knowledge engineering and has a basic legal background. Chris is also known to have good social skills. Chris will research the legal task because he thinks he might be able to understand the task and he has dealt with legal experts before, with success.

Methods and techniques

Before the KM project is started, it should be clear whether there are methods and techniques available which might be used during the project. When this is not the case, it should be agreed whether a specific method or technique will be developed, and conditions have to be formulated. For a KM project for the entire organisation, global knowledge on which methods and techniques are available may be relevant. For a KM project for the support of a legal task, detailed knowledge on the availability and use of methods and techniques may be more relevant.

For the development and use of methods and techniques equipped for law practice, elements stemming from the field of AI and law may be useful. This field has been occupied with the analysis and application of legal knowledge for decades. This resulted in the development of several (knowledge based) system development methods [37], [21], ontology techniques [30], [31], [33], argumentation and reasoning techniques [26], [17], [11], [14], [32]. It can be questioned though whether these methods and techniques, which are aimed at the development of legal knowledge (based) systems, are sufficient for the development and deployment of a KM method for the legal practice. Their focus is on (legal) knowledge, usually related to a small domain. We believe that we can benefit in a great deal from the AI&Law research which has been focussed on methods and techniques for working with (legal) knowledge. But data and information are also part of managing knowledge, and an important part. Methods and techniques dealing with data and information may differ from methods dealing with knowledge. Another point of attention is that most of AI&Law research may be too theoretical to be used for the support of practical knowledge management.[7] That is, to actually support the execution of legal tasks. The differences between methods and techniques and the analysis of the parts that are suitable for KM, is part of our future research.

In this stage of research however, we found that it is difficult to give clear guidelines on which technique is best suitable in a certain situation [36]. The use of techniques depends a.o. on the task and the domain. In some (legal) domains statistical analyses are important while in other domains observations or interviews play an important role [34]. The following criteria may be useful [36]: When the technique is common in a certain legal domain and is used by the domain expert [5] this implies he has experience with this technique, and consequently it will be easier for him to transfer his knowledge. Another criterion is that it has to be clear what kind of knowledge the domain contains. One type of knowledge (e.g. procedural knowledge) may need another approach than another type of knowledge (e.g. declarative knowledge). Finally, it needs to be clear what kind of problems play a role for the domain expert. For several problems (e.g. diagnosis), specific techniques have been developed which can thus be used.

For example a specific law domain contains a lot of procedural knowledge. The knowledge has a hierarchical structure. The problem the expert has to deal with is that the law contains one major exemption which states that the law is in a certain situation not applicable. But in a typical session, this rare exception can be ignored temporarily by the expert. The expert is used to talk with clients in the form of a interview.

Based on this, Chris the knowledge engineer decides upon the techniques which he could

[7]This is certainly true for AI&Law research on legal argumentation, the development of legal knowledge based systems on the other hand proved to be more practical [27].

use best. The expert has experiences with interviewing and interviewing is a common technique in the domain. Chris decides to prepare a interview. Because the domain contains procedural knowledge and has a hierarchical structure, Chris thinks that he might use a classification network to structure the domain and task and use forward or backward reasoning techniques. By preparing more than one technique, Chris decreases chances on failure.

Equipment

To be able to perform the KM project, some major elements need to be present. First of all, knowledge sources are necessary. Secondly, IT may be necessary to process data and to create milestones. Knowledge sources are those sources in which the knowledge engineer can find knowledge. The amount, diversity and availability of sources can be big [25]. Knowledge sources can be divided in the human as a source of knowledge (e.g. experts or end-users), writings as a source of knowledge (e.g. AI&Law literature) and information technology (e.g. databases containing cases or legislation).[8]

As a preparation to the KM project, it should be clear which knowledge sources can be approached in what way. For a KM project for the entire organisation it is relevant to have global knowledge on the knowledge sources available within the organisation. For a KM project for the support of a legal task it is necessary to have detailed knowledge on the availability and use of knowledge sources.

Knowledge sources can be approached directly (knowledge engineer – human, knowledge engineer – writings and knowledge engineer – IT) and indirectly (knowledge engineer – IT – human and knowledge engineer – IT- IT). Each approach needs its own technique.

Chris for example obtains knowledge from the legal expert Charlotte by using interview techniques. Chris knows Charlotte deals with liability law. Knowledge on this domain can be found in various knowledge sources. A human knowledge source is the expert, Charlotte. Other human knowledge sources are other employees of the law firm or experts of other legal organisations who deal with the same task. Writings as a source of knowledge are various publications on liability law. Chris finds these publication in the local library. Nowadays, various other publications on liability law are also available as an IT source of knowledge and information in legal databases available through the internet and available on CD-ROM's. Chris knows this because of his experience and because his interviews with Charlotte who pointed out some of these.

To access the knowledge information sources and to process the knowledge and information obtained, IT can be useful. Popular forms of IT are text editors and databases. For the KM project for the support of use will be made for example of a text editor to type the results (e.g. the results of an interview or decision tables), internet and CD-ROM's for searching legal databases, an e-mail application to send and receive information and a drawing application for the construction of networks.

Milestones

Milestones are products resulting during the KM project. These milestones are for example reports on the current situation or evaluation reports or models. Milestones are necessary for the continuation of the project. This is relevant to both the KM project for the entire organisation as to the KM project for the support of a legal task. The type of milestone may be

[8]Many examples of (legal) knowledge sources exist [21], [37], [34], [13].

different though. One could imagine that evaluation reports are of more importance to a KM project for the entire organisation than a specific decision table used for the support of a legal task.

When a milestone does not meet the demands as made clear at the start of the project, a decision can be made to stop the entire project or to take a step back to improve the delivered milestone(s). During the project the following milestones could be produced; a report of the current situation and a model of the future KM architecture.

Activities

In this part of the KM project plan the main activities of the KM project are described and planned. This means that a planning is given in which it becomes clear which activity leads to a certain milestone within a certain period of time. Planning and descriptions of activities are both relevant to the KM project for the entire organisation and to the KM project for the support of a legal task. The KM project for the entire organisation may use a global planning and description of activities in opposite to the KM project for the support of a legal task, which needs a detailed planning and description. For planning several (standard) techniques can be used. Examples of activities which will be executed after there has been an agreement on this project plan are 'describing and analysing the current situation and current use of IT' and 'developing KM architecture'.

Reports

In this part of the KM project plan it becomes clear when reports on the forthcoming of the KM project are discussed and by whom.[9] This is may be especially important to the KM project for the support of a legal task and more than to the KM project for the entire organisation.

Educational plan

Members of the project group may need to know more about for example task analysis and knowledge management.

Costs and means

In this part of the plan it becomes clear how much time will be spend on the project by members of the project group. It should clarify if the entire project can be financed. This is both important to the KM project for the entire organisation and the KM project for the support of a legal task. For the KM project for the entire organisation it is important to have global knowledge on how much a certain KM project costs, while for the KM project for the support of a legal task it clarifies precisely what each of the parties will earn by their involvement in the project.

By filling in of one or more of these elements a decision can be made whether to proceed with the KM project. To structure the filling in of the plan, knowledge management might also be helpful.

---

[9]To gain insight in planning and costs, several techniques are available. See for example [10].

4 Conclusions and Future Research

This paper showed some of our ideas on knowledge management for law practice. These ideas are based on the first explorations of a PhD. research performed by the first author since March 2001.

In this paper we explored the idea that knowledge management could be used in more ways *(see section 2)*. Not only can KM be deployed to entire organisations, but also to divisions and legal employees who perform legal tasks. Each of these groups has its own characteristics and to successfully perform KM projects, they should be approached according to their characteristics. Many KM methods also lack a preparation; they are developed and applied on the basis of the presumption that KM is useful. To increase the chance of success of a KM project we believe that a good preparation, including a project plan, should be applied *(see section 3)*. This idea is not new; it is based on years of research in the area of software engineering. For the filling in of a KM project plan, it should also be kept in mind that we have to deal with different groups involved (e.g. the entire organisation or employees performing a legal task).

Because the PhD. research has started this year, we are still exploring (new) ways of KM for law practice. Our future research will look more closely at subjects like the practical use of linking KM support for a legal task to the KM support of an entire organisation, methods for the preparation of a KM project, other phases necessary for a KM method to support legal tasks and AI&Law methods and techniques suitable and necessary for use in such a method. At the moment the idea is to put the results of the PhD. research into law practice (e.g. a law firm) and to find out whether (AI&Law) methods, techniques and IT for example, are suitable for KM. On basis of the results, a KM method for law practice could be developed.

References

[1] Apistola, M., Juridisch kennismanagement in de praktijk: Advocatenkantoor Stibbe, in: BNVKI Newsletter, vol. 18, No. 3, June, 2000.

[2] Avison, D.E., Fitzgerald, G., Information systems development- methodologies, techniques and tools, London, McGraw-Hill, 1995 p.205.

[3] Cawsey, A., The essence of Artificial Intelligence, Prentice Hall Europe, 1998.

[4] De Veij Mestdagh, C.N.J., Juridische kennissystemen, Rekentuig of rekenmeester?, dissertation Groningen, Deventer, Kluwer, 1997.

[5] Doukidis, G.I., Whitley, E.A., Developing Expert Systems, Chartwell-Bratt, 1988 pp. 20-29.

[6] Duivenboden, H. van, Lips, M., Frissen, P (red.), Kennismanagement in de publieke sector, Elsevier Bedrijfsinformatie, Den Haag, 1999.

[7] Edwards, D.L., Mahling, D.E., Toward Knowledge Management Systems in the Legal Domain, ACM, 1997.

[8] Eilers, H.B., Systeemontwikkeling volgens SDM, Academic Service, Schoonhoven, 1991.

[9] Florijn, R., Gurchom, M. van, Meulen, M. van der, Kennis leren managen – de theorie en praktijk van kennismanagement, Ten Hagen & Stam, Den Haag, 2000.

[10] Ghezzi, C., Jazayeri, M., Mandrioli, D., Fundamentals of software engineering, Prentice-Hall, 1991 pp. 427-437.

[11] Gordon, T.F., The pleadings game, Dordrecht, Kluwer Academic Publishers, 1995.

[12] Gottschalk, P., Use of IT for Knowledge Management in Law Firms, The Journal of Information, Law and Technology (JILT), vol. 3, http://www.law.warwick.ac.uk/jilt/99-3/gottschalk.html, 1999.

[13] Gurchom, M. van, Florijn, R., Meulen, M. van der (red.), Kennis leren managen, Ten Hagen & Stam

uitgevers, Den Haag, 1999 42.
[14] Hage, J., Reasoning with rules, An essay on legal reasoning reasoning and its underlying logic, Kluwer Academic Publishers, 1997.
[15] Keil, M., Cule, P.C., Lyytinen, K., Schmidt, R.C., A framework for identifying software project risks, in: Communications of the ACM, Vol. 41, No. 11, November, 1998.
[16] Konstantinou, V., Sykes, J., Yannopoulos, G.N., Can legal knowledge be derived from legal texts?, in: ACM, London, 1993.
[17] Lodder, A.R., DiaLaw – On legal justification and dialog games, dissertation University Maastricht, Maastricht, 1998.
[18] Matthijssen, L., Kennismanagement: B there or B2 , in: R&EM, nr. 3, December, 2000.
[19] Morabito, J., Sack, I., Bhate, A., Organization modeling, innovative architectures for the 21st century, Prentice Hall, 1999.
[20] Nonaka, I., Takeuchi, H., De kenniscreërende onderneming- hoe Japanse bedrijven innovatieprocessen in gang zetten, Scriptum Management, Schiedam, 1999.
[21] Oskamp, A., Het ontwikkelen van juridische expertsystemen – een theoretische beschouwing, dissertation Vrije Universiteit Amsterdam, Kluwer, Deventer, 1990 pp. 30-91.
[22] Oskamp, A., Tragter, M., Knowledge for automated legal problem solving: theory versus practice, ICAIL-97, ACM, Australia, 1997.
[23] Oskamp, A., Rechtsinformatica: Vooruitzien in de informatiemaatschappij, oratie Katholieke Universiteit Nijmegen, Kluwer, Deventer, 1998 6.
[24] Oskamp, A., Lodder, A.R., Tragter, M., Mutual benefits for AI & Law and Knowledge Management, Proceedings of the Seventh International Conference on Artificial Intelligence and Law, ACM, New York, 1999.
[25] Oskamp, A., Beheer van juridische kennis in het IT tijdperk, in: Onderneming en ICT, Berkvens, J.M.A., Faber, N.E.D., Kortmann, S.C.J.J., Oskamp, A., (red.), W.E.J. Tjeenk Willink, Deventer, 2000 301-305.
[26] Prakken, H., Logical tools for modelling legal argument, Dordrecht, Kluwer, 1997.
[27] Prakken, H., Argumentatieonderzoek in de rechtsinformatica, mogelijke toepassingen, Jurix meeting May 11, 2001.
[28] Samson, E.P., Organisatie, besturing en informatie, Kluwer Bedrijfswetenschappen, Deventer, 1993 p.21.
[29] Scott, A.C., Clayton, J.E., Gibson, E.L., A practical guide to knowledge acquisition, Addison-Wesley Publishing Company, 1991.
[30] Valente, A., Legal Knowledge Engineering – A Modelling Approach, dissertation University of Amsterdam, IOS Press, Amsterdam, 1995.
[31] Van Kralingen, R., Frame-based conceptual models of statute law, dissertation University Leiden, 1995.
[32] Verheij, B., Rules, Reasons and Arguments, A study of defeasible reasoning in law, dissertation Maastricht, 1996.
[33] Visser, P.R.S., Knowledge specification for multiple legal tasks: A case study of the interaction problem in the legal domain, dissertation Leiden, Den Haag, Kluwer Law International, 1995.
[34] Wahlgren, P., Automation of Legal Reasoning – A study on Artificial Intelligence and Law, Kluwer, Deventer, 1992 pp. 256-259.
[35] Weggeman, M., Kennismanagement – inrichting en besturing van kennisintensieve organisaties, Scriptum Management, Schiedam, 1997 p.67.
[36] Werff, B.M. van der, Methoden van kennisacquisitie, in: Kennis in organisaties – toepassingen en theorie van kennissystemen, Jorna, R.J., Simons, J.L. (red), Dick Coutinho, Muiderberg, 1992 pp.145-146.
[37] Weusten, M.C.M., De bouw van juridische kennissystemen – KRT methodologie en gereedschap, dissertation Universiteit Utrecht, Kluwer, Deventer, 1999 p. 50.
[38] Wiig, K.M., Knowledge Management: Where did it come from and where will it go?, in: Expert systems with applications, Vol. 13, Nr. 1, Liebowitz, J., Hoog, R. de, Spek, R. van der (eds.), Elsevier, 1997.

The Dialectics of Case Comparison: a Formal Reconstruction

Bram Roth
Department of Metajuridica
Faculty of Law
Universiteit Maastricht
The Netherlands
bram.roth@metajur.unimaas.nl

Abstract. This paper is about the dialectics of case comparison as it unfolds in legal case-based reasoning, and its aim is to provide a representation of the phenomenon in formal terms. This is done by formalising argument moves in case comparison concisely in *argument schemes*, and specifying *attack relations* between the arguments and their corresponding counterarguments. A feature that is new in research on case comparison is, that in these argument schemes *dedicated case denotations* are used to refer to the cases under consideration, and that set-theoretic operations on cases appear in the formalised arguments.

1 Introduction

Legal case-based reasoning is an argumentation strategy in which a legal claim is supported by citing a favourable precedent and subsequently comparing it to the current fact situation. If one is able to establish a 'sufficiently good' analogy between a precedent and the present case, then according to the principle of *stare decisis* the past case should be followed and the same conclusion should hold. For this reason a legal debate will often focus on the issue how good the analogy between the past and present case actually is. The party who has cited the precedent will try to *support* the analogy by emphasising the similarities between the past and the present case, a move that is often called 'analogising'. The other party will instead *attack* the analogy by pointing out relevant differences, and this is usually called 'distinguishing'. Thus the legal debate between both parties will involve both arguments for the analogy, and counterarguments against it. The debate on the quality of the analogy can therefore be seen as a *dialectical* process, and it is the purpose of this paper to propose a way to represent the dialectics of case comparison explicitly in formal terms.

The present paper extends the work in past publications (Roth 2000 [14], Roth 2001 [15]) in two respects. First, case comparison is presently treated as a dialectical process involving argument attack, while in earlier work only the possible types of argument move were studied, with no specification at all of attack relations between them. Second, the present paper provides a fully formalised representation of argument moves in case comparison, while

Bram Roth, 'The Dialectics of Case Comparison: a Formal Reconstruction' in Bart Verheij, Arno R. Lodder, Ronald P. Loui and Antoinette J. Muntjewerff (eds.), *Legal Knowledge and Information Systems. Jurix 2001: The Fourteenth Annual Conference*. Amsterdam: IOS Press, 2001, pp. 29-40.

in past publications this representation was done semi-formally. However, due to space and time limitations the present paper has to restrict itself to arguments on *analogy* between cases, while in Roth 2001 [15] more possible outcomes of case comparison were considered.

2 Dialectics in General: a Simple Model

Suppose a bank employee is dismissed and challenges his dismissal in court, arguing that he should keep his job. Furthermore, suppose that the facts of the case are as follows, where each fact formulation is preceded by an abbreviation as a capital letter:

C : the employee insulted the employer
D : the employee is highly esteemed as a colleague
E : the employee has children to raise
F : the employee once committed fraud
G : the employee's wife has got a good income
H : the employee once deceived his employer with a forged diploma
I : the diploma was not relevant for the job
J : the employee works for a bank and should therefore be trustworthy

Moreover, suppose that in this dismissal case the issue arises whether the worker "has always behaved like a good employee" (a general obligation for employees that is codified in article 6:611 Dutch civil code), and let the sentence expressing that this is the case be abbreviated as 'A'. Then the employee will obviously argue in favour of conclusion A, while the employer will try to establish the opposite conclusion. This results in a process in which a number of arguments and counterarguments is exchanged, and it is the purpose of this section to provide an abstract formal account of this process.

For dialectics in general and for case comparison in particular, it is crucial that facts are not neutral but can play certain *roles* as *reasons*[1]. In the following, facts will be assumed to play one of two basic roles, namely that of a reason *supporting* a conclusion and that of a reason *detracting from* a conclusion. To express this supporting and this detracting role, respectively, the connectives '$\nearrow$' and '$\searrow$' are introduced. Suppose, for instance, that being highly esteemed as a colleague (D) 'supports' the conclusion A. Then this supporting role can be expressed as '$D \nearrow A$'. Furthermore, suppose that if one has once deceived one's employer with a forged diploma (H), then this 'detracts from' A. Then one can express by '$H \searrow A$' that the fact expressed by 'H' plays this detracting role.

The supporting or detracting roles of facts can *themselves* in turn be *supported* or *detracted from* by other facts[2]. For instance, suppose that if it is known that (I) an employee's forged diploma was not relevant for the job, then this detracts from the role of H as a reason

[1] In this section the complication is ignored that often more than one fact go into a reason (see e.g. Hage 1997 [8], p. 13-14). See, however, the discussion on *compound* reasons as they appear below in the formalisation of arguments in case comparison.

[2] Verheij includes comparable mechanisms in what he calls 'naïve dialectical arguments'. See the draft of 'DefLog-a logic of dialectical justification and defeat', to be found at http://www.metajur.unimaas.nl/~bart/publications.htm. See also Verheij 2000 [18], p. 212 or Verheij 2001 [19].

detracting from A. Then by introducing brackets in the notation this role of I can be expressed straightforwardly by means of the nested construction 'I$\searrow$(H$\searrow$A)'. This mechanism of detracting from another fact's role as a reason underlies the undercutting type of attack on arguments, which will be introduced below.

As an example of a fact supporting another fact's role[3], let us suppose that if the person is a bank employee (J) and should therefore be trustworthy, then this supports the role of H as a reason detracting from A. Then by using brackets once again this supporting role of J can be expressed straightforwardly by means of the nested construction 'J$\nearrow$(H$\searrow$A)'.

To specify the syntax of the sentences that are allowed under the present model in a concise way, let us adopt the convention to write metavariables for sentences as strings of characters in italics, starting with an uppercase (so as '*Fact*', for instance). Now all sentences must either be atomic or composite, where the composite sentences can be specified recursively as sentences of the form (*Fact1*)$\nearrow$(*Conclusion1*) or (*Fact2*)$\searrow$(*Conclusion2*). Here *Fact1* and *Fact2* are atomic sentences while *Conclusion1* and *Conclusion2* can be either atomic, or be of a composite form themselves. Moreover, brackets will be omitted if there is no danger of ambiguities, just as was done in the examples above.

It must be noted that the notions of 'support' and 'detraction from' were only introduced informally above and will not be specified any further here. Accordingly, no semantics will be formulated for the connectives '$\nearrow$' and '$\searrow$' that are used to express these mechanisms. The reason for this is, that the present account merely aims at formally *representing* the dialectics of case comparison, and that the status of legal claims is not evaluated. It therefore suffices here to have an intuitive understanding of the two mechanisms, so that the examples can serve as an explication of their intended meaning.

Still it must be said, however, that the aforementioned notions should not be construed as stating necessary or sufficient conditions for a conclusion or for its negation (see for a similar remark Aleven 1997 [2] p. 46 or Ashley 1991 [4] p. 757). The statement that D 'supports' the conclusion A, for instance, does not mean that D alone would be a sufficient condition for A. Likewise, if H 'detracts from' the same conclusion (A), then this does not mean that a necessary condition for A would be that H is not the case.

In the following it will be assumed that the *roles* of facts as supporting conclusions or detracting from them, are known in advance. In other words, these roles are assumed to be given as *background knowledge* that can be represented as a set of sentences of the formal language. It can also be made explicit by representing it graphically, however, as in Figure 2 below[4]. The representation in that figure constitutes a small part of what may be called an 'Entangled Factor Hierarchy' after the term 'Factor Hierarchy' used in CATO (Aleven 1997 [2], p. 44/5). It is called 'entangled' because unlike CATO's Factor Hierarchy, it contains arrows that point at other arrows, thus representing the mechanisms of supporting or detracting from other facts' roles.

With this background knowledge of the roles of facts as reasons, the following formalisation of dialectics can now be given.

[3]Cf. Toulmin's 'backings' of 'warrants' (Toulmin 1958 [16], p. 98f.).

[4]When inspecting this figure it may seem that the Entangled Factor Hierarchy is not a general representation of the domain under consideration, because it contains relatively factual expressions like "the employee insulted the employer." It must be noted, however, that each of these expressions can apply to a whole *class* of *different* cases, just as CATO's and HYPO's factors.

Arguments will be formally treated as sentences that are selected from the background knowledge. There are two possible ways in which arguments can *attack* each other. First, one can put forward a reason for a conclusion that is *incompatible* to the conclusion of the original argument. Suppose, for example, that an argument involves a fact D which *supports* the conclusion A: D↗A. Then this argument can be attacked by putting forward the fact H, given that this *detracts from* the conclusion A: H↘A. As another example, consider an argument involving a fact I which *detracts from* the role of H as a reason detracting from A: I↘(H↘A). This argument can be attacked by putting forward the fact J, given that this *supports* the role of H as a reason detracting from A: J↗(H↘A). In the literature (Pollock 1995 [11] p. 40 and 85, Hage 1997 [8] p. 167f., Verheij 1996 [17] p. 121/2) such an attack strategy is often called *rebutting*, and this term will be adopted here as well.

More generally, rebutting attacks can be represented as follows. An argument of the form

Fact1↗*Conclusion*

can be rebutted by the corresponding argument of the form

Fact2↘*Conclusion*,

and vice versa. Note that if rebutting is formalised in this way, this results in a symmetric attack relation[5].

A second way of attacking an argument[6] is by detracting from the role of the fact involved in it. Consider, for example, an argument involving a fact H which detracts from the conclusion A: H↘A. This argument can be attacked by putting forward the fact I which detracts from the role of H as a reason detracting from A: I↘(H↘A). This attack strategy is often called *undercutting* in the literature (Pollock 1995 [11] p. 41 and 86, Hage 1997 [8] p. 166, Verheij 1996 [17] p. 120/1), and this term will be used here as well. Note that this undercutting attack relation is an asymmetric one.

To represent undercutting attacks in a concise way, it is convenient to have a dedicated metavariable for the two connectives expressing the roles of 'support' and 'detraction from'. To this end the small italicised letter '*r*' is used (for 'role'), which can be instantiated either as ↗, or as ↘. Then any argument of the form

(*Fact3*) *r* (*Conclusion*)

can be undercut by the corresponding argument of the form

Fact4 ↘((*Fact3*) *r* (*Conclusion*)).

[5] In the present account no weighing (Hage 1997 [8], p. 140f.) or priority (Prakken and Sartor 1998 [13], p. 254) information can be taken into account. Such information cannot be used here for dialectical purposes either.

[6] A third possibility would be to detract from the fact is put forward as a reason (see Roth 2001 [15] for a semi-formal account). This attack strategy is ignored in the present formal treatment, however.

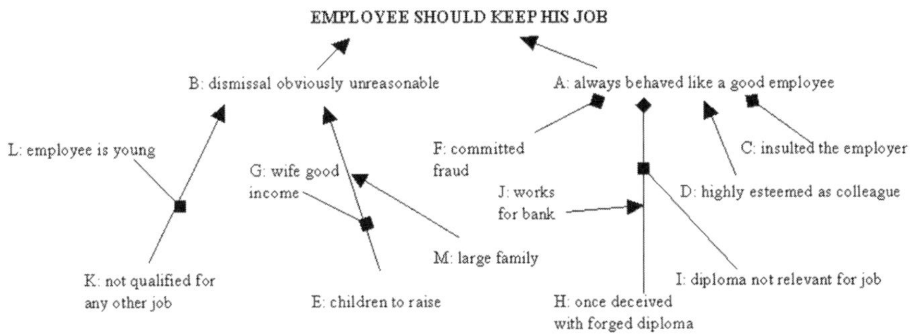

Figure 1: A portion of an 'Entangled Factor Hierarchy', a possible graphical representation of background knowledge. At the top of the picture one finds the main issue in bold capitals, that is, whether the employee should keep his job. Normal arrows stand for 'support', while arrows ending in a solid square stand for 'detraction from'. Note in particular the arrows pointing at other arrows, the graphical equivalent of nested sentences.

3 The Dialectics of Case Comparison: a Formal Reconstruction

In the following the dialectics of case comparison is formally accounted for by specifying attack relations between (schemes of) argument moves in case comparison and their corresponding (schemes of) counterarguments (viz. *rebutting* and *undercutting* attack, see previous section). The representation is not done in the form of a dialogue game (see for dialogue games, e.g., Lodder 1998 [10], Gordon 1995 [9]).

The syntax of the formal language has to be extended first. As remarked in the introduction, case comparison is treated as a debate on the analogy between cases. For a start one should therefore be able to express that two cases are analogous, and to this end cases will be denoted as terms[7] in the formal language. By convention these terms are (strings of) characters in bold type, starting with an uppercase. Thus, for instance, the expressions '**PastCase**' and '**PresentCase**' can denote the past and the present case under consideration, respectively. Moreover, to express that two cases are analogous the symbol '$\approx$' is introduced, so that the formula '**PastCase** $\approx$ **PresentCase**', for instance, says that the present and past case are analogous[8]. The analogy relation is assumed to be symmetric, so that formulas like '**Case1** $\approx$ **Case2**' and '**Case2** $\approx$ **Case1**' are equivalent.

Analogising moves can be treated formally as arguments in *support* of the conclusion *that two cases are analogous*, while distinguishing moves can be formalised as arguments *detracting from* that conclusion. As a result, the connectives '$\nearrow$' and '$\searrow$' can also be used in the present formal treatment of arguments in case comparison.

However, if one treats analogising and distinguishing as putting forward reasons in support of and detracting from the analogy, respectively, then the question arises which fact types

[7]Cf. the use of terms to denote cases in Reason-Based Logic (Hage 1997 [8], p.133/4).

[8]The establishment of an analogy may depend on the particular conclusion at stake. One could account for this by adding the disputed conclusion, say C, as a subscript: '$\approx_C$'. Presently this complication is ignored, however.

can actually play these roles as reasons. As will become clear from the informal examples below, the role in case comparison of individual case facts is partly determined by their *role as a reason* according to the background knowledge. This means that in formalising argument moves as reasons affecting the analogy, in these reasons reference must be made to the supporting or detracting role of the individual case fact involved.

The examples below will also show that for argument moves on analogy it is relevant whether an individual fact occurs in *only one* of the cases or in *both*, because this partly determines whether this fact can be used to distinguish or to analogise. This means that in the reasons in support of or detracting from the analogy, one must also specify the *precise origin* of the case fact involved.

To accomplish this, cases will be treated simply as collections of facts from now on. Using standard set-theoretic notation the formula 'X ∈ **Case1**', for instance, then says that the fact expressed by 'X' is present in the case denoted as **Case1**. Furthermore, in order to be able to say that a fact is present in one case but not in the other, the set-theoretic symbol '\' is introduced. This symbol stands for *set difference*, and the expression '**Case1****Case2**', for instance, represents the set of all the facts that occur in **Case1** and *not* in **Case2**. The formula 'X ∈ **Case1****Case2**', for instance, then says that X occurs in **Case1** and not in **Case2**. Moreover, the set-theoretic symbol '∩' for intersection is used to express that a fact is shared. The expression '**Case2**∩**Case3**', for instance, then represents the set of all the facts that occur both in **Case1** and in **Case2**. Accordingly, a formula 'X ∈ **Case2**∩**Case3**' says that X is there in both **Case2** and **Case3**.

Argument moves on analogy can now be expressed as ones in which a *compound* reason is put forward which involves both the location of a case fact, and this fact's role as a reason according to the background knowledge[9]. Naturally enough, the representation of a compound reason will therefore contain two expressions, one for the case fact's location and one for its role as a reason. By convention both expressions will be separated by a comma and placed between brackets. In this way an expression like '(X ∈ **PresentCase****PastCase**, X↗Z)', for instance, represents a compound reason that is made up by two states of affairs. The first of these is that the fact expressed by 'X' occurs in the *present* case *only*, while the second is that this fact gives support to the conclusion expressed by 'Z'. Given this representation for this particular compound reason, the formula

$$(\mathrm{X} \in \mathbf{PresentCase} \backslash \mathbf{PastCase},\ \mathrm{X} \nearrow \mathrm{Z}) \searrow (\mathbf{PresentCase} \approx \mathbf{PastCase})$$

then expresses that this reason detracts from the analogy between the past and the present case. In other words, the formula says that the two cases are *distinguished* by pointing out X in the *present* case *only*.

Metavariables for case denotations will be written in italics and remain written in bold type, just as the case denotations themselves. As an example, the expression '***Case1***' can thus be used as a metavariable for case denotations. As the examples below suggest, it comes in handy to be able to refer to the *same* and the *other* case. To accomplish this the two metavariables ***Case1*** and ***Case2*** will be used as denotations of the two cases involved in the comparison process, with the additional convention that these metavariables will always stand

[9]One of the referees suggested that by including *values* in the representation, the present model can very readily be extended for *teleological* reasoning with cases (see, e.g., Bench-Capon and Sartor 2001 [7]).

for *different* cases. Thus, if ***Case1*** is instantiated by the denotation **PastCase** for the cited past case, then ***Case2*** stands for **PresentCase** for the case at hand, and vice versa.

Finally, as was done above, the small italicised letter 'r' is used as a metavariable for the two connectives '$\nearrow$' and '$\searrow$'.

Suppose one has to deal with the same dismissal case as in the previous section (see the list of facts on the first page), but suppose that the employee now cites a similar dismissal case to support the claim that he should keep his job. Let the facts of the past case be as follows, where each fact formulation is again preceded by its abbreviation as a capital letter:

C : the employee insulted the employer
D : the employee is highly esteemed as a colleague
E : the employee has children to raise
K : the employee is not qualified for any other job
L : the employee is still young and capable of retraining
M : the employee has a large family

Regarding the question whether the employee should keep his job, one issue is once again that which was abbreviated above as 'A'. Another issue is, whether "the dismissal was obviously unreasonable" (7: 681 paragraph 2 Dutch Civil Code), and the sentence expressing this will be abbreviated as 'B'.

As the past case is cited by the employee, his employer will now seek to distinguish both cases. This can be done, for instance, by pointing out the fact (F) that there is a case of fraud in the *present* case *only*. This fact is a relevant distinction because it *detracts from* the legally relevant conclusion A: F$\searrow$A. Another way to distinguish both cases is to point out the fact (K) that the bank employee was not qualified for any other job, which occurs in the *past* case *only*. This fact also constitutes a relevant distinction because it *supports* the legally relevant conclusion B: K$\nearrow$B.

This pattern of distinguishing can be generalised and formalised as follows. Let ***Case1*** and ***Case2*** be the denotations of the two cases involved in the comparison, and let *Fact1* be a fact that occurs in ***Case1***$\setminus$***Case2*** and that plays role r as a reason relative to some conclusion *Conclusion*. Then one can take

$$(\mathit{Fact1} \in \boldsymbol{Case1}\setminus\boldsymbol{Case2}, (\mathit{Fact1})r(\mathit{Conclusion})) \searrow (\boldsymbol{Case1} \approx \boldsymbol{Case2})$$

as a general scheme of distinguishing arguments of the kind that is presently under consideration.

The employee can now respond to the distinguishing move involving C by pointing out that in *both cases* the employer was insulted (C), a fact which *detracts from* A in the *past case as well*: C$\searrow$A. And the distinguishing move involving K can be attacked by pointing out that in *both cases* there were children to raise (E), a fact which provides *support for* B in the *present case as well*: E$\nearrow$B.

More generally, one can attack a distinguishing move by pointing out a fact which occurs in *both* cases and which plays the *same* supporting or detracting role as the fact involved in the original distinguishing move. More formally, if the original distinguishing move involves a fact occurring in ***Case1***$\setminus$***Case2*** and playing role r as a reason relative to conclusion *Conclusion*, then the response makes use of a fact (*Fact2*), which occurs in ***Case1***$\cap$***Case2*** and plays role r as a reason relative to conclusion *Conclusion* as well. Since this way of attacking involves a shared fact it will be formalised as an analogising move, and since analogising is presently treated as supporting the analogy, the present attack strategy is a *rebutter*. Formally, this means that if

$$(\mathit{Fact1} \in \textbf{\textit{Case1}}\backslash\textbf{\textit{Case2}}, (\mathit{Fact1})r(\mathit{Conclusion})) \searrow (\textbf{\textit{Case1}} \approx \textbf{\textit{Case2}})$$

is once again a scheme of distinguishing arguments, then

$$(\mathit{Fact2} \in \textbf{\textit{Case1}}\cap\textbf{\textit{Case2}}, (\mathit{Fact2})r(\mathit{Conclusion})) \nearrow (\textbf{\textit{Case1}} \approx \textbf{\textit{Case2}})$$

is a scheme representing the corresponding rebutting analogising counterarguments.

If the employee uses E to analogise the cases in response to a distinguishing move, then the employer can in turn distinguish in two different ways. The first way is by pointing out that although E occurs in both cases, its role as a reason supporting B is *detracted from* by the fact (G) that the wife of employee has a good income, which occurs in the *present* case *only*: G$\searrow$(E$\nearrow$B). Another way of distinguishing at this point is to point out that while E is shared by both cases, its role as a reason supporting B is itself *supported* in the *past* case *only* by the fact (M) that the employee had a large family: M$\nearrow$(E$\nearrow$B).

The employee can also attack his employer's distinguishing argument by pointing out the fact (L) that the employee was young and capable of retraining, which also occurs in the *past* case and which *detracts from* the role of K as a reason supporting B: L$\searrow$(K$\nearrow$B).

More generally, if the two cases are analogised in response to a distinguishing move by pointing out a shared fact, then one can in turn distinguish in two ways. The first is by pointing out a fact, which *only* occurs in the *same* case as the fact involved in the original distinguishing argument and which *supports* the role of the shared fact that is pointed out in the analogising response. The second way of distinguishing involves a fact which *only* occurs in the *other* case than the fact involved in the original distinguishing argument and which *detracts from* the role of the shared fact used in the analogising move. More formally, if the original distinguishing move involves a fact (*Fact1*) occurring in ***Case1***$\backslash$***Case2*** and playing role$r$ as a reason relative to conclusion *Conclusion*, and the analogising response makes use of a fact (*Fact2*) which occurs in ***Case1***$\cap$***Case2*** and plays role r as a reason relative to conclusion *Conclusion* as well, then one can in turn distinguish in two ways. The first is by pointing out a fact (*Fact3*) which occurs in ***Case1***$\backslash$***Case2*** and which *supports* the role of *Fact2* as a reason. The second way of distinguishing involves a fact (*Fact3*) which occurs in ***Case2***$\backslash$***Case1*** and which *detracts from* the role of *Fact2* as a reason.

Formally, this means that if

$$(\mathit{Fact1} \in \textbf{\textit{Case1}}\backslash\textbf{\textit{Case2}}, (\mathit{Fact1})r(\mathit{Conclusion})) \searrow (\textbf{\textit{Case1}} \approx \textbf{\textit{Case2}})$$

is once again a scheme of distinguishing arguments, and

$$(\mathit{Fact2} \in \textbf{\textit{Case1}}\cap\textbf{\textit{Case2}}, (\mathit{Fact2})r(\mathit{Conclusion})) \nearrow (\textbf{\textit{Case1}} \approx \textbf{\textit{Case2}})$$

is the scheme for the corresponding analogising counterarguments, then

$$(\mathit{Fact3} \in \textbf{\textit{Case1}}\backslash\textbf{\textit{Case2}}, \mathit{Fact3} \nearrow ((\mathit{Fact2})r(\mathit{Conclusion}))) \searrow (\textbf{\textit{Case1}} \approx \textbf{\textit{Case2}})$$

and

$$(\mathit{Fact3} \in \textbf{\textit{Case2}} \backslash \textbf{\textit{Case1}}, \mathit{Fact3} \searrow ((\mathit{Fact2})r(\mathit{Conclusion}))) \searrow (\textbf{\textit{Case1}} \approx \textbf{\textit{Case2}})$$

are schemes representing the corresponding distinguishing counterarguments.

If, as above, the employer distinguishes by pointing out K in the *past* case *only*, then the employee can also respond by pointing out a fact L which also occurs in the *past* case and which *detracts from* the role of K as a reason supporting B: L$\searrow$(K$\nearrow$B).

Another strategy to distinguish the two cases is to point out the fact H, which occurs in the *present* case *only*. This fact can also be used to distinguish because it *detracts from* the legally relevant conclusion A: H$\searrow$A. If the employer distinguishes in this way, then the employee can in turn attack this distinguishing argument by pointing out the fact I which also occurs in the *present* case and which *detracts from* the role of H as a reason detracting from A: I$\searrow$(H$\searrow$A).

More generally, one can always attack a distinguishing move by pointing out a fact which occurs in the *same* case as the fact involved in the original distinguishing argument and which *detracts from* the latter's role as a reason. More formally, if the original distinguishing move involves a fact (*Fact1*) occurring in ***Case1\Case2*** and playing role r as a reason relative to conclusion *Conclusion*, then the present way of attacking involves a fact (*Fact2*) occurring in ***Case1*** and detracting from this role of *Fact1* as a reason. Furthermore, for reasons to be explained below this way of attacking will presently be treated as an *undercutting* attack on the original distinguishing move, and not as an analogising move in its own right. This means that if

$$(\mathit{Fact1} \in \textbf{\textit{Case1}} \backslash \textbf{\textit{Case2}}, (\mathit{Fact1})r(\mathit{Conclusion})) \searrow (\textbf{\textit{Case1}} \approx \textbf{\textit{Case2}})$$

is once again a scheme of distinguishing arguments, then

$$(\mathit{Fact2} \in \textbf{\textit{Case1}}, \mathit{Fact2} \searrow ((\mathit{Fact1})r(\mathit{Conclusion}))) \searrow \\ ((\mathit{Fact1} \in \textbf{\textit{Case1}} \backslash \textbf{\textit{Case2}}, (\mathit{Fact1})r(\mathit{Conclusion})) \searrow (\textbf{\textit{Case1}} \approx \textbf{\textit{Case2}}))$$

is the corresponding scheme of undercutting counterarguments.

The reason for treating this attack strategy as undercutting is, that it involves compound reasons in which reference is made to only one of the cases, while it does not matter at all whether or not the fact is also present in the other case. This suggests that these attacking moves be not treated as analogising arguments. However, because they do attack the role of the fact involved in some distinguishing argument, they can be interpreted sensibly as undercutters of this distinguishing move.

At this point one reservation has yet to be made. As remarked above, the aim of this paper is to propose a way to represent the dialectics of case comparison in formal terms, and this was done in the form of argument schemes. This does not imply any claim, however, that the given schemes make up an exhaustive list.

4 Related Work[10]

Probably the most important accounts of dialectical case comparison are those in the work on HYPO (Ashley 1990 [3], Ashley 1991 [4]) and CATO (Aleven 1996 [1], Aleven 1997 [2]). HYPO makes use of pre-stored background knowledge on the tendency of factors to favour a certain party (Ashley 1991 [4], p. 775). CATO exploits a more sophisticated body of background knowledge in its 'Factor Hierarchy' (Aleven 1997 [2], p. 44/5). From the present perspective this Factor Hierarchy is a representation of the roles that case facts can play as reasons. However, these roles are assumed as self-evident background knowledge (Aleven 1997 [2], p. 46), so that no arguments *on* the roles of facts are possible. In contrast, in the present approach such arguments are possible, thanks to the mechanisms affecting other facts' roles. These mechanisms appear as the 'entanglement' of factors in the Entangled Factor Hierarchy that represents the background knowledge as it is presently used (see Figure 2 above).

Using its Factor Hierarchy, the CATO system can produce special arguments about the significance of a distinction, such as 'downplaying a distinction' (Aleven 1997 [2] p. 58). In the present framework these special CATO moves cannot yet be accommodated, but in Roth 2001 [15] a semi-formal account was given. This account relied on other possible outcomes of case comparison than that studied here, such as that one case is overall 'more favourable' to a conclusion than another one. A full formalisation of these ideas has to be left for future research, however.

Prakken and Sartor (Prakken and Sartor 1998 [13]) give an account of case-based reasoning within the framework of their formal dialogue game. The following features of this approach are most relevant to the present discussion.

The representation of precedents reflects their dialectical structure, that is, the arguments pro and con that appear in them. This is accomplished by representing past cases as collections of rules from which the arguments pro and con can be constructed (p. 256). The model allows for the following argument moves: *analogizing* and *distinguishing*.

Analogizing is treated as the extraction of a rule from a past case and making this rule applicable to the present case by omitting unfulfilled conditions. The resulting rule is then said to *broaden* the original one.

Distinguishing is only possible after a rule has been broadened. It can take place in two ways, viz. *strong* and *weak*. *Strong* distinguishing is treated as the introduction of a rule which states as its conditions that the ones omitted from the broadened rule are not explicitly satisfied, and which has an *opposite* conclusion.

Weak distinguishing is treated as the introduction of a rule that concludes to the *inapplicability* of the broadening rule on the basis of that rule's unfulfilled conditions.

As an account of case comparison, this approach has two shortcomings. The first is, that while the present model requires the establishment of an analogy *before* a legal conclusion can be drawn on the basis of some past case, in Prakken and Sartor's approach much more *direct* arguments are produced. Their analogizing move, for instance, provides an argument that pleads directly for the conclusion for which the past case is cited.

[10] Due to space limitations the discussion of a lot of relevant work has to be omitted (Bench-Capon and Sartor 2000 [5], Bench-Capon and Sartor 2001 [6], Henderson and Bench-Capon 2001 [7], Prakken 2000 [12]).

The second shortcoming is that Prakken and Sartor's model *abstracts* from the concrete cases by extracting rules from them, while in the present approach they are recognised as entities that can stand on their own. Accordingly, their special 'analogizing' and 'distinguishing' moves are treated as operations on *rules*, and no reference at all is made to the *cases* involved in the comparison process. In contrast, in the present account of the comparison process cases play a role in their own right, and a dedicated denotation is therefore used for them in the formal representation of this process.

5 Conclusion and Future Research

In this paper a very abstract and simple model of dialectics was taken as a background to give a formal account of the dialectics of case comparison, by specifying attack relations between arguments. Moreover, these argument moves were represented in a concise way by means of schemes of arguments and their corresponding counterarguments.

There are a number of shortcomings, leaving some problems for future research. First, in the present paper only reasoning by analogy was studied, and the moves in case comparison were treated accordingly as ones affecting the quality of analogy. As I suggested in earlier work (Roth 2001 [15]), though, it may be necessary to recognise more relations that may come to hold between cases once the comparison process is completed. One such relation, for example, may be that the present case is overall 'more favourable' to a legal conclusion than the past case, in which situation one can make an *a fortiori* argument. It is left for future research to extend the formal language in such a way that more relationships between cases can be represented, in order to accommodate the corresponding patterns of arguing with past cases.

The present framework allows for considering only one past case regarding its similarity with the present one, while in practice often more than one past case is cited. In the HYPO model (Ashley 1991 [4]), for example, one can 'trump' (p. 760, 761) one precedent by citing a 'better' (in the sense of the 'on pointness' ordering) one with an opposite outcome. A formal treatment of arguing with more than one past case has to be left for future research as well, however.

Acknowledgements

The author thanks Bart Verheij and Jaap Hage for comments and discussion, and three anonymous referees for their suggestions.

References

[1] Aleven, Vincent (1996). How Different Is Different? Arguing about the Significance of Similarities and Differences. *Proceedings of the Third European Workshop, EWCBR-96*, 1-15.

[2] Aleven, Vincent (1997). *Teaching Case-Based Reasoning Through a Model and Examples*. Ph.D. dissertation University of Pittsburgh.

[3] Ashley, K.D. (1990). *Modeling Legal Argument: Reasoning with Cases and Hypotheticals*. Cambridge, MA: MIT Press/Bradford Books.

[4] Ashley, K.D. (1991). Reasoning with cases and hypotheticals in HYPO. *International Journal of Man-Machine Studies* **34**: 753-796, 1991

[5] Bench-Capon, T.J.M. and Sartor, G. (2000). Using values and theories to resolve disagreement in law. *Proceedings of the Thirteenth Annual Jurix Conference* (eds. Joost Breuker, Ronald Leenes and Radboud Winkels), 73-84.

[6] Bench-Capon, T.J.M. and Sartor, G. (2001). Theory Based Explanation of Case Law Domains. *Proceedings of the 8th International Conference on Artificial Intelligence and Law*, 12-21.

[7] Henderson, J. and Bench-Capon, T.J.M. (2001). Dynamic Arguments in a Case Law Domain. *Proceedings of the 8th International Conference on Artificial Intelligence and Law*, 60-69.

[8] Hage, J.C. (1997). *Reasoning with Rules. An Essay on Legal Reasoning and Its Underlying Logic.* Dordrecht: Kluwer Law and Philosophy Library.

[9] Prakken, H. and Sartor, G. (1998). Modelling Reasoning with Precedents in a Formal Dialogue Game. *Artificial Intelligence and Law* **6**: 231-287.

[10] Gordon T.F. (1995). *The Pleadings Game. An Artificial Intelligence Model of Procedural Justice.* Dordrecht: Kluwer Academic Publishers.

[11] Lodder, A.R. (1998). *DiaLaw. On legal justification and diolog games.* Doctoral dissertation Universiteit Maastricht.

[12] Pollock, J.L. (1995). *Cognitive Carpentry: A Blueprint for How to Build a Person.* The MIT Press, Cambridge (Massachusetts).

[13] Prakken, H (2000). An exercise in formalising teleological case-based reasoning. *Proceedings of the Thirteenth Annual Jurix Conference* (eds. Joost Breuker, Ronald Leenes and Radboud Winkels), 49-57.

[14] Roth, A.C. (2000). New reasoning patterns in analogical legal case-based reasoning: an informal investigation. *Proceedings of the Thirteenth Annual Jurix Conference* (eds. Joost Breuker, Ronald Leenes and Radboud Winkels), 113-122.

[15] Roth, A.C. (2001). A Typology of Moves Involved in Case Comparison. *Proceedings of the 8th International Conference on Artificial Intelligence and Law*, 129-138.

[16] Toulmin, S.E. (1958). *The uses of argument.* University Press, Cambridge.

[17] Verheij, B. (1996). *Rules, Reasons, Arguments. Formal Studies of Argumentation and Defeat.* Doctoral dissertation Universiteit Maastricht.

[18] Verheij, B. (2000). Dialectical Argumentation as a Heuristic for Courtroom Decision Making. *Rationality, Information and Progress in Law and Psychology* (eds. Peter J. van Koppen and Nikolas H.M. Roos): 203-226, 2000. Universitaire Pers Maastricht.

[19] Verheij, B. (2001). Legal decision making as dialectical theory construction with argumentation schemes. *Proceedings of the 8th International Conference on Artificial Intelligence and Law*, 225-226.

Back to the Future: Dimensions Revisited

Trevor J.M. Bench-Capon
Department of Computer Science
The University of Liverpool
Liverpool
UK
t.j.m.bench-capon@csc.liv.ac.uk

Edwina L. Rissland
Department of Computer Science
University of Massachusetts
Amherst, MA
USA
rissland@cs.umass.edu

Abstract. Most recent work on reasoning with cases in law has taken the style of reasoning used in the CATO system as its model, and uses the notion of factors, as found in that system. Fundamental to CATO, a successor the HYPO system, were factors, which are closely related to HYPO-style dimensions. In this paper, we will argue that the simplification involved in using factors, while it has proved pragmatically useful both for clarifying understanding of certain aspects of reasoning with cases and for implementation, causes problems with domain analysis and precludes certain kinds of argument that we would wish to model. We therefore believe that the time is now ripe to go back to the original notion of dimensions, while retaining the insights that have been gained from working with the simpler notion of factors. The paper uses two case studies to argue that this is so.

1 Introduction

[5] gives an account of reasoning with cases as a process involving the construction, evaluation and application of theories. It attempts to articulate the relationship between decided cases, defeasible rules explaining the outcomes of those cases, and societal values promoted by those rules, so as to provide a theory that explains past decisions and that can be applied to as yet unresolved cases. In that paper, cases are taken to be described using *factors*, broadly following work such as that of [7], the CATO project ([1]) and [8]. The set of such factors, and decisions as to whether or not they apply to cases, is taken as being the product of some prior analysis of cases. All of this builds on ideas from the HYPO system (e.g., [2], [3]). In the HYPO system, however, a more sophisticated notion of factor—called a *dimension*—was used. In keeping with the terminology suggested recently by [10], we will refer to the type of factor used by Berman & Hafner, Sartor & Bench-Capon, and others, as CATO-style factors. By comparison, the original conception of dimensions ([13]) was used in other progeny of HYPO, such as CABARET ([11]) and BankXX ([12]).

HYPO-style dimensions allow finer grained comparison of cases than do CATO-style factors. They thus enable closer argumentation about relevant similarities and differences between cases. We believe that it is important that this potential should be available, since otherwise much of the creative reasoning with cases is placed outside the system. From the perspective of theory construction as described in [5], recognition of dimensions allows us

Trevor J.M. Bench-Capon and Edwina L. Rissland, 'Back to the Future: Dimensions Revisited' in Bart Verheij, Arno R. Lodder, Ronald P. Loui and Antoinette J. Muntjewerff (eds.), *Legal Knowledge and Information Systems. Jurix 2001: The Fourteenth Annual Conference.* Amsterdam: IOS Press, 2001, pp. 41-52.

to make explicit an additional stage in theory construction. Rather than taking factors as simply given in the background, and so not subject to discussion, we can see the move from dimensions to factors as being a topic within the theory construction process. We believe that the time is ripe to return to thinking in terms of dimensions rather than factors, and the primary purpose of this paper is to argue for that belief.

In section 2 we discuss the relationship between factors and dimensions. In section 3 we give two case studies which show the importance of starting from dimensions rather than factors if we are to capture some important aspects of reasoning with cases. In section 4 we draw some conclusions from the case studies and suggest directions for future work.

2 Dimensions and Factors

As used in the work referred to in section 1, a *factor* is:

- some feature of a case which may be present or absent. This is an all or nothing matter; there is no notion of an extent to which the factor is present. We say that a factor that is present is *applicable*;
- if present, a factor always strengthens the case for the same disputant, either the plaintiff or the defendant.

Dimensions are designed to capture the knowledge that a legal problem can be approached in a certain way. They represent a *range* of possible positions that a case can exhibit with regard to the aspect of the problem represented by the dimension. Dimensions have three elements:

- one or more *prerequisites*: some fact or facts of the case that make the dimension applicable to the case;
- one or more *focal slots*: some fact or facts of the case that determine the position in the range applicable to this case;
- a *direction*: one extreme of the range of positions favours the plaintiff, and the other extreme, the defendant. As one moves towards an extreme the appropriate party is increasingly more favoured, *ceteris paribus*.

These three elements are part of the original HYPO definition of a dimension [3]. In addition in HYPO—but not in CABARET or BankXX—factors were grouped into those that generally favoured the plaintiff and those that generally favoured the defendant.

In many of these systems, cases are described in terms of either the collection of factors applicable in them (e.g., in CATO), or the collection of facts (e.g., in HYPO, CABARET), from which it is possible to compute which dimensions are applicable. BankXX represented a case both by its facts and by the set of applicable dimensions and the case's values on them.

Two important contrasts between factors and dimensions emerge from this:

- Whereas the presence of a factor is an all or nothing affair; a case's strength, or value, on the dimension is a matter of more or less. In trade secrets law, the number of outsiders to whom the secret has been divulged is a relevant consideration. The defendant's case is strengthened according to the number of disclosures made. If this dimension were treated as a factor, a decision would need to be made as to precisely how many disclosures were required for the factor to be present, which might mean that a single disclosure had the same effect as ten million;

- Dimensions are *per se* neither pro-plaintiff nor pro-defendant; a dimension can potentially favour either of the parties depending on which position on its range is occupied. No disclosures can be regarded as a strong position for a pro-plaintiff argument, whereas a significant number of disclosures can be a strong position for a pro-defendant argument. One way to represent this with CATO-style factors, would be to have two factors: one, favouring the plaintiff, that applied when there were no disclosures, and another, favouring the defendant, when there were any, even just one, disclosures. Note, however, that CATO did not actually create such a "No-Secrets-Disclosed-Outsiders", because Ashley and Aleven could not find any court cases where a judge had said that an absence of disclosures was a positive strength for the plaintiff. Another way to split this dimension would be to use some intermediate number (N) of disclosures to create two factors, one, favouring the plaintiff, for less than N disclosures and one, favouring the defendant, for greater or equal than N. Again, Ashley and Aleven did not do this because they could not find any court opinion that mandated such a split. Even though CATO might not have used this approach of splitting a (numerical) dimension into two factors, creating CATO-style factors in this way is not precluded. A more typical split occurs when a dimension with only two values is split into two factors; for example, what was done for land in [7], where the land was classified as either "open" or "owned" (by the plaintiff).

In the next section we consider two case studies, both derived from work that uses the notion of factors rather than dimensions. In each case we consider the impact of using dimensions rather than factors, to explore the gains that result in terms of richness of representation and bringing within the system considerations that must otherwise be left to the knowledge engineer.

3 Case Studies

In this section we consider two case studies. The first is from [8] in which they use an artificial example concerning change of domicile. Here we use the simplest form of their example; they also developed a more elaborate example to explore issues relating to a factor hierarchy, which is not relevant to this paper. The second is the set of wild animals cases, used in [7], but since used also by other authors, including Bench-Capon and Sartor ([4],[5]), and Prakken ([9]). Here we extend the example of the wild animal cases by the inclusion of some other related cases not discussed in Berman and Hafner.

3.1 Prakken and Sartor's Domicile Example

The aim of the example used in Prakken and Sartor is to show how it is possible to reconstruct a case-based reasoning system, specifically HYPO, in terms of the framework provided by the defeasible logic developed in their earlier work. The issue is whether a stay in another country changes one's fiscal domicile with respect to income tax. They begin by identifying three dimensions:

- whether the applicant gave up his house in his original country of domicile;
- whether the applicant's company is based in the old or the new country;
- whether the applicant's stay in the new country has been long or short.

At this point they explicitly simplify matters by restricting each of these dimensions to two positions, one extreme value favouring the interpretation of change of fiscal domicile and the other extreme value favouring no change of fiscal domicile. They then make the move to factors. They make no use of prerequisites, and so all three dimensions seem to be taken as applicable to all cases, and each case will take one of the two positions. They thus get six factors:

- Pro change is that the old house was given up; con change is that it was kept.
- Pro change is that the taxpayer's company is based in the new country; con change, that it is based in the old country.
- Pro change is that stay is long; con change, that it is short.

In each instance, however, the dimension could have been seen as having a spectrum of values. Certainly the facts of the cases may exhibit variation. For example:

- gave up house: *sold-house, house-kept-occupied-by-family* [this could be made finer grain if we thought the relationship mattered], *rented-out-house, house-kept-unoccupied;*
- foreign company: *foreign-company, multi-national, foreign-subsidiary-of-domestic-company, domestic-company-with-foreign-offices, domestic-company;*
- duration: *number-of-months*.

An immediate problem arises. Once it is recognised that the situation may not fall at either of the two extremes, the knowledge engineer must decide *whether*, in such cases, one of the factors applies, and also *which* factor applies. Suppose the house has been rented out: should this be taken as giving up the house, and so a point *pro change*; as not giving up the house, and so *con change*; or should it be taken as neither, rendering the dimension inapplicable? It is understandable that Prakken and Sartor do not discuss this issue, since their concern is to illustrate a technical point, but were we building a practical system, we would have to answer such questions. In order to represent cases in terms of the dimensions, the knowledge engineer must be in a position to allocate these intermediate positions to one or other of the factors. But this is precisely the kind of point that might be raised in a case, and which therefore needs to be decided on the basis of authority. This then is the first problem: to use factors, the positions on the range of the dimension must be shoehorned into one of two factors. Once this is done in the representation, it cannot be undone or questioned in the operation of the system. Yet deciding where the line should be drawn seems to be a part of theory construction—certainly, courts are involved in this sort of theory construction—and something we would like to be an explicit subject of debate *within the system*.

The 1998 paper by Prakken and Sartor [8] makes use of factors to construct defeasible rules and to enable cases to establish priorities between rules. Essentially any case will give rise to three rules:

R1 : conjunction of pro-change factors present implies change

R2 : conjunction of con-change factors present implies no change

R3 : if decision was change, R1 > R2, otherwise R2 > R1

This is an appealing and simple way of deriving a set of rules and priorities among them from decided cases. But problems arise if we consider that the intermediate points on a dimension may mean that an outcome is favoured *to a certain extent*.

This presents a second problem. Suppose we draw the line for gave up house at *sold-house*, so that anything else will be a con-change factor. Now suppose we have a case with *house-kept-unoccupied* and *foreign-company*, decided no change. (Ignore for the moment duration: it may be intermediate so that neither duration factor applies). We would conclude that

$$\textit{kept-house-unoccupied} \rightarrow \textit{no change} > \textit{foreign-company} \rightarrow \textit{change}$$

Given a new case where the company was foreign and the house was kept occupied by adult children, we would have to conclude that again there was no change, since the cases cannot be distinguished on their factors. But we might not want to do that. Does this simply mean that we drew the line between *kept house* and *gave up house* in the wrong place, and that *occupied by adult children* should be treated as *gave up house*? We would say not; if we think of *gave up house* as actually selling the house, then

$$\textit{gave-up house} \rightarrow \textit{change} > \textit{short-duration} \rightarrow \textit{no change}$$

looks plausible. But, where *gave-up-house* is only to the extent that it is occupied by adult children, this might not be considered enough to defeat *short-duration*. In other words, in this comparison it seems that we should split the dimension differently, so that occupied by adult children counts as *kept-house-unoccupied*. Ignoring the possibility of several positions within the dimension means that we have to lump together distinguishable situations *in the same way in all comparisons*. But a given position in the range might favour a side sufficiently to defeat some rules but insufficiently to defeat others.

The third problem is factors in combination. If someone has been abroad for only a short time, the fact that the house is rented perhaps should not count against them. It takes time to sell a house, and it is perhaps sensible to rent it for a short period while arrangements for sale are made. If, however, the person has been abroad for a longer period, holding on to a property useable in the event of return suggests some possibility of return. Thus renting a house should count against change when, *but only when*, the duration exceeds a certain limit. Again there is a need to draw the line once, to cover all situations, whereas it may be appropriate to draw it differently in the context supplied by other factors.

There are therefore three reasons for preferring the analysis to recognise dimensions:

- The split into two positions may be hard to motivate: without an appropriate case we may not be able to justify drawing the line at any particular point;
- By conflating several positions along the dimension together we may get contradictory rule preferences;
- By conflating several positions together we are unable to give the factor a different import in different contexts.

3.2 The Wild Animal Cases

[7] discusses three cases concerning the interrupted pursuit of wild animals. These cases have also been used by Bench-Capon and Sartor (e.g. [4],[5]) and Prakken (e.g. [9]), as well as by [10]. A brief summary of these cases can be given as follows.

In all three cases, the plaintiff (P) was chasing wild animals, and the defendant (D) interrupted the chase, preventing P from capturing those animals. The issue to be decided is whether or not P has a legal remedy (a right to be compensated for the loss of the game) against D. In the first case, *Pierson v Post*, P was hunting a fox on open land in the traditional manner using horse and hound, when D killed and carried off the fox. In this case P was held to have no right to the fox because he had gained no possession of it. In the second case, *Keeble v Hickeringill*, P owned a pond and made his living by luring wild ducks there with decoys, shooting them, and selling them for food. Out of malice, D used guns to scare the ducks away from the pond. Here P won. In the third case, *Young v Hitchens*, both parties were commercial fisherman. While P was closing his nets, D sped into the gap, spread his own net and caught the fish. In this case P won.

Berman and Hafner identify five factors:

1. whether P had not gained possession of the animal (favours D);
2. whether the land was open (favours D);
3. whether the land was owned by P (favours P);
4. whether P was attempting to earn his living (favours P);
5. whether D was in competition with P (favours D).

Note that the second and third factors could be seen as the two extremes of a single dimension, as in Prakken and Sartor. The other three factors seem to come from different dimensions (although the presence of the fourth might be seen as a prerequisite for the fifth).

Using these factors, *Pierson* contains 1 and 2, *Keeble* contains 1, 3 and 4, and *Young* contains 1,2,4 and 5. On this analysis it seems odd that *Pierson* was litigated at all: surely the plaintiff must have thought there was something in his favour? Perhaps we should suspect that the statement in terms of factors has obliterated some important information? Let us look at the cases more closely.

In fact *Keeble* was the first case to be decided (in England, in 1707). Here the ownership of the land was considered crucial. Keeble could be said to own the ducks by "occupancy" even though he could not prevent them from leaving (until he had shot them). As quotations in Berman and Hafner make clear, factor 4 was also considered and used by the judges to support the plaintiff.

Pierson was tried in 1805 in New York. The decisions make it clear that P's claim was that pursuit gave him a right to the fox. Consider first the *Per Curiam* opinion by Tompkins in *Pierson v. Post*, 3 Caines 175 (N.Y.S.Ct. 1805), which was couched in terms of 'occupancy'; it suggests that *Keeble* had been introduced as a precedent. This opinion cites Justinian in saying "pursuit alone vests no property or right for the huntsman," and "even pursuit, accompanied by actual wounding" is not enough, "unless the animal be actually taken." It further cites Pufendorf: "a beast mortally wounded, or greatly maimed, cannot be fairly intercepted by another, whilst the pursuit of the person inflicting the wound continues" and concludes that "The foregoing authorities are decisive to shew, that mere pursuit gave Post no legal right to the fox."

Some contrary authorities are considered. Most past cases "have arisen between the huntsman and the owner of the land upon which beast *ferae naturae* have been apprehended" and are thus not relevant. (But note that this means in effect that the open land is favouring the plaintiff, not the defendant, since it excludes some potentially damaging precedents). It also cites Barbeyrac, who counters Pufendorf with : "actual bodily seizure is not... necessary to constitute possession of wild animals." The opinion agrees with Barbeyrac in so far as "actual bodily seizure is not indispensable" as a condition for possession, speculating that "on the contrary, mortal wounding... by one not abandoning pursuit, may,... be deemed possession..." since the pursuer "manifests an unequivocal intention of appropriating the animal..., has deprived him of his natural liberty, and brought him within his certain control." "So also, encompassing and securing animals with nets and toils, or otherwise intercepting them, in such a manner as to deprive them of their natural liberty, and render escape impossible, may justly be deemed to give possession of them to those persons who, by their industry and labour, have used such means of apprehending them." Finally it distinguishes *Keeble*: "in the report of the same case, 3 Salk. 9. Holt, Chief Justice, states that the ducks were in the plaintiff's decoy pond and *so in his possession*, from which it is obvious the court laid much stress in their opinion upon the plaintiff's possession of the ducks, *ratione soli*."

We should also consider the opinion of Livingston, who favoured the plaintiff. He held that if "on waste and uninhabited ground" then "in full pursuit" would be enough to count as possession, "so as to give greatest encouragement to the destruction of an animal, so cunning and ruthless". Livingston rejects Justinian as simply too old—Justinian was a Byzantine Emperor circa A.D. 550—an authority to carry weight, and acknowledges the difficulty in deciding where possession should begin: "I... feel great difficulty in determining, whether to acquire dominion over a thing, before in common, it be sufficient that we barely see it, or know where it is,... or whether, in the case of wild beasts, setting a trap, or lying in wait, or starting, or pursuing, be enough; or if actual wounding, or killing, or bodily tact and occupation be necessary." Finally he agrees with Barbeyrac: "[P]roperty in animals *ferae naturae*, may be acquired without bodily touch or manucaption, provided that the pursuer be within reach, or have *a reasonable prospect (which certainly existed here) of taking*" the beast. [our emphasis]

What does this tell us? First that Berman and Hafner were right to identify the failure of Pierson to gain possession as the decisive factor. On the other hand they cannot do justice to the range of positions that were considered; *bodily seizure* (from Barbeyrac), *mortal wounding* or *great maiming* (Pufendorf), *encompassing and securing animals with nets and toils* and *within certain control* (Tompkins), *in full pursuit* (Livingston), *setting a trap*, or *lying in wait*, or *starting* (Livingston). Both Tompkins and Livingston felt the need to draw a line along this range of possibilities. Both felt difficulty; Tompkin is sure that pursuit is not enough, but does not need to pronounce on wounding and maiming, since this did not apply in this case. Livingston, on the other hand will allow full pursuit, but refuses to be drawn on lesser degrees of contact. Where the line was to be drawn between possession and no possession was a central feature of the reasoning of both Tompkins and Livingston, but *they did not draw it*, contenting themselves with a conviction that the particular case was inside it. Confronted with a case featuring great maiming we would need to draw it ourselves. But this is precisely what we cannot do within the five factor framework; the line is drawn when the case is represented and removed from discussion.

A second feature is the question of the open land. First we should note that this was not seen as favouring the defendant. Second, we should see that the possibility of the defendant owning the land was raised by some past cases which were discounted on this ground. Third, in *Keeble*, land ownership was important, not because of the land itself, (since the defendant operated remotely and committed no trespass) but because it conferred possession of the ducks alighting on it. Thus to determine possession, as well as the hunting considerations conferring degrees of possession in *Pierson*, we need to consider also the property considerations that conferred possession in *Keeble*. Following [10], a dimension for possession might then look like:

- Extreme PRO-D = feral & free: under no control by P or anyone else
- animal is seen or started by P
- animal happens to be on P's site (walks through, alights, swims)
- animal is attracted onto P's site (e.g., to visit deerlicks, birdfeeders, food-left-by-P)
- animal is lured onto P's site (e.g., decoys)
- P sets a trap or lies in wait for animal
- animal is hotly pursued by P (e.g., fox/hare/deer hunting)

- animal temporarily confined by P (e.g., in paddock)
- animal wounded by P (e.g., shot, stunned)
- animal is mortally wounded or maimed
- animal caught by P (e.g., in net, trap, toils)
- Extreme PRO-P= animal is killed or totally controlled by P (e.g., in P's gunny bag)

Obviously both the positions and their ordering is something of a matter of conjecture; we would need some more decisions with more definite pronouncements to have any confidence in this ordering. We can, however, say that *Keeble* and *Pierson* together suggest that we have ordered hot pursuit and attracted to the plaintiff's site correctly.

If we still want to include land as a consideration separate from its impact on ownership, we probably need a range of positions here, starting from the extreme pro-d position where the defendant holds the freehold and progressing towards the extreme pro-p position where the plaintiff holds the freehold through a variety of leasehold arrangements and degrees of common and state ownership.

We can also see intermediate positions in the fourth factor. The court was well disposed towards Keeble because he was pursuing his livelihood and the defendant was acting out of malice. But Livingston was disposed towards the fox hunter because he was doing something beneficial to the livelihood of others. Perhaps we need a dimension to capture a range of motives here, ranging from the economic, through the socially beneficial and innocent pleasure, through to malice.

We will not say much about *Young*, except to note that if we use the dimension for possession above, whether factor 1 applies to this case or not seems to depend on whether the fish could have escaped him if not intercepted by Hitchens.

None of this is intended to suggest that Berman and Hafner's analysis was incorrect or superficial. They have chosen their factors and used them to construct a theory, which is both explanatory of the cases and plausibly based on the decisions. This is exactly what we believe reasoning with cases to be about. The point is, however, that other theories can be constructed, but this possibility depends critically on the availability of the dimensions, so that we can describe the cases differently rather than limiting our arguments to what is available from the factors presented in their theory. Thus a good deal of the reasoning has been pre-empted once we have selected the factors and applied them to the cases. We need something like dimensions if this part of the theory construction is to be brought out into the open.

We will conclude this section by mentioning some other cases that have some bearing on the issues involved in this domain.

Consider first *Ghen v Rich* (Mass 1881). Here a finback whale washed ashore at Brewster, Mass. Ellis found it, and sold it by auction to Rich, who stripped off the blubber and tried out the oil. According to local custom, Ellis should have sent word to Provincetown, where Ghen would have identified his bomb-lance, claimed his whale, and paid Ellis a fee. The courts found for the plaintiff here on the basis of established custom in the whaling industry: "[T]he iron holds the whale... a custom which embraced an entire business, and had been concurred in for a long time by every one engaged in the trade." The result differs from *Young*, where it appears no established custom existed in that trade. Customs are, however, important in other areas. For example, in England all swans and sturgeons are the property of the monarch, and must be offered to the monarch if caught by accident or design. Where customs exist, different considerations relating to the possession dimension clearly apply: this could be reflected through the prerequisite slots in a dimension based system.

Consider next *Conti v ASPCA* (NY 1974). Chester, a parrot used by ASPCA for educational exhibits, flew the coop, was offered food by P and finally entered P's home, where P placed it in a cage. D removed parrot from P's home. Here it was held that Chester was a domesticated animal and thus the rule of ferae naturae did not apply and ASPCA was the true owner with the right to regain possession. This gives us another consideration for our possession dimension: possession through domestication. This suggests a certain pessimism with respect to ever fully articulating the positions on a dimension: the next case may always throw up a new, unanticipated, position.

In our discussion of the wild animals cases we have concentrated on the difficulty in drawing the line through a range of positions, which is necessary if we are to work with factors. As we have seen, drawing this line is regarded by judges as a central part of their responsibility; and also, once drawn, it greatly limits the theories that can be constructed.

4 Discussion

A major difficulty with reasoning with cases is that we need to compare cases so that we can apply conclusions from one case to another case. But the facts of each case are really unique. So we have to find a way of assimilating unlike cases to give a basis of comparison. In the animals cases we have a fox, fowl and fish in disputed possession. When we construct a dimension of possession, we say that any kind of animal may be treated in the same way (even though we may later have to exclude whales and domesticated parrots). But a dimension has a range of positions, and constructing and ordering this range involves classifying different situations into the same position within that range. When we move to factors we map this range of possibilities into an even smaller range, thus grouping several positions on a dimension together. When we use the flexibility of dimensions, we avoid the coalescing and washing out of distinctions that happen with factors. If we go on to allow factors to be mapped into societal values, as in [5], we can, assuming different factors can promote the same societal values, treat cases with different factors promoting the same values as comparable, erasing the differences between cases still further, but again requiring different situations to be treated as if they were alike. Since the smaller the range of the items we map the cases into, the more definite are the comparisons that can be made, the temptation is to aim for the smallest set of items one can get away with in a particular situation. Constructing a theory is in part just making such a set of decisions about what can be compared, and on what basis. But each mapping involves some compression of information, elimination of distinctions, and judgement as to where a line is to be drawn; therefore if we wish to allow a fuller range of alternative theories to be constructed we need to retain the ability to draw the lines differently. Our view is that starting from dimensions rather than factors is essential if we are to retain that ability.

Dimensions, we believe, make possible the following desirable things not possible with factors:

- The same fact situation can be used by both parties to a dispute. Recall that in *Pierson*, Livingston argued for the plaintiff because he was in pursuit of the fox, whereas Tompkins argued against the plaintiff because he was *only* in pursuit of the fox. If we had a factor to represent the situation, it could favour one side only.
- We can choose whether we think a situation should be treated like another or not: for example whether we believe maiming is enough to count as possession, or whether we think mortal wounding is required. With factors these decisions are made for us.
- We can ascribe different degrees of strength to different positions within the dimension. Earning one's living might overcome lack of possession, whereas altruism might not, even if in other contexts a factor *acting from a socially beneficial motive* might be what was wanted. Once both positions have been classified as making a factor present, the possibly to distinguish these different strengths is lost.

We believe that these are significant benefits, but there is a price to pay. Factors are very much simpler to handle than dimensions, and, when producing an implementation, this is an important consideration. Moreover the investigation of other features, such as the factor hierarchy of CATO and the mapping from cases to rules of [8] is facilitated by working with the simpler notion. Once, however, the insights have been gained from working with the simpler model, we are in position to re-introduce the complications. For example Bench-Capon and Sartor ([6]) provides an extension of the model of [5] that brings dimensions within the theory construction process. This exercise could not have been done without first constructing the simpler model, and it also serves to indicate the considerable complications that using dimensions introduces if an explicit set of defeasible rules is to be derived from precedent cases.

5 Conclusion

In order to understand an area it is often necessary to simplify so that the various difficulties can be attacked one by one. That we learn logic by first understanding propositional calculus, then first order predicate calculus, and only then approach exotic and modal logics, is a good example of this. Only when one stage has been thoroughly understood can we move on to the next. Moreover, each of the simplifications is *useful*: for some purposes propositional calculus suffices, and for many purposes predicate calculus is enough. Only when we need to address particular problems do we need our most elaborate machinery.

Reasoning with cases is a similarly complicated affair, which would inevitably overwhelm us were we to attempt to capture all its richness at once. Over the last decade much progress has been made in modelling reasoning with cases, and the simplification of dimensions into factors has played an important role in moving the area forward. Also, for some purposes, the simplification may be benign; for example factors may be adequate if we wish to build a system that will apply a settled theory. To the extent that we can be confident that the knowledge engineer is in a position to make the right decisions as to the factors to use and the conditions for their presence, to that extent we have no need to require dimensions to be manipulated. But if we want to capture some aspects of reasoning with cases, factors are, as we hope we have shown, no substitute for dimensions. Just as some kinds of sound logical argument cannot be expressed in propositional calculus, so some kinds of legal argument turn on handling dimensions. It is the very usefulness of factors, in permitting our current level of understanding of the aspects of reasoning with cases that they can capture, that allows for the reintroduction of the associated with dimensions that will allow us to explore these additional aspects of the problem.

As an idea, dimensions have a long history, although they have been little explored in most recent years. They should not be seen as part of the history of the subject—we see the future of modelling reasoning with cases as beginning with their revival.

References

[1] Aleven, V. Teaching Case Based Argumentation Through an Example and Models. PhD Thesis. The University of Pittsburgh,1997.

[2] Ashley, K.D., and Rissland, E.L.. A Case Based Approach to Modelling Legal Expertise. *IEEE Expert*, (1988). pp. 70-77.

[3] Ashley, K. D. Modeling Legal Reasoning, MIT Press, Cambridge.

[4] Bench-Capon, T.J.M., and Sartor, G. Using Values and Theories to Resolve Disagreement in Law. In J. Breuker, R. Leenes and R. Winkels (eds),Legal Knowledge and Information Systems: Jurix 2000. IOS Press, Amsterdam (2000). pp. 73-84.

[5] Bench-Capon, T.J.M., and Sartor, G. Theory Based Explanation of Case Law Domains. In Proceedings of the Eighth International Conference on AI and Law. ACM Press: New York, (2000). pp.12-21.

[6] Bench-Capon, T.J.M. and Sartor, G., (submitted). A Model of Legal Reasoning with Cases Incorporating Theories and Values. Submitted to *Artificial Intelligence*.

[7] Berman, D.H., and Hafner, C.L. Representing Teleological Structure in Case Based Reasoning: The Missing Link. In Proceedings of the Fourth International Conference on AI and Law. (1993). ACM Press, New York.pp. 50-59.

[8] Prakken, H. & Sartor, G. Modelling Reasoning with Precedents in a Formal Dialogue Game. *Artificial Intelligence and Law*, **6**: (1998). 231-287.

[9] Prakken, H. (2000). An exercise in formalising teleological case based reasoning. In J. Breuker, R. Leenes, and R. Winkels (eds.),Legal Knowledge and Information Systems: Jurix 2000,IOS Press, Amsterdam (2000). pp. 49-57.

[10] Rissland, E.L., & Ashley, K.D. A Note on Dimensions and Factors. To appear in *Artificial Intelligence and Law* (2001).

[11] Rissland, E.L., & Skalak, D.B. CABARET: Statutory Interpretation in a Hybrid Architecture,*International Journal of Man-Machine Studies (IJMMS)*, **34** , (1991) 839-887..

[12] Rissland, E.L., Skalak, D.B., & Friedman, M.T. BankXX: Supporting Legal Arguments through Heuristic Retrieval. *Artificial Intelligence and Law*. **4**, (1996) 1-71.

[13] Rissland, E.L., Valcarce, E.M., & Ashley, K.D. (1984). Explaining and Arguing with Examples. Proceedings Fourth National on Artificial Intelligence (AAAI-84), Austin, TX,. (1984) pp. 288-294.

A Quantitative Approach to Theory Coherence

Trevor J.M. Bench-Capon
Department of Computer Science
The University of Liverpool
Liverpool
UK
t.j.m.bench-capon@csc.liv.ac.uk

Giovanni Sartor
Department of Law
The Queen's University of Belfast
Belfast
Northern Ireland
sartor@cirfid.unibo.it

Abstract. In this paper we describe an approach which can attempt to give a quantitative measure of the coherence of legal theories. Starting from the notion of a theory as described in [3], we show how some ideas of Thagard can be adapted to give a measure of how coherent such a theory is. Some experiments, using the wild animals domain and theories concerning it discussed in [3] are described. We then identify some issues, both of detail and principle, that are raised by this work.

1 Introduction

In [3] we articulated a view of reasoning with cases as a process of theory construction, evaluation and application. On this view, reasoning with cases involves the construction of competing theories to explain the body of decided cases, evaluating these theories to select the best, and then applying that theory to new cases. That paper focussed primarily on the components of theories and how they could be constructed, but we did offer also a brief discussion of what made one theory better than another, detailing several aspects which together make up the *coherence* of a theory. That discussion, however, used only qualitative considerations. In this paper we will explore an approach to providing a quantitative measure of theory coherence.

Our approach is inspired by the work of [5]. In that book Thagard attempts to account for concept change in science in terms of more coherent theories replacing less coherent ones. His essential idea is to represent the evidence to be accounted for by a theory and the tenets of a theory as nodes connected by links representing support and conflict. A set of initial values (between 1 and -1) is assigned to these nodes, and these values are then propagated, support links increasing the values of nodes, and conflict links decreasing them. Moreover, links are subject to a rate of decay so that isolated nodes decrease in value. This propagation is continued through a number of cycles, until the values of the nodes stabilise. In Thagard's interpretation of this process, nodes which end with a high activation can be considered part of a coherent, and hence acceptable theory, while those with a low activation do not form part, and so should be rejected. In this paper we will follow a slightly different approach, which is

Trevor J.M. Bench-Capon and Giovanni Sartor, 'A Quantitative Approach to Theory Coherence' in Bart Verheij, Arno R. Lodder, Ronald P. Loui and Antoinette J. Muntjewerff (eds.), *Legal Knowledge and Information Systems. Jurix 2001: The Fourteenth Annual Conference.* Amsterdam: IOS Press, 2001, pp. 53-62.

more in line with our adversarial view of legal argument. Our purpose is not to extract the best theory out of the body of existing evidence and hypotheses, but to measure the comparative coherence of competing theories. Therefore, we do not see nodes in a theory having a low level of activation as rejected: they remain in the theory but lower its overall coherence.

We will adapt this idea to legal theories as described in [3]. In section 2 we will recapitulate some of the essential ideas of that paper, the example cases used and some of the example theories concerning them given there. Section 3 will give details of the nodes links that need to be included to provide a graph structure representing a theory, and the program used to propagate support and conflict through these nodes and links. Section 4 will describe the behaviour of the program with respect to the theories given in section 2. This work throws up a numbers of issues of detail and principle. These will be discussed in the concluding section.

2 The Example Domain

The example used in [3] was based on three example cases concerning the pursuit of wild animals used in [4]. In all three cases, the plaintiff (π) was chasing wild animals, and the defendant (δ) interrupted the chase, preventing π from capturing those animals. The issue to be decided is whether π has a legal remedy (a right to be compensated for the loss of the game) against δr not. In the first case, *Pierson v Post*, π was hunting a fox on open land in the traditional manner using horse and hound when δ killed and carried off the fox. In this case π was held to have no right to the fox because he had gained no possession of it. In the second case, *Keeble v Hickeringill*, π owned a pond and made his living by luring wild ducks there with decoys, shooting them, and selling them for food. Out of malice δ used guns to scare the ducks away from the pond. Here π won. In the third case, *Young v Hitchens*, both parties were commercial fisherman. While π was closing his nets, δ sped into the gap, spread his own net and caught the fish. In this case δ on.

A theory can be seen [3] as consisting of five elements; a set of cases, a set of factors (in the sense used in CATO [1]) used to describe those cases, a set of defeasible rules relating those factors to case outcomes, a set of preferences between the rules, and a set of preferences between values justifying the rule preferences.

We used four factors in the construction of our theories:

- πLiv = π was pursuing his livelihood (Keeble, Young), favouring Π
- $\pi Land$ = π was on his own land (Keeble), favouring Π
- $\pi Nposs$ = π was not in possession of the animal (Pierson, Keeble and Young), favouring Δ
- δLiv = δ was pursuing his livelihood (Young), favouring Δ

The factors were based of three values:

Llit = Less Litigation, promoted by $\pi Nposs$
Prop = Enjoyment of property rights, promoted by $\pi Land$
Mprod = More productivity, promoted by πLiv and δLiv.

On this basis we constructed a number of possible theories to explain the domain. The assumption here is that *Young* is as yet undecided, so we are trying to explain different outcomes for *Young*. Four of these theories are summarised in Table 3. The outcome for Young is shown in brackets in the cases column; arbitrary preferences are marked with an asterisk.

Our assessment of the theories was that T4 was best, followed by T3, which makes arbitrary assumptions, followed by T2, which is unsafe because it includes too few factors, followed by T1, which includes too few cases. This qualitative assessment will be used as the basis for discussion of the quantitative assessments in the experiments below.

3 Implementation of the Approach

In order to apply Thagard's method, we need to represent theories as graphs. The nodes of these graphs will correspond to certain elements of theories, cases, rules, preferences between rules, and preferences between values. Factors and values themselves are not included in the graphs, since they are intended to be not the propositions of a theory, but rather the vocabulary out of which the theory is constructed.

Table 1: Summary of Theories in [3]

Theory	Cases	Factors	Rules	Rule Prefs	Value Prefs
T1	Pierson Young (d)	$\pi Nposs$	r1: $\pi Nposs \rightarrow \Delta$		
T2	Pierson Keeble Young (p)	$\pi Nposs$ πLiv	r1: $\pi Nposs \rightarrow \Delta$ r2: $\pi Liv \rightarrow \Pi$	r2 > r1	Mprod> LLit
T3	Pierson Keeble Young (d)	$\pi Nposs$ πLiv $\pi Land$	r1: $\pi Nposs \rightarrow \Delta$ r2: $\pi Liv \rightarrow \Pi$ r3: $\pi Land \rightarrow \Pi$ r4: πLiv & $\pi Land \rightarrow \Pi$	r4 > r1 r1 > r2*	Llit > Mprod* Mprod + Msec > LLit
T4	Pierson Keeble Young (d)	$\pi Nposs$ πLiv δLiv	r1: $\pi Nposs \rightarrow \Delta$ r2: $\pi Liv \rightarrow \Pi$ r5: δLiv $\rightarrow \Delta$ r6: $\pi Nposs$ & δLiv $\rightarrow \Delta$	r2 > r1 r6 > r2	Llit > Mprod Mprod + Llit > Mprod

The nodes will be connected according to whether they are used together in theory construction or application. Rules are constructed from, and applied in, cases. Rule preferences are constructed from cases and used to defeat the application of rules in particular cases. Value preferences are derived from, and allow the derivation of rule preferences. All these therefore represent connections.

We also need to recognise that connections may have different strengths. First, Thagard suggests that conflicting links should be given a higher strength than supporting links [5], if convergence is to be achieved. Second, if a factor contains several factors for the same side, it could support several rules. For example, if a case contains factors A and B and was decided for the plaintiff, then it could be explained by any of the three rules A→P, B → P or A&B→P. Clearly the case will give full support to the inclusive rule, which is entailed by the other two rules, but its support for the two primitive rules must be divided between them. In all these cases, support is considered bi-directional. Finally we note that the rule A→P logically implies A&B→P. Therefore there should be a very strong connection between them, but running only in that direction.

The program was implemented in two parts. One part holds a model of a particular theory, describing the nodes, the connections between them and the strength of these connections. Two lists of connections are maintained for each node, one containing the positive connections, and one containing the hostile connections. Note that in the case of a hostile connection between a rule and a case, the connection can itself be in conflict with a rule preference. These connections need therefore to be also modelled as nodes, supported by their rule, and attacked by the preference which defeats them. Again these links are uni-directional. The second part was a generic program to propagate values through these models. The algorithm is fairly straightforward. Its psuedo-code is as follows:

```
For each node
    find current node value
    set temp node value := node value
    find connections
    apply decay factor
    for each supporting node
      temp node value := temp node value +
              connected node value * strength
    for each hostile node
      temp node value := temp node value -
              connected node value * strength
    if temp node value > 1 then temp node value := 1
    if temp node value ¡ -1 then temp node value := -1
    if node is hostile link and temp node value ¡ 0 then
              temp node value = 0
    store temp node value
for each node
    node value := temp node value
```

Note that the values of hostile links can never drop below 0; a defeated rule cannot support a case.

The above algorithm was embedded in a simple interface, which after each cycle displays the node values, and executes another cycle or halts as the user requires. A history list of all node values is maintained. After the last cycle a number of statistics such as the average node value is produced.

4 Experimental Results

The program was executed on four models of theories, representing the four theories in Table 3.

We needed to choose a number of specific values to represent connection strengths. The values used are shown in Table 2.

In all cases, except where mentioned below, nodes representing decided cases were initialised to 1, and all other nodes to 0.

Table 2: Parameters Used in the Experiments

Parameter	Value
Decay factor	0.1
Normal Support Link	0.4
Entailment support Link	0.8
Conflict Link	0.6

4.1 Theory 1

This is the simplest theory comprising only two cases and a single rule. The connections and their initial weights are shown in Table 3:

Table 3: Connections in Theory 1

Nodes	Pierson	Young	r1
Pierson			0.4
Young			0.4
r1	0.4	0.4	

Table 3 shows the initial weights of the connections in Theory 1. Each row shows the connections from the node in the left hand column from the nodes in the column header. An empty cell indicates no connection. Tables 4-6 provide similar information for theories 2-4 respectively.

Executing this model results in all 3 nodes attaining the value 1 in seven cycles. This suggests that the theory is entirely coherent. We should expect this, since the problem with this theory is not in how well it hangs together, but that is does not account for some of the cases.

4.2 Theory 2

Theory 2 introduces the third case, and an additional rule. There is now a conflict between the rules which is resolved by a rule preference, and a corresponding value preference.

The connections, and their initial values is shown in Table 4

This model converges after 10 cycles. All the nodes achieve 1, except the hostile connections between r1 and Keeble and Young, resulting in an average activation of 0.8. Essentially the theory is can be seen as coherent, but requiring a rule to be defeated in two of its applications.

4.3 Theory 3

Theory 3 improves on Theory 2 by including an extra factor, and hence extra rules. It contains 3 cases, 4 rules, 2 rule preferences (one of which is arbitrary) and two value preferences (again, one arbitrary). The connections and their initial weights in theory 3 are shown in

Table 4: Connections in Theory 2

Nodes	Pierson	Keeble	Young	r1	r2	r2>r1	Mprod > Llit	r1→ -Keeble	r1→ -Young
Pierson				0.4					
Keeble				0.6	0.4	0.4			
Young				0.6	0.4				
r1	0.4	0.6	0.6						
r2		0.4	0.4						
r2>r1		0.4					0.4	0.6	0.6
Mprod > Llit						0.4			
r1→ -Keeble						0.6			
r1→ -Young						0.6			

Table 5. Note here we have some uni-directional columns: thus, for example, a connection runes from r2 to r4, but not *vice versa.*

The execution of this model converges in 11 cycles. 3 nodes, the two arbitrary preferences and Young, end as -1. Two nodes, the attack of r1 on Keeble and attack of the arbitrary preference on the attack of r2 on Young become 0. All others become 1. The overall activation is 0.5.

From this we can see that the resort to arbitrary preferences has made the theory much less coherent than its predecessors. Indeed the preferred nodes of the theory after propagation suggest a victory for the plaintiff in Young.

Table 5: Connections in Theory 3

Nodes	Pie	Kee	You	r1	r2	r3	r4	r4 > r1	r1 > r2	L > Mp	Mp + Ms > L
Pie				0.4							
Kee				0.6	0.2	0.2	0.4	0.4			
You				0.4	0.6						
r1	0.4		0.4								
r2		0.4									
r3		0.4									
r4		0.4			0.8	0.8					
r4 > r1		0.4									0.4
r1 > r2										0.4	
L > Mp									0.4		
MP +Ms > LL		0.4						0.4			
r1→ -Kee								0.6			
r2→ -You									0.6		

4.4 *Theory 4*

The final, and most elaborate theory is Theory 4. This theory contains 3 cases, 4 rules, two preferences and two value preferences. In this case the value preference is not arbitrary, but rather is taken as axiomatic, since the less preferred value is a proper subset of the preferred value. This time, therefore, this value preference will be initialised as 1. The connections and their initial weights are shown in Table 6.

If we run this model it converges after 8 cycles, with an average activation of only 0.47. In this case two nodes, those representing the defeated applications of r1 to Keeble and r2 to Young go to zero. The rule preferences are enough to defeat these. However, r5 , r6 and Young also go to -1, which is not what we anticipated. The reason for this is that the decay factor is such that r1 does not grow sufficiently quickly to counter the negative impact of the decay on Young, on r5 and r6. Because there is no independent evidence for r5, its impact on r6 and Young is rather negative. This could be interpreted as suggesting that a factor introduced solely to explain the current case is detrimental to the theory. (An alternative suggestion would be that values should be included in the model to support the introduction of new factors, but this would require a different approach to representing the theories as graphs from that taken in this paper).

The crucial element in producing this behaviour is the decay factor. This can be seen as representing the degree of intrinsic believability or otherwise of propositions. The higher the decay factor the closer must be the connection of a proposition with some evidence, otherwise the scepticism represented by the decay factor will overcome the distant evidence.

Table 6: Connections in Theory 4

Nodes	Pie	Kee	You	r1	r2	r5	r6	r2 > r1	r6 > r2	Mp > L	Mp+L > Mp
Pie				0.4							
Kee				0.6	0.4			0.4			
You				0.2	0.6	0.2	0.4				
r1	0.4		0.4								
r2		0.4									
r5			0.4								
r6			0.4	0.8		0.8					
r2 > r1		0.4								0.4	
r6 > r2											0.4
L > Mp		0.4						0.4			
MP +Ms > LL									0,4		
r1→ -Kee								0.6			
r2→ -You									0.6		

Suppose, however, that we are somewhat less sceptical, and more prepared to take beliefs on trust. This would mean a smaller decay factor. If we reduce the decay factor to 0.05, we find that all of Young, r5 and r6 go to 1 after 18 cycles, with an average activation of 0.87. This highlights the significance of the precise choice of parameters, but given this choice this theory comes out as superior to theories 2 and 3.

4.5 *A Final Experiment*

For our last experiment we constructed a model which contained essentially the union of all the preceding theories. As well as Keeble and Pierson it contained two versions of Young, one with the outcome π and one with the outcome δ. All six rules were included, together with the possible preferences between them, and the various value preferences which would licence them. All rules were connected to the cases according to their applicability to the cases.

In this model cases were set to 1, and value preferences to 1 if the lesser value was a proper subset of the preferred value, to -1 if the preferred value was a proper subset of the lesser value, and 0 otherwise. Connections were given values as in Table 2.

Obviously the theory represented by this model is *not* coherent. The idea here was to step through the model to see which cases and rules were believed and which disbelieved. In some ways this is closer to Thagrard's original use of the technique, in which he always represented competing theories in a single model.

Two runs were performed, one with a decay factor of 0.1 and one with a decay factor of 0.5.

The results for the cases and rules are given in Table 7.

Table 7: Results for Combined Model

Node	decay = 0.1: 15 iterations	decay = 0.05: 15 iterations
Pierson	1	1
Keeble	1	1
Young(π)	-1	-1
Young(δ)	-1	1
r1	0.33	1
r2	1	1
r3	-1	-1
r4	-1	1
r5	1	1
r6	-1	1

Consider first the sceptical version. Here we end up disbelieving both outcomes for Young. Moreover, the disbelief in Young extends itself to the rules which could establish the conclusion. Doubt is even present in case of the perfectly well founded r1, despite the presence of Pierson. Note also that it is r2, that the land is owned which is held to explain Pierson; r3 is doubted by its contamination from Young.

The less sceptical version gives a theory we might prefer. Now we believe the outcome δ or Young. Note, however, that again r2 is the key element in Keeble: r3, the plaintiff earning his livelihood, is not considered sufficient to explain Keeble for π. Is this reasonable? It probably does go against the analysis of [4], but does accord with some readings of the original decisions (see [2]).

Probably we should not try to draw very definite conclusions from this small experiment, but it does suggest intriguing possibilities which would need to explored in the context of larger models.

5 Issues and Future Work

From a limited set of experiments performed on a small domain, probably not too much can be concluded. None the less, two surprising (at least to the experimenters) points arose.

- The issue relating to the decay factor called into question the practice of using a factor present only in the current case;

- The final experiment suggested that it was the ownership of the land which was crucial in Keeble. Our original theories did not take this view, but it is arguable, and worthy of consideration.

This work raises a number of questions which require further exploration:

- The program requires us to choose a number of values for certain parameters; the decay factor, the weights initially assigned to support and conflict links, and the initial values for our case nodes. Changing these parameters can significantly affect the outcome. We need to do some systematic investigation of these effects.

- We have a number of different types of link. In our initial study we used a higher value for conflict links that normal support links, and a higher value still where support can be seen as logical inference. Again there is scope for distinguishing more kinds of link, and changing these relative weights.

- In a large body of cases there will be cases which do not fit with the theory, either because the decisions have been superseded, or because they were "rogue" decisions. For our initial experiment, we used only a consistent set of cases. We need to further explore the effects of aberrant cases. We also need to consider setting different initial values to represent the different importance of cases, according to their recently, the seniority of the court and the like.

- Considering activation alone seems not to reflect adequately the explanatory power of the theory, or the simplicity of the theory. We need to consider how we can combine the activation measure with measures of these aspects; for example a positive effects from the number of cases nodes included in the theory, and an adverse effect from the total number of nodes.

- The models used in the experiments derive their connections from an idea of which nodes are used to construct other nodes in theory construction, and which nodes are applied to explain and derive other nodes during theory application. We have already begun work on a more formal and disciplined account of how theories can be transformed into graphs representing the theory and the explanation and inference relations within it. This account will be used to give a stronger rationale for the connections in the theory models.

- In general we need to conduct further exploration through experiments on larger models, on models constructed with different views on connections, and with different values for the various parameters.

We find this approach interesting and holding promise of more interesting results. The question, of course, arises as to whether the approach has any cognitive validity with respect to the ways in which lawyers evaluate theories. Once the technical questions above have been answered, some kind of empirical study will be required to see how far the judgements on theories given by this approach can be seen as reflecting a legal consensus.

References

[1] Aleven, V. (1997). *Teaching Case Based Argumentation Through an Example and Models.* PhD Thesis. The University of Pittsburgh.

[2] Bench-Capon and Rissland (2001) *Back to the Future: Dimensions Revisited.* Submitted to JURIX 2001.

[3] Bench-Capon, T.J.M., and Sartor, G., (2001). Theory Based Explanation of Case Law Domains. In *Proceedings of the Eighth International Conference on AI and Law,* 12-21. ACM Press: New York.

[4] Berman, D.H., and Hafner, C.L., (1993). Representing Teleological Structure in Case Based Reasoning: The Missing Link. In *Proceedings of the Fourth International Conference on AI and Law,* 50-59. ACM Press, New York.

[5] Thagard, P. 1992. *Conceptual Revolutions.* Princeton (NJ): Princeton University Press.

Towards the Application of Association Rules for Defeasible Rule Discovery

Guido Governatori
Cooperative Information Systems Research Centre, Queensland University of Technology, Brisbane, Queensland, Australia
g.governatori@qut.edu.au

Andrew Stranieri
Donald Berman Laboratory for Information Technology and Law, La Trobe University, Bundoora, Victoria, Australia
stranier@cs.latrobe.edu.au

Abstract. In this paper we investigate the feasibility of Knowledge Discovery from Databases (KDD) in order to facilitate the discovery of defeasible rules that represent the ratio decidendi underpinning legal decision making. Moreover we will argue in favour of Defeasible Logic as an appropriate formal system in which the extracted principles should be encoded.

1 Introduction

One of the main and most controversial issues in the legal domain is the identification of the ratio decidendi. In other words, given a collection of similar cases we want to determine the principles (rules) leading to the adjudication of the cases. On the other hand the defeasibility of normative reasoning is a very well established phenomenon, so the rules (principles) extracted from the cases should be defeasible and we have to identify the appropriate non-monotonic reasoning mechanism.

The central aim of this paper is to demonstrate that the field of knowledge discovery from databases (KDD) can be applied to facilitate the discovery of defeasible rules that represent the ratio decidendi underpinning legal decision making. According to [13] KDD techniques can be grouped into four categories;

- Classification. The aim of classification techniques is to group data into predefined categories such as 'pro-plaintiff' or 'pro-defendant'. KDD classification techniques have been applied to law by [33], [32], [35], [20] and [5].
- Clustering. The aim of clustering techniques is to analyze data in order to group the data meaningfully. Clustering techniques have been applied to the law by [29], [27], [19], [31], [8], [34], [24] and [10].
- Series Analysis. The aim of series analysis to discover sequences within the data. Very few studies have been performed that analyze sequences of data in law. The study by [28] is an exception.

Guido Governatori and Andrew Stranieri, 'Towards the Application of Association Rules for Defeasible Rule Discovery' in Bart Verheij, Arno R. Lodder, Ronald P. Loui and Antoinette J. Muntjewerff (eds.), *Legal Knowledge and Information Systems. Jurix 2001: The Fourteenth Annual Conference*. Amsterdam: IOS Press, 2001, pp. 63-75.

- Association. The objective of association techniques is to discover ways in which data elements are associated with other data elements. For example, an association between the gender of litigants and the outcome of their cases may surprise analysts and stimulate hypotheses to explain the phenomena. Association techniques have not been applied to law to the same extent as classification and clustering techniques. [30] have illustrated that association rule generators can highlight interesting associations in a small dataset in family law. In that study, the Apriori algorithm advanced by [1] was applied to suggest hypotheses for future investigation. The present study differs in that it applies association rules generated directly from data to facilitate the discovery of defeasible rules.

One of the main applications of the KDD process is the discovery of rules (principles) from a set of relevant cases. It is indeed customary in Common Law to examine precedents in order to extract the ratio decidendi, and very often the principles leading to the adjudication can be expressed as a set of defeasible rules. However, it is seldom the case that precedents consist only of facts; more often the facts are supplemented by some principles. In some cases the explicitly listed principles are not enough to justify the conclusions. Thus the proposed methodology can be used to identify hidden principles.

In this study we represent legal reasoning using defeasible logic. First of all Defeasible Logic has been developed by Nute [25, 26] over several years with a particular concern about computational efficiency (indeed, its efficiency is linear cf. [22]) and ease of implementation (nowadays several implementations exist [9, 23] and some of them can deal with theories consisting of over 100,000 propositional rules [23]). In [3] it was shown that Defeasible logic is flexible enough to deal with several intuitions of non-monotonic reasoning, and it has been applied to legal reasoning [4] and legal negotiation [16]. Moreover various variants of Defeasible Logic have been characterised in terms of argumentation semantics [17, 18]; thus it is possible to establish correspondences with other non-monotonic systems for legal reasoning.

Defeasible rules are sourced from regulations, statutes, precedents and expert heuristics. This is a very manually intensive task that involves skilled knowledge engineers and experts. As a consequence, the knowledge acquisition phase is typically extensive. The objective of the present study is to apply KDD so as to automatically suggest plausible defeasible rules. This will facilitate knowledge engineer-expert interaction and lead to the development of improved knowledge bases in less time.

Often, in the knowledge acquisition phase, the focus is not on the discovery of rules. The principles are known, but we have to identify the most appropriate rules for the case at hand, especially when the rules are conflicting. In such cases we have to establish a preference order among available rules. KDD techniques explored in this study can help to identify rule preferences.

Another benefit in the application of KDD to facilitate the generation of defeasible rules involves the validation of decision making practice against explicitly given normative codes. Both precedents and statutes are frequently subject to opposite interpretations; thus a method to determine rules from cases can be used to see whether an interpretation corresponds to actual legal practice. Finally the same approach can be applied to the measure the degree of legal efficacy.

[21] describes the application of KDD in the form of inductive logic programming (ILP) to learning in two settings, predictive and descriptive. The aim of an ILP approach for predictive discovery is to induce a theory that explains positive and negative examples and background knowledge. This has been applied to learning default rules by [12]. The descriptive setting usually includes only positive examples and relaxes the strict notion of explanation. This enables ILP to be applied to describe patterns in a dataset that meet criteria such as associativity by enhancing algorithms for generating association rules [11]. Although ILP has been applied to discover default rules and also to enhance the discovery of association rules, ILP is not used in this study. Instead, association rules that are discovered using conventional algorithms are applied to help identify plausible groups of defeasible rules.

The KDD technique known as Association Rules is described in the next section of this paper. Following that, Defeasible Logic is described. In the subsequent section the application of association rules to facilitate the identification of useful defeasible rules will be discussed with examples from a hypothetical data set constructed for the purpose.

2 Association Rules

An association rule identifies a link between two or more attributes in a dataset. A famous, yet unsubstantiated example of an association rule that is generated from a supermarket database of purchases is:

$$Nappies \rightarrow Beer\ (Support = 30\%,\ Confidence = 75\%)$$

The support represents the number of times Nappies and Beer are purchased together as a proportion of the total transactions. The support for Nappies and Beer is the proportion of itemsets (Nappies, Beer) in the dataset, i.e., frequency $(Nappies, Beer)/n$ where an itemset is a group of items such as (Nappies, Beer) within a transaction.

The confidence is interpreted as the percentage of transactions where Beer is purchased given that Nappies are purchased. For example, of the 10 transactions four involved Nappies and, of those 3 also purchased Beer then the confidence is 75%. The confidence of a rule $A \rightarrow B$ is the conditional probability that a transaction contains B given that it contains A and is calculated as $Support(A \cup B)/Support(A)$

An association rule is drawn directly from data. It is not a generalization from the data but merely identifies an association between the purchase of features. As such, association rules are typically used to identify patterns in data-sets that can be used to suggest hypotheses.

Difficulties in the generation of association rules in large datasets involve the combinatorial explosion in the number of rules to be assessed. For example, if a database has only 2 boolean attributes A, B then the support of 6 itemsets representing the following rules need to be calculated:

$$A \rightarrow; A \rightarrow B; A \rightarrow A; B \rightarrow; B \rightarrow A; B \rightarrow B;$$

If the the database has 3 boolean attributes the support of 25 itemsets need to be calculated. In a real world database containing many multi-valued attributes, and large numbers of records, the support calculations become extremely demanding of memory and processor resources.

[1] first described the Apriori algorithm for discovering association rules from large databases. This algorithm reduced the computational complexity by avoiding the exploration

of all rules. This was achieved by inviting the user to specify threshold confidence and support values. If a rule $A, B \rightarrow D$ did not meet the threshold values then the Apriori algorithm avoids an analysis of the rule $A, B, C \rightarrow D$ and all other rules that have A, B in the antecedent.

The application of association rules to facilitate the discovery of defeasible rules advanced in this paper, relies on the calculation of a support for every itemset in a database. For the trials performed in this study, the Apriori implementation by Christian Borgelt (http://www.cs.uni-magdeburg.de/~borgelt) was used with the support and confidence thresholds set to 0. This did not present a resource problem because the data set was small. However, for the method advanced here to scale to large datasets an approach that can generate the support of all itemsets in real time must be adopted. Fortunately, [15] has recently advanced brute force algorithms that are tractable in large datasets.

3 Defeasible Logic

In this section we describe Defeasible Logic formally following the presentation of [6]. Defeasible logic is a sceptical formalism, meaning that it does not support contradictory conclusions. Instead it seeks to resolve differences. In cases where there is some support for concluding A but also support for concluding *not* A ($\neg A$), the logic does not conclude either of them (thus the name "sceptical"). If the support for A has priority over the support for $\neg A$ then A would be concluded. Sceptical reasoning, in general, is appropriate for the study of normative reasoning.

A set of norms (rules) will be represented as a defeasible theory. A defeasible theory, i.e., a knowledge base in Defeasible Logic, consists of five different kinds of knowledge: facts, strict rules, defeasible rules, defeaters, and a superiority relation defined over the rules.

Facts denote simple pieces of information that are deemed to be true regardless of other knowledge items. A typical fact is that John is a minor: $minor(John)$.

Briefly, strict and defeasible rules are represented, respectively, by expressions of the form $A_1, \ldots, A_n \rightarrow B$ and $A_1, \ldots, A_n \Rightarrow B$, where $A_1, \ldots, A_n$ is a possibly empty set of prerequisites and B is the conclusion of the rule.

Strict rules are rules in the classical sense: whenever the premises of a rule are given, we are allowed to apply the rule and get a conclusion. When the premises are indisputable (e.g., facts) then so is the conclusion. An example of a strict rule is "every minor is a person". Written formally: $minor(X) \rightarrow person(X)$.

Defeasible rules are rules that can be defeated by contrary evidence. An example of such a rule is "every person has the capacity to perform legal acts to the extent that the law does not provide otherwise"; written formally: $person(X) \Rightarrow hasLegalCapacity(X)$.

The idea is that if we know that someone is a person, then we may conclude that he/she has legal capacity, *unless there is other evidence suggesting that he/she has not.*

Defeaters are a special kind of rules. They are used to prevent conclusions not to support them. For example: $WeakEvidence \rightsquigarrow \neg guilty$ This rule states that if pieces of evidence are assessed as weak, then they can prevent the derivation of a "guilty" verdict; on the other hand they cannot be used to support a "not guilty" conclusion.

The *superiority relation* among rules is used to define priorities among rules, that is, where one rule may override the conclusion of another rule. For example, given the defeasible rules

$$\begin{aligned} r: &\quad person(X) \Rightarrow hasLegalCapacity(X) \\ r': &\quad minor(X) \Rightarrow \neg hasLegalCapacity(X) \end{aligned}$$

which contradict one another, no conclusive decision can be made about whether a minor has legal capacity. But if we introduce a superiority relation $>$ with $r' > r$, then we can indeed conclude that the minor does not have legal capacity.

It turns out that we only need to define the superiority relation over rules with contradictory conclusions. Also notice that a cycle in the superiority relation is counter-intuitive from the knowledge representation perspective. In the above example, it makes no sense to have both $r > r'$ and $r' > r$. Consequently, the defeasible logic we discuss requires an acyclic superiority relation.

Now we present formally defeasible logics. A *rule* r consists of its *antecedents* (or *body*) $A(r)$ which is a finite set of literals, an arrow, and its *consequent* (or *head*) $C(r)$ which is a literal. There are three kinds of arrows, $\rightarrow$, $\Rightarrow$ and $\leadsto$ which correspond, respectively, to strict rules, defeasible rules and defeaters. Where the body of a rule is empty or consists of one formula only, set notation may be omitted in examples.

Given a set R of rules, we denote the set of all strict rules in R by R_s, the set of strict and defeasible rules in R by R_{sd}, the set of defeasible rules in R by R_d, and the set of defeaters in R by R_{dft}. $R[q]$ denotes the set of rules in R with consequent q.

A *defeasible theory* D is a structure $D = (F, R, >)$ where F is a finite set of facts, R is a finite set of rules, $>$ is a binary relation over R.

A *conclusion* of D is a tagged literal, where a tag is either ∂ or Δ, that may have positive or negative polarity.

$+\Delta q$ which is intended to mean that q is definitely provable in D (i.e., using only strict rules).

$-\Delta q$ which is intended to mean that we have proved that q is not definitely provable in D.

$+\partial q$ which is intended to mean that q is defeasibly provable in D.

$-\partial q$ which is intended to mean that we have proved that q is not defeasibly provable in D.

Basically a conclusion B is supported if there is a rule whose conclusion is B, the prerequisites are either supported or given in the case at hand, and a stronger rule whose conclusion is *not* B has prerequisites that fail to be supported.

Provability is based on the concept of a *derivation* (or *proof*) in $D = R$. A derivation is a finite sequence $P = (P(1), \ldots, P(n))$ of tagged literals satisfying four conditions (which correspond to inference rules for each of the four kinds of conclusion). In the following $P(1..i)$ denotes the initial part of the sequence P of length i.

$+\Delta$:
If $P(i+1) = +\Delta q$ then
  $\exists r \in R_s[q]$
    $\forall a \in A(r) : +\Delta a \in P(1..i)$

$-\Delta$:
If $P(i+1) = -\Delta q$ then
  $\forall r \in R_s[q]$
    $\exists a \in A(r) : -\Delta a \in P(1..i)$

The definition of Δ describes just forward chaining of strict rules. For a literal q to be definitely provable we need to find a strict rule with head q, of which all antecedents have been definitely proved previously. And to establish that q cannot be proven definitely we must establish that for every strict rule with head q there is at least one antecedent which has been shown to be non-provable.

Now we turn to the more complex case of defeasible provability. Before giving its formal definition we provide the idea behind such a notion. A defeasible proof of a literal p consists of three phases. In the first phase either a strict or defeasible rule is put forth in order to support a conclusion p; then we consider an attack on this conclusion using the rules for its negation $\neg p$. The attack fails if each rule for $\neg p$ is either discarded (it is possible to prove that part of the antecedent is not defeasibly provable) or if we can provide a stronger counterattack, that is, if there is an applicable strict or defeasible rule stronger than the rule attacking p. It is worth noting that defeaters cannot be used in the last phase.

$+\partial$:
If $P(i+1) = +\partial q$ then either
$+\Delta q \in P(1..i)$ or
(1) $\exists r \in R_{sd}[q] \forall a \in A(r) : +\partial a \in P(1..i)$ and
(2) $-\Delta{\sim}q \in P(1..i)$ and
(3) $\forall s \in R[{\sim}q]$ either
(a) $\exists a \in A(s) : -\partial a \in P(1..i)$ or
(b) $\exists t \in R_{sd}[q]$ such that
$\forall a \in A(t) : +\partial a \in P(1..i)$ and $t > s$.

$-\partial$:
If $P(i+1) = -\partial q$ then
$-\Delta q \in P(1..i)$ and
(1) $\forall r \in R_{sd}[q]\ \exists a \in A(r) : -\partial a \in P(1..i)$ or
(2) $+\Delta{\sim}q \in P(1..i)$ or
(3) $\exists s \in R[{\sim}q]$ such that
(a) $\forall a \in A(s) : +\partial a \in P(1..i)$ and
(b) $\forall t \in R_{sd}[q]$ either
$\exists a \in A(t) : -\partial a \in P(1..i)$ or $t \not> s$.

Let us work through the condition for $+\partial$, an analogous explanation holds for $-\partial$. To show that q is provable defeasibly we have two choices: (1) We show that q is already definitely provable; or (2) we need to argue using the defeasible part of D as well. In particular, we require that there must be a strict or defeasible rule with head q which can be applied (2.1). But now we need to consider possible "attacks", that is, reasoning chains in support of a complementary of q. To be more specific: to prove q defeasibly we must show that every complementary literal is not definitely provable (2.2). Also (2.3) we must consider the set of all rules for ${\sim}q$ which are not known to be inapplicable (note that here we consider defeaters, too, whereas they could not be used to support the conclusion q; this is in line with the motivation of defeaters. Essentially each such rule s attacks the conclusion q. For q to be provable, each such rule s must be counterattacked by a rule t with head q with the following properties: (i) t must be applicable at this point, and (ii) t must be stronger than s. Thus each attack on the conclusion q must be counterattacked by a stronger rule.

It is worth noting that defeaters can be simulated in term of the other elements of Defeasible Logic [2], thus we can consider theories without defeaters.

To explain the mechanism of defeasible derivations –showing at the same time the appropriateness of Defeasible Logic for normative reasoning– we consider rule 162 of the Australian Civil Aviation Regulations 1988: "When two aircraft are on converging headings at approximately the same height, the aircraft that has the other on its right shall give way, except that (a) power-driven heavier-than-air aircraft shall give way to airships, gliders and balloons; ...” This norm can be represented in defeasible logic as follows:

$$r_1 : \neg rightOfWay(Y, X) \Rightarrow rightOfWay(X, Y)$$
$$r_2 : onTheRightOf(X, Y) \Rightarrow rightOfWay(X, Y)$$

The first rule states that, given two aircraft, if one of the aircraft does not have right of way then the other aircraft does, while the second states that the aircraft X has right of way over the aircraft Y if X is on the right of Y;

$$r_3 : \; powerDriven(X), \neg powerDriven(Y) \Rightarrow \neg rightOfWay(X, Y)$$

The idea of the above rules is that a power-driven aircraft does not have right of way over a non-power-driven one.

$$r_4 : balloon(X) \rightarrow \neg powerDriven(X)$$
$$r_5 : glider(X) \rightarrow \neg powerDriven(X)$$

r_4 and r_5 classify balloons and gliders as non-power-driven aircraft and

$$r_6 : \; \Rightarrow powerDriven(X)$$

assumes aircraft to be power-driven unless further information is given. The superiority relation is determined as follows: $r_3 > r_2$ because r_3 is an exception to r_2. By specificity $r_4 > r_6$ and $r_5 > r_6$. Moreover $r_1 > r_3$.

Let us examine the following cases: 1) two aircraft of the same type (power-driven, non-power-driven) are converging 2) a power-driven aircraft and a non-power-driven aircraft are converging. In the first case we can apply r_2 since the prerequisites of r_3 do not hold and we cannot prove the antecedent of r_1. In the second case we can apply r_3 given that both of the two prerequisites hold, and after the conclusion of r_3 has been established we can apply r_1 to derive that the non-power-driven aircraft has the right of way over the power-drive one.

It is worth noting that in this example all the rules have been drawn from the same normative code, and the superiority relation is explicitly given. However, the first is not a serious limitation in so far as it is possible to merge several codes in the same defeasible theory; for the second [7] proposed a variant of Defeasible Logic where the superiority relation is computed dynamically according to some principles encoded as defeasible rules.

4 Identifying Defeasible Rule Sets using Association Rules

Association rules automatically generated from a dataset can facilitate the discovery of strict rules, defeasible rules and rule preferences. We must assume that the data set is a high quality set in that there are no missing values and all values present are correctly recorded (i.e., no noise). The extent to which these assumptions can be violated is left to future research.

In order to illustrate the application of association rules to the discovery of defeasible rule, we adopt a hypothetical sample dataset that relates to the aircraft example illustrated in the previous section. Table 1 represents three records from 36 situations that were regarded as plausible recordings of air traffic data. For example, Case 1 illustrates a situation in which

Table 1: Sample data for aircraft data set

Case	Right of way	Y power driven	X power driven	position	x Type	y Type
1	rightOfWayX	yPowerDriven	xPowerDriven	X_on_right	Xairship	Yairship
2	rightOfWayY	yPowerDriven	xPowerDriven	Y_on_right	Xairship	Yairship
3	rightOfWayX	yPowerDriven	-xPowerDriven	X_on_right	Xglider	Yairship

Table 2: Sample itemsets for aircraft data set

Itemset	Attribute	Attribute	Attribute	Support
1.	X_on_right			0.49
2.	X_on_right	¬ yPowerDriven		0.22
3.	rightOfWayX	X_on_right		0.405
4.	rightOfWayX	X_on_right	¬ yPowerDriven	0.135
5.	¬ yPowerDriven	X_on_right	rightOfWayX	0

aircraft X was granted right of way over Y. In that situation both X and Y were power driven and X was on the right of Y.

As discussed above, association rules are typically deployed to suggest hypotheses with datasets so large that the generation of all possible rules is not normally feasible in real time. Instead, a threshold level of support and confidence are set by the user, so that only those rules that exceed the thresholds are sought. However, for the purposes of this study, the confidence and support thresholds are set to 0 in order to generate all itemsets.

Table 2 illustrates a sample of the 1057 itemsets with up to four antecedent and one consequent attribute (rightOfWay) generated from the aircraft dataset. Itemset 1 in that table indicates that 49% of records in the set included the attribute X_on_right; Itemset 4 reflects that 13.5% of records contains the itemset triplet (rightOfWayX, X_on_right, -yPowerDriven).

Recall that the confidence of a rule is the conditional probability that the consequent will occur given the antecedent has been observed. The confidence of the rule $A \Rightarrow B$ is

$$\frac{Support(A, B)}{Support(A).}$$

Table 3 lists two rules along with their confidence, support and a measure called interest.

According to [14] the "interestingness" of a rule refers to the degree to which a discovered pattern is of interest to the user. The interest metric aims to highlight those rules that are more interesting than others. Various metrics have been advanced but a conventional metric for the calculation of interest for the rule $A \rightarrow B$ is the

$$\frac{Support(A, B)}{Support(A) * Support(B)}.$$

Although the mere generation of association rules may arguably be a useful tool for the engagement of a domain expert in the process of eliciting defeasible rules, the sheer number of rules generated mitigates against this. A closer analysis of the itemsets and rules may go some way toward facilitating the automatic generation of strict and defeasible rules from association rules.

Table 3: Sample rules from aircraft data set

Rule	Rule	Confidence	Support	Interest
ar1.	$X\_on\_right \Rightarrow rightOfWayX$	0.68	0.405	1.15
ar2.	$X\_on\_right, -yPowerDriven \Rightarrow \neg rightOfWayX$	0.62	0.135	1.63

For the association rule $A \rightarrow B$ generated from a non-noisy data-set, to be interpreted as a Strict rule in defeasible reasoning, we assume the confidence of the rule to be 100%. Every time A is observed B is also observed. For example, itemsets $(A, \neg B)$, $(A, C, \neg B)$, are not present in the data-set. We assume the closed world assumption and conclude that these itemsets do not exist because their presence could represent exceptions to the $A \rightarrow B$ rule and render it defeasible.

For the association rule $A \rightarrow B$ generated from a non-noisy data-set, to be interpreted as a defeasible rule the confidence of the rule $A \rightarrow B$ is greater than 0 but less than 100%. On some occasions that A is also observed, B is observed and on others $\neg B$ is observed.

There are typically many rules with a confidence between 0 and 100 so additional effort is required in order to identify rules that may be considered meaningful in a defeasible rule set. To identify plausible defeasible rules we look for groups of rules that represent the following situations: Simple Exceptions; Separate Vs. Aggregate rules; General Vs. Specific rules; and Apparent irrelevance.

A simple exception occurs when a rule is an exception to a base rule that results in the opposite conclusion. Consider two defeasible rules, $ar3 : \ A \Rightarrow P$ and $ar4 : A, B \Rightarrow \neg P$. $ar4$ is an exception to $ar3$ because A is associated with P unless in the presence of B, it is associated with $\neg P$. The necessary conditions for this situation to be identified using association rules are:

- the support for the itemsets (A, P), and $(A, B, \neg P)$ is greater than 0. This indicates that there the rules $A \Rightarrow P$ and $A, B \Rightarrow \neg P$ are represented in the dataset

- the support for the itemset (A, B, P) should be 0. This confirms that A, in the presence of B never leads to P.

The rules illustrated in Table 3 meet the criteria of a simple exception group. The rule $ar1$ in that table is taken to be the base rule and $ar2$ is the exception.

If these conditions are met we identify the base rule and determine a rule preference using the "interestingness" metric where the exception rule has a higher preference than the rule. In the example above $ar1$ is the base rule so the preference relation is $ar1 < ar2$.

A variant of simple exception, refers to the situation where there is a clear defeasible rule say, $ar5 : A \Rightarrow P$ and many different exceptions such as $ar6 : A, B \Rightarrow \neg P$, $ar7 : A, C \Rightarrow \neg P$, $ar8 : \ A, D \Rightarrow \neg P$. Each single exception has a very limited distribution. The necessary conditions above still apply to identify these rules as a group with a base rule and several exceptions.

The procedure for identifying rule pairs (or groups) that meet simple exception criteria is currently performed using a brute force approach on the small hypothetical dataset. This procedure is cumbersome in that any defeasible rule (i.e., those that correspond to association rules with a confidence between 0 and 100) could be a base rule in an exception group.

Therefore, rules that may be exceptions to the base candidate must be sought according to the criteria above. This task explodes combinatorially with large numbers of candidate rules. Future research aims to develop more effective mechanisms than brute force that can be applied to large datasets in real time.

Another situation that association rules can help to automatically identify involves separate and aggregate rules. In this situation A and B are, independently, sufficient reasons for P, but, very often they occur simultaneously. In this case we want to conclude that there are two rules for P, i.e., $A \Rightarrow P$ and $B \Rightarrow P$ instead of $A, B \Rightarrow P$. We identify this situation from the support of itemsets as follows:

$$\frac{Support(A, P) * Support(B, P)}{Support(A, B, P)} > t$$

where t is the aggregate threshold defined by an user.

The next situation addressed involves general vs specific rules. Consider two defeasible rules, $ar8 : A \Rightarrow P$ and $ar9 : A, B \Rightarrow P$. Rule $ar9$ is more specific than $ar8$ because it applies to fewer cases than $ar8$ does. However, in some contexts the more specific (and complex) defeasible rule is preferred and in others the more general (and simpler) rule is preferred. Here again, we include a user defined minimum threshold support for the general rule. If the minimum support is reached then the rule with the highest confidence is selected. For example, the rule $ar10 : X\_on\_right \Rightarrow rightOfWayX$ has a support of 40.5% and confidence 83% the rule $ar11 : X\_on\_right$ and $\neg yPowerDriven \Rightarrow rightOfWayX$ has a support of 13.5% and confidence 62%. If the minimum support for a general rule is set by the user to less than 40% then $ar10$ is preferred because the confidence of $ar10$ is greater than that for $ar11$. However, if the minimum support is greater than 40.5% the general rule does not reach the minimum support for general rules and $ar11$ is selected. A preference for a more general rule over a specific rule underpins the situation we call Apparent irrelevance.

Let us suppose that A alone is not a sufficient reason for D, but together with B it is: the general rule $ar12 : A \Rightarrow D$ does not prevail over the more specific rule $ar13 : A, B \Rightarrow D$. At the same time C alone is not enough to conclude $\neg D$, but $\neg D$ follows from B and C together: $ar13 : C, B \Rightarrow \neg D$ prevails over $ar14 : C \Rightarrow \neg D$.

The use of association rules to facilitate the discovery of defeasible rules is limited in a number of ways. If the antecedent and consequent are not in the same record in the dataset then no association rule corresponding to the desired defeasible rule can be found. For example r_1 above cannot be discovered by association rules because the antecedent and consequent are not separate attributes in the sample dataset:

$$r_1 : \neg rightOfWay(Y, X) \Rightarrow rightOfWay(X, Y)$$
$$r_2 : onTheRightOf(X, Y) \Rightarrow rightOfWay(X, Y)$$

$$r_3 : \ powerDriven(X), \neg powerDriven(Y) \Rightarrow \neg rightOfWay(X, Y)$$

$$r_4 : balloon(X) \rightarrow \neg powerDriven(X)$$
$$r_5 : glider(X) \rightarrow \neg powerDriven(X)$$

The defeasible rules r_2, r_3, r_4, r_5 and r_6 were discovered with confidence levels of 68%, 35%, 100%, 100% and 32%. The rules r_4 and r_5 were discovered as strict rules because their confidence is 100%.

Preference relations identified as appropriate for the aircraft defeasible rules do not seem to be readily derived in a general way from confidence, interest or support measures. This illustrates a further limitation. In addition, the application of any KDD technique including association rules is limited by the coverage of the dataset. Currently, datasets that represent key attributes of the ratio decidendi of human decision making do not readily exist in the legal domain. However, as case management systems become prevalent in Courts across many jurisdictions this is likely to change.

5 Conclusion

In this paper we have noted that although considerable research has been done in the application of Knowledge discovery from database (KDD) techniques to law, the majority of attempts have focused on classification and clustering KDD studies. Few applications of KDD have applied association rules to discover potentially interesting patterns from a dataset.

Metrics of confidence, support and interest that association rule algorithms calculate are suited to the task of discovering patterns from a dataset that suggest appropriate rules for the Defeasible Logic formalism. This non-monotonic logic has been shown to have elegant properties that make it very suitable for practical application in modelling legal reasoning.

Strict rules can be discovered by a direct application of the confidence metric. Defeasible rules can similarly be identified. However, typically too many plausible rules emerge. The number of candidate rules can be reduced by applying support, confidence and interest metrics to the discovery of known types of Defeasible rule groupings. The ones explored in the present study include simple exceptions, separate Vs. aggregate rules, general Vs. specific rules and apparent irrelevance. Future research is aimed at identifying additional rule groupings.

Future research is also aimed at the development of a search algorithm that can scan a set of candidate Defeasible rules more effectively than the brute force method adopted in this toy dataset. Once this is achieved a more rigorous empirical trial can be performed to evaluate the approach advanced here.

References

[1] R. Agrawal, T. Imielinski, and A. Swami. Mining association rules between sets of items in large databases. In *Proceedings of ACM Sigmod Conference*, pages 207–216. ACM Press, 1993.

[2] G. Antoniou, D. Billington, G. Governatori, and M.J. Maher. Representation results for defeasible logic. *ACM Transaction on Computational Logic*, 2:255–287, 2001.

[3] G. Antoniou, D. Billington, G. Governatori, M.J. Maher, and A. Rock. A family of defeasible reasoning logics and its implementation. In W. Horn (Ed.) *ECAI 2000. Proceedings of the 14th European Conference on Artificial Intelligence*, Amsterdam, 2000. IOS Press.

[4] G. Antonious, D. Billington, G. Governatori, and M.J. Maher. On the modelling and analysis of regulations. In *AAAI-2000 Proceedings of the Australian Conference on Information Systems*, pages 401–405, 1999.

[5] T. Bench-Capon. Neural networks and open texture. In *Proceedings of the Fourth International Conference on Artificial Intelligence and Law. ICAIL'93*, pages 292–297. ACM Press, 1993.

[6] D. Billington. Defeasible logic is stable. *Journal of Logic and Computation*, 3:370–400, 1993.

[7] D. Billington and G. Antoniou. A plausible logic with dynamic priorities. In G. Antoniou and G. Governatori (Eds.) *Proceedings of the 2nd Australasian Workshop on Computational Logic*, pages 11–20. QUT Press, 2001.

[8] S. Bruninghaus and K. Ashley. Improving the representation of legal case texts with information extraction methods. In *ICAIL'01. Proceedings of the 8th International Conference on Artificial Intelligence and Law*, pages 42–51. ACM Press, 2001.

[9] M. Covington, D. Nute, and A. Vellino. *Prolog Programming in Depth.* Prentice Hall, 1997.

[10] J. Daniels and E. Rissland. Finding legally relevant passages in case opinions. In *ICAIL'97. Proceedings of the Sixth International Conference on Artificial Intelligence and Law.*, pages 39–46. ACM Press, 1997.

[11] L DeHaspe and L de Raedt Mining Association Rules in Multiple Relations *Proceedings of the 7th International Workshop on Inductive Logic Programming.* Springer-Verlaf. pages 125-132. 1997

[12] B. Duval and P. Nicolas. Learning Default Theories In S. Parsons and A. Hunter (Eds)*Qualitative and Quantitative Approaches to Reasoning with Uncertainty. Lecture Notes in Artificial Intelligence* . Springer-Verlag, pages 148-159.

[13] U. Fayyad, G. Piatetsky-Shapiro, P. Smyth, and R. Uthurusamy, editors. *Advances in Knowledge Discovery and Data mining.* 1996.

[14] W.J. Frawley, G. Piatetsky-Shapiro, and C.J. Matheus. Knowledge discovery in databases: an overview. *Knowledge discovery in databases*, pages 1–27, 1991. AAAI/MIT.

[15] G. Goulbourne, F. Coenen, and P. Leng. Algorithms for computing association rules using a partial support tree. *Journal of Knowledge Based Systems*, 13:141–149, 2000.

[16] G. Governatori, M. Dumas, A.H.M. ter Hofstede, and P. Oaks. A formal approach to protocols and strategies for (legal) negotiation. In *ICAIL'01. Proceedings of the 8th International Conference on Artificial Intelligence and Law*, pages 168–177. ACM Press, 2001.

[17] G. Governatori and M.J. Maher. An argumentation theoretic characterization of defeasible logic. In W. Horn (Ed.) *ECAI 2000. Proceedings of the 14th European Conference on Artificial Intelligence*, Amsterdam, 2000. IOS Press.

[18] G. Governatori, M.J. Maher, G. Antoniou and D. Billington. Argumeantation semantics for defeasible logics. In *Pacific Rim Internatinal Conference on Artificial Intelligence*. Springer-Verlag, 2000.

[19] P. Hayes. Intelligent high volume text processing using shallow, domain specific techniques. In P. Jacobs (Ed.) *Text-Based Intelligent Systems: Current Research and Practice in Information Extraction and Retrieval*, pages 227–241. Lawrence Erlbaum, Hillsdale, NJ, 1992.

[20] J. Hobson and D. Slee. Indexing the theft act 1968 for case based reasoning and artificial neural networks. In *Proceedings of the Fourth National Conference on Law, Computers and Artificial Intelligence*, Exeter, 1994.

[21] N. Lavrac *Computational Logic and Machine Learning: A Roadmap for Inductive Logic Programming* Technical Report, J. Stefan Institute, Ljubljana, Slovenia, 1998.

[22] M.J. Maher. Propositional defeasible logic has linear complexity. Technical report, Department of Mathematical and Computer Sciences, Loyola University, Chicago, 2000.

[23] M.J. Maher, A. Rock, G. Antoniou, D. Billignton, and T. Miller. Efficient defeasible reasoning systems. In *Proc. International Conference on Tool in Artificial Intelligence*. EEEI Computer Society Press, 2000.

[24] M. Moens, C. Uyttendaele, and J. Dumortier. Abstracting of legal cases: The salomon experience. In *ICAIL'97. Proceedings of the Sixth International Conference on Artificial Intelligence and Law.*, pages 114–122. ACM Press, 1997.

[25] D. Nute. Defeasible reasoning. In *Proc. 20th Hawaii International Conference on System Science*, pages 470–477. IEEE Press, 1987.

[26] D. Nute. *Handbook of Logic in Artificial Intelligence and Logic Programming*, volume 3, chapter Defeasible Logic, pages 353–395. Oxford University Press, Oxford, 1994.

[27] A. Pannu. Using genetic algorithms to inductively reason with cases in the legal domain. In *ICAIL'95 Proceedings of the Fifth International Conference on Artificial Intelligence and Law*, pages 175–184. ACM Press., 1995.

[28] E. Rissland and T. Friedman. Detecting change in legal concepts. In *ICAIL'95. Proceedings of the Fifth International Conference on Artificial Intelligence and Law*, pages 127–136. ACM Press, 1995.

[29] E. Schweighofer. The revolution in legal information retrieval or: The empire strikes back. *Journal of*

Information, Law and Technology, 1, 1999.

[30] A. Stranieri, J. Zeleznikow, and H. Turner. Data mining in law with association rules. In *Proceedings of IASTED International conference on Law and Technology*, pages 129–135, 2000.

[31] P. Thompson. Automatic categorisation of case law. In *ICAIL'01. Proceedings of the 8th International Conference on Artificial Intelligence and Law*, pages 70–77. ACM Press, 2001.

[32] G. Vossos, J. Zeleznikow, A. Moore, and D. Hunter. The credit act advisory system (caas): Conversion from an expert system prototype to a c++ commercial system. In *ICAIOL'93. Fourth International Conference on Artificial Intelligence and Law*, page 180. ACM Press, 1993.

[33] D. Wilkins and K. Pillaipakkamnatt. The effectiveness of machine learning techniques for predicting time to case disposition. In *ICAIL'97. Proceedings of the Sixth International Conference on Artificial Intelligence and Law*, pages 106–113. ACM Press, 1997.

[34] J. Yearwood, A. Stranieri, and J. Zeleznikow. Case-based retrieval of refugee review tribunal text cases. In A. Oskamp, R.V. De Mulder, C. van Noortwijk, C.A.F.M. Grtters, K. Ashley, and T. Gordon, editors, *Legal Knowledge Based Systems. JURIX: The Tenth Conference*, pages 67–83, 1997.

[35] J. Zeleznikow, G. Vossos, and D. Hunter. The ikbals project: Multi-modal reasoning in legal knowledge based systems. *Artificial Intelligence and Law*, 2:169–203, 1994.

What to Expect from Legal Logic?

Jaap Hage
Department of Metajuridica
Faculty of Law
Universiteit Maastricht
The Netherlands
jaap.hage@metajur.unimaas.nl

Abstract. This paper argues for a proper position for legal logic in between a general theory of *legal* reasoning and a general theory of *valid* reasoning. In discussion with McCarty it argues that legal logic should not be seen as a general theory of legal reasoning, but rather as a theory of what counts as valid reasoning in the legal field. In discussion with earlier work by Verheij and the author himself, and of Prakken and Sartor, the paper argues that legal logic should employ a conceptual framework that is as close to that of the legal domain as possible. A simpler logic, how attractive as it might seem at first sight, has the disadvantage that it leads to problematic formalizations of the domain theory and to marginalization of the logic as means to evaluate the validity of informal arguments.

1 What Legal *Logic* is not

In his paper *Some Arguments About Legal Arguments*, Thorne McCarty [7] did something which is regrettably seldom done in the publications on Law and Artificial Intelligence. He attacked the work of other authors and thereby made an end to what seemed to be a silent convention, namely that researchers merely continue their own research and only address the work of others to show that they are familiar with the recent literature in their field. Science progresses through criticism (Popper) and overpoliteness does not contribute to such progress. In this paper I intend to continue the polemical spirit in which McCarty so boldly advanced his paper. And which publication would be a more worthy candidate for being the first object of criticism than McCarty's own paper?

In the already mentioned paper, McCarty launched an attack against, amongst others, rule-based theories of legal argument. In fact, he only discusses argument-based approaches, but I suspect that his criticisms would also apply to other rule-based approaches, such as Reason-based Logic, which McCarty seems to have overlooked. The precise nature of McCarty's attack is not easy to determine, since his argument against rule-based theories consists mainly of examples, but I think that the following adequately rephrases his point in the form of an argument.

1. A lawyer who makes an argument before a real judge will use a simple and clear set of rules which favor his client.

Jaap Hage, 'What to Expect from Legal Logic?' in Bart Verheij, Arno R. Lodder, Ronald P. Loui and Antoinette J. Muntjewerff (eds.), *Legal Knowledge and Information Systems. Jurix 2001: The Fourteenth Annual Conference*. Amsterdam: IOS Press, 2001, pp. 77-87.

2. Arguments as discussed by the authors of rule-based systems are rather complex, featuring for example priorities on rules. Moreover, it is sometimes an issue for discussion between the theoreticians themselves what the outcomes of these arguments should be.
3. Therefore, arguments as they occur in rule-based systems are unlike the arguments that are used by lawyers who argue for real judges.
4. Therefore, rule-based systems are 'wrong'.

The final conclusion of this argument is formulated so vaguely on purpose, because McCarty himself does not really draw a conclusion at all in the section of his paper devoted to rule-based systems. In a later section, under the optimistic heading 'The Correct Theory' McCarty emphasizes that legal reasoning is a form of theory construction. Maybe his criticism of rule-based approaches should therefore be formulated as the objection that these approaches do not address theory construction, and therefore misconstrue the nature of legal reasoning.

Although I agree with McCarty's point that legal reasoning is (to some extent) theory construction, I heartily disagree with his attempt to adduce this observation as an objection to rule-based theories of legal argument. It seems, at least at first sight, that McCarty fell victim to a popular error in thinking about legal logic, namely that legal logic should solve the problems with which a lawyer who has to 'solve' a case, is wrestling. A logic which does not support a lawyer in fulfilling his reasoning tasks would for this reason be defective. Obviously this criticism of legal logic is wrong, because it overlooks that legal logic aims to provide standards for evaluating the logical qualities of legal arguments, and does not pretend to be a tool to solve legal problems. I cannot imagine that McCarty would adhere to this mistaken view of legal logic, but it seems to me that he has overlooked that the rule-based theories of legal argument were intended as logical theories and not as theories about how to solve legal problems. As a consequence, he seems to adduce reasons against theories of legal logic, which would be forceful against theories about legal problem solving.

McCarty might defend himself by pointing out that his criticism is not directed at legal logic as a theory of legal problem solving but, on the contrary, at 'grossly exaggerated, and seriously mistaken' claims about the nature of these legal logics. In fact, he quoted Prakken and Sartor in his paper to support the view that these authors made such claims.

Personally I cannot see that the quotation at issue supports the view that Prakken and Sartor made such wrong claims for their logic. But that is not the main point. Even if Prakken and Sartor would have made such exaggerated claims, this would not be a ground to criticize rule-based theories of legal argument, but only a ground to criticize exaggerated claims for such logics and those who made those claims. The main line of McCarty's 'argument' is directed against the rule-based theories of legal reasoning themselves, however, and not against wrongly made claims about them.

What then about McCarty's point that a lawyer who makes an argument before a real judge will use a simple and clear set of rules and that the arguments dealt with by rule-based systems are often highly complex? It seems to me that this point may be inspired by the common law background of McCarty, where the materials that form the input of legal decision making consist to a large extent of case law which is, in comparison to statutory regulations, little structured. Case law asks for much more reconstruction than statutory law, before it can be applied to new cases. To be convincing, reconstructions need to be relatively simple, given the constraints on judicial information processing capabilities. That the arguments leading to such reconstructions need not be simple at all, is illustrated by, for instance, the work of Dworkin on constitutional interpretation [1].

Statutory regulations are meant to be applied to concrete cases without additional reconstruction. That it is, at least in theory, always possible to reconstruct statutory law from an interpretation at first sight into an interpretation in the light of all the rest of the law and its underlying values, policies etc. [Peczenik and Hage 2000], does not subtract from this. Working with statutory law in its prima facie interpretation sometimes involves the complications dealt with by rule-based theories of legal reasoning and these theories therefore rightly deal with these complications. That doctrinal literature often redescribes statutory law with as one of its purposes to lessen these complications, does not take anything away from this observation, because the reconstructions given in this literature are based on the same complex reasoning patterns that should be used by legal decision makers if the literature had not 'compiled the complications out', to use a computational expression.

My critical evaluation of McCarty's criticism on rule-based theories of legal reasoning can be summarized in two points: First it seems, despite the above-mentioned counterindications, that McCarty unjustly expects from logical theories of legal reasoning that they are tools for legal problem solving, and in this light scorns them for not paying attention to theory construction. And second, McCarty seems to undervalue the role of logic in both legal decision making and theory construction. This may be caused by his background in the common law tradition, where the materials that go into theory construction are less structured than the statutory regulations that are all important in the civil law tradition.

2 What *Legal* Logic should be

It seems that McCarty's expectancies with regard to legal *logic* are too high, because he expects more form logic than it is meant to do. Arguably some modern theories of legal logic succumb to the opposite mistake by setting their demands on *legal* logic too low. In the rest of this paper I will try to formulate some objections against earlier work by Verheij and myself, and work by Prakken and Sartor. My argument against these logics boils down to it that

1. There are many viable logics, and none of them is a priori better than the others.
2. Which logic is the best, depends on the purpose for which the logic is to be used, including the knowledge domain in question.
3. A logic for a particular domain should use a conceptual framework that is as close as possible to that of the domain in question. Logics that fail in this respect are not useful for testing the validity of arguments.
4. The logics in question do not take sufficient characteristics of the legal domain into account.

Since my argument deals amongst others with philosophical questions about the nature of logic, it pays attention to some elementary logical issues which will be familiar to those who are well acquainted with formal logic and its philosophy. Nevertheless, I feel that even some of those readers might benefit from re-thinking what they already felt to know.

2.1 The Purpose of Logic

I will take logic to be a theory that provides standards to evaluate arguments on their logical validity.[1] Modern versions of logic tend to be formal in two senses. The first sense is that they are concerned with the form, rather than the content of arguments, on the assumption that it is the form, not the content which determines whether an argument is valid. The second sense is that modern logics tend to be developed by means of so-called logical languages, which are defined precisely. These languages are called formal, presumably because they use meaningless characters to represent meaningful elements of natural language. In this way, the formal nature (in the first sense) of logical appraisal is emphasized.

Logics tend to provide procedures by means of which the validity of arguments in their formal language can be tested. In propositional logic this procedure consists, for instance, of drawing up a truth table. To evaluate an argument in natural language, the argument must first be formalized, that is, translated into the language of some formal logic. The resulting formal argument can then be tested, and the outcome of this test is applied to the original informal argument.

Regrettably, the exactness with which the quality of formalized arguments can be tested is not available for the translation of the natural language argument into the formal argument. As a consequence, there is some room for gerrymandering. If an intuitively valid argument comes out invalid, or the other way round, this can be interpreted as a reason why the argument was incorrectly formalized. As we will see, there is also room for choosing a logic, where some arguments come out as invalid under one logic, while they come out as valid under another logic. In my opinion this room for choosing a formalization should be minimized, and this leads me, in the end, to the conclusion that the language of logic should be as close *as viable* to the informal language which it is meant to formalize.

2.2 Logical Form

A logic should provide tests for the validity of arguments. In theory, a logic might consist of an enumeration of all arguments which it considers to be valid. In practice this is not viable, and therefore logics tend to characterize arguments by means of some abstract properties and these properties are the basis of the evaluation of these arguments as valid or invalid. Traditionally these abstract properties concern what is called the 'form' of the argument, and therefore it is the form of an argument, and not its content, that determines whether an argument is valid. For instance, arguments of the form '$p \rightarrow q$, p therefore q' are valid, while arguments of the form '$p \rightarrow q$, q, therefore p' are invalid.

Attractive as this simple theory about logical validity may seem at first sight, it has the drawback that the notion of logical form is not so clear. Take the following informal argument:

All thieves are punishable
John is a thief
Therefore: John is punishable

[1] In this characterisation, I use the word 'valid' not in the strict sense of deductive validity, but in the broad sense of 'good from a logical point of view', where the standards for goodness remain largely unspecified.

Formalized in propositional logic it has the form:
'p, q therefore r' and this form is invalid. The informal argument is therefore classified as invalid under propositional logic. But formalized in predicate logic it becomes

$$\forall x(\text{Thief}(x) \rightarrow \text{Punishable}(x)), \text{Thief}(a), \text{therefore Punishable}(a)$$

and this form is valid.[2] The same argument that was invalid under propositional logic turns out to be valid under predicate logic. This phenomenon is explained by the fact that predicate logic recognizes more as logical form. In particular it recognizes the universal quantifier as a logical expression, that is as something that determines the logical form of the sentence, while propositional logic does not recognize quantifiers as determiners of logical form.

In general it may be said that a logic is more powerful (stronger) if it recognizes more logical form and abstracts less away as 'mere content'.[3] In this sense modal propositional logic is more powerful than 'mere' propositional logic, because it recognizes modal words like 'necessarily' and 'possibly' as determinative of logical form. Deontic logics are more powerful than their non-deontic counterparts, because they recognize the words 'ought' and 'permitted' as determining logical form, etc. It depends on the logic what counts as logical form.[4] It is, for example, possible to develop a logic of love and hate that recognizes the validity of arguments of the form $x$hates y,therefore: $x$does not love$y$[14]. An understandable question in this connection is whether it makes sense to develop such a logic.

2.3 *From Strong Logic to Weak Logic*

To see the importance of the issue how strong a logic is, I will pay special attention to what seem to me to be the strongest and the weakest possible logic. Given my starting point, according to which logic should provide standards for evaluating arguments as to their validity, a logic should ex hypothesi deal with arguments and formulate standards for their validity.

The strongest possible logic consists of a list of all valid arguments. If an argument is taken to be a set of premises and a conclusion, the list should specify for every combination of a set of premises and a conclusion whether the conclusion 'logically follows from' the premises in the set.[5] Every item in the list can be seen as an inference rule of the logic, and this logic has an inference rule for every individual valid argument. This logic is the strongest possible logic, since it recognizes everything as logical form. In fact it does not distinguish between form and content, and nothing of an argument is left out of consideration in determining its validity.

---

[2]One might object that the first 'formalisation' of the argument is not a proper formalisation at all, because it neglects the logical structure available in the informal argument. This objection misses the point however, the point being that there is no such thing as inherent logical structure, but merely something which we choose to treat as logical structure. The adoption of a particular system of formal logic is implicitly a choice about what we want to recognize as logical structure.

[3]One can think of different ways to characterize the 'power' of a logic. One other characterisation would be in terms of the number of theorems a logic has, another one in terms of the expressiveness of the logical language used. My characterisation should be distinguished from these other ones.

[4]Related themes are explored in [14, 15 and 16].

[5]Since it is not necessarily the case that a conclusion that follows from a set of premises also follows from each superset, this logic need not be monotonic.

The weakest possible logic looks, strange enough, very much like the strongest possible one. This is easily seen if the list that specifies the strongest logic is written down as follows, where A ... A" represent sets of premises and p ... p" represent conclusions:

$$A \mid\!- p\ ,\ A' \mid\!- p'\ ,\ A'' \mid\!- p''\ , \ldots$$

Notice that the items in this list are not sentences of the logical language, but inference rules of the metalanguage in which it is specified which arguments are valid ones.

The weakest possible logic, which is essentially a stripped down version of propositional logic, only recognizes arguments of the form '$P \rightarrow q$, P, therefore q' as valid, where P stands for (the truth of) a set of sentences. For every argument of the list above, an additional premise would be needed to be valid under this weak logic:

$$A \rightarrow p\ ,\ A' \rightarrow p'\ ,\ A'' \rightarrow p''\ , \ldots.$$

As is clear from this example, the additional premise specifies by means of (the truth of) a sentence of the object language that the argument from the rest of the premises to the conclusion is valid. The inference rules of the strongest possible logic are replaced by object language sentences, but otherwise the logics are very much alike.

Nevertheless there is an important difference between the logics, because the strongest logic recognizes everything as logical form, while the weakest logic hardly recognizes any logical form. In the weakest logic every valid argument must contain a premise of the form $P \rightarrow q$, in order to specify that the conclusion q follows from the other premises of the argument. In other words, all valid arguments have the 'validity' of the argument as one of their premises.[6] There is hardly a task left over for the logic, because the validity of the argument comes down to the truth of the premise that declares the argument to be valid.

2.4 Pragmatism and the Choice of a Logic

The strongest possible logic is impracticable, because it presupposes an exhaustive list of all valid arguments. The weakest possible logic is almost useless, because it leaves the judgment on the validity of an argument to one of the premises of the argument. Any realistic logic should be somewhere in between these extremes. However, there appears to be no hard and fast standard to determine where precisely one should be in between these extremes. Apparently there is no such thing as THE logic. There are merely many different logics, and it is a matter of choice which one would like to use.

There is a trade-off here. The weaker a logic is, the simpler it tends to be, and simplicity is often considered to be a virtue in science (and in real life law, if we may believe McCarty). We have already seen, however, that too much weakness goes at the cost of usefulness. Stronger logics are more useful to test arguments for their validity, but they tend to be more complex. Given this trade-off, I therefore propose to use those logics (it is improbable that there is only one) which are most suited for the domain (and within the domain: the reasoning task) in question.

[6]The word 'validity' is placed between quotes, because it is not exactly the validity of the argument that is stated in the premise, but rather the truth of a conditional sentence that corresponds to the validity of the argument.

In my opinion a logic should be adapted to the way in which the domain to which it is applied, is conceptualized. To be more specific, a logic for the use in legal reasoning systems should exhibit *as many as possible* characteristics of the legal domain *that are relevant for the validity of legal reasoning* as logical form. And if it turns out that for reasoning purposes it is useful to distinguish more than one legal domain, the logic should exhibit as many as possible characteristics of the subdomain in question. In the following two subsections I will give two examples of logics that in my opinion exhibit too little of the structure of the domain that they attempt to capture.

2.5 Rules and Principles in Reason-based Logic

Let me start with what I now regard as a mistake of my own. In our work on Reason-based Logic of about 1995 [3, 12, 13], Verheij and I defended an integrated view on rules and principles. That is, we took principles as logical primitives and expressed rules in terms of them.

Our argument was basically as follows. Legal principles have the structure of conditionals. They differ from traditional conditionals in two ways. First, if their condition part is satisfied, this does not allow the derivation of the conclusion, but merely the derivation of a reason for the conclusion. Whether the conclusion follows depends on all reasons pro and con this conclusion. In short the application of a principle merely contributes to the derivation of a conclusion. Principles should therefore never be considered on their own, but always in combination with other reasons, or generators of reasons.

Second, principles differ from traditional conditionals in that their operation can be shut out. If there is an exception to a principle, the fact that the condition part of the principle is satisfied does not make the principle generate a reason for its conclusion anymore.

Legal rules seem to be different from principles in that their application guarantees their conclusions. So, where principles only generate reasons which must be considered in combination with possible other reasons, rules guarantee their conclusions when they are applied.

In the work mentioned at the beginning of this section, Verheij and I simulated the operation of legal rules, by treating them as principles which not only provided reasons for their conclusions, but also created exceptions to (almost) all competing principles. If a principle generates exceptions to its competitors, the reason for its conclusion has no competition anymore. So, even though this reason should in principle be balanced against other reasons, these other reasons are in fact absent. The effect of this is that the single reason based upon the principle determines the conclusion on its own, and this is very similar to the operation of a legal rule that guarantees its conclusion. On this analysis, legal rules are principles which block the operation of all competing principles.

This approach has the advantage of a simpler logic, because it is not necessary anymore to distinguish both principles and rules in the logical language. Moreover, it opens the way for a gradual transition between principles and rules, by considering principles that shut out the operation of more and more of their competitors. It has the disadvantage that the logical behavior of legal rules is not part of the logic anymore, but must be simulated by adding to the premises of rule-based arguments that the principle that takes the logical role of the rule must make exceptions to all competing principles. Presently I would consider this as a reason against the *legal* logic which makes such a simulation necessary. In *Reasoning with Rules* [4], I therefore proposed a version of Reason-based Logic in which rules and principles are given different logical characteristics.[7]

2.6 Misrepresenting the Weighing of Reasons as Rule-based Arguments

As my second example of a theory that buys logical simplicity at the cost of misrepresenting the legal domain I will take the system popularized by Prakken and Sartor [e.g. 9]. I will call this system PS-logic. I expect that most readers are sufficiently familiar with it to make extensive exposition superfluous.

An argument in PS logic is a sequence of instantiated rules, where the rules are chained by their conclusions and conditions. Arguments can attack each other. One argument is for instance said to *rebut* another argument if the conclusions of the two arguments are complementary. In case of two arguments which rebut each other, the *stronger* argument of the two defeats the other one. Which argument is the stronger is determined by priority relations over the rules on which the arguments are based.

The idea of arguments that attack each other is quite alien to the legal domain, especially in the civil law areas, which rather deals with rules, principles, rights, values and exceptions. Whether somebody has a right, or is liable to be punished, ideally depends on the facts of the case and the law in question, and not on the arguments which lawyers might make to support the conclusions that such a right or liability exists. That reality is in this respect less than ideal, and that arguments can influence the outcome of legal cases does not show that the law is about arguments, but rather that our *views about the law* can be *influenced* by arguments. It is important to recognize that the questions what the law is and what we are justified to believe that the law is are, at least in principle, very different.[8]

This does not imply that PS logic is useless in connection with legal arguments. As Prakken and Sartor have shown frequently, the contrary is true. With some ingenuity it is possible to translate many different kinds of legal arguments into the conceptual framework of PS logic. My point here is that this translation is sometimes quite counterintuitive, as a consequence of the difference in conceptual framework employed by the law and PS logic. Since I do not have much space here, I will illustrate my point with a single example[9]:

A case exhibits three factors, say a, b, and c. The factors a and b plead for decision D, while c pleads for decision ¬D. Let us assume that the factors a and b are individually outweighed by c, but that together they outweigh c. Since all three factors are available in our example case, the solution is simple: decision D is the appropriate one.

[7]Reconsidering this issue again, about a year after writing the first version of this paper, I would say that the hybrid construction of our early work has some advantages that make it worthwhile to maintain the construction. It should not be used as an alternative for the logical representation of rules, however. In this respect I stick to the criticism ventilated in this paper.

[8]There is still a complication here, which was emphasized in [2, 6, and 8]. Because the law is an open system, the distinction between what the law is, and between what the best theory of the law says the law is, is not so sharp, to say the least. As a consequence legal arguments *that are actually adduced* (and not merely the possible ones on the basis of a set of premises; see [5]) can change the law, and thereby determine what the law *is*.

[9]The example has on purpose some similarity with the arguments discussed in [11]. Another example concerning oversimplification in PS-logic would be that (legal) rules are represented as sentences of the object language. See [14] for - in my opinion well-founded - criticism on this approach.

How should this be formalized in PS-logic? First the factors must be translated in to instantiated rules:

$$a \rightarrow D, b \rightarrow D, c \rightarrow \neg D.$$

Second priorities should be assigned to these instantiated rules:

$$c \rightarrow \neg D > a \rightarrow D$$

$$c \rightarrow \neg D > b \rightarrow D$$

Unhappily, given these priorities, the argument based on the rule $c \rightarrow \neg D$ defeats the arguments based on the rules $a \rightarrow D$ and $b \rightarrow D$, and the seeming conclusion should be that $\neg D$. Because the factors a and b together outweigh c, this is undesirable, and to avoid this undesirable conclusion, a new rule must be introduced, namely the rule $(a \,\&\, b) \rightarrow D$. This rule has priority over the rule $c \rightarrow \neg D$, and this solves the logical problem.

However, this solution introduces a conceptual problem, because the legal problem as stated originally did not mention the new rule at all. In fact it did not mention rules at all, only factors. Because of the universalizability of factors, the step from factors to rules has something to be said for it. But universalization from sets of factors to rules with compound conditions is a far cry from what happens in legal thinking. This step is a purely artificial one, only defensible because of the need to obtain the correct logical result. It is only necessary because PS-logic works with rules, rather than factors or reasons, and therefore needs a separate rule for every set of reasons. Again we see that the lack of logical power must be compensated for by introducing additional premises which seem to have no counterpart in the original domain theory.

The same point can be made in a slightly different way, namely by observing that if a logic is too weak, the validity of an argument must be coded into its (hidden) premises. Intuitively if the two factors a and b are both present, the decision should be D, even in the presence of factor c. Although the original theory does not contain a premise that would make the necessary derivation of the conclusion D possible, the desirability of this conclusion 'shows' that the premises

$(a \,\&\, b) \rightarrow D$, and
$(a \,\&\, b) \rightarrow D > c \rightarrow \neg D$

'must' be true and can therefore be added to the premises of the argument. This is a perfect example of the point made in section 2.3 that premises often are nothing else than coding an argument's intuitive validity into the premises of the argument. Unnecessary to say that the possibility to do this makes the logic almost useless as a test for the argument's validity.

The 'poor' conceptualization of the legal domain in PS-logic, which has no place for the weighing of reasons, makes this logic relatively simple and maybe therefore attractive at first sight. But the gain in simplicity goes at the cost of more difficult formalization and the introduction of unnatural premises, as was illustrated by the example above. Obviously, one example is not sufficient to reject PS-logic. However, in my opinion, this example illustrates a fundamental point, namely that if a logic for a domain does not use the conceptualization of the domain itself, the gain in logical simplicity must be bought at the cost of more complex and often unnatural formalizations of the domain knowledge. The disadvantage of this becomes clear from the above example, in which the formalization of the argument is adapted to make the formalized argument logically valid, as the informal argument intuitively seems to be.

3 What to Expect from Legal Logic?

In the above sections I developed two lines of thought that I want to tie together as a partial answer to the question what to expect from legal logic. First I argued that we should not expect from legal logic that it is a full theory of legal problem solving. It is merely a theory of valid legal reasoning in a broad sense. Such a theory is relevant for legal problem solving because legal problem solving involves legal reasoning. But the ability to reason validly is not sufficient to solve legal problems. Theories of legal logic can and should not be blamed for that, however.

Our expectations from legal logic should not be exaggerated, but they should not be too modest either. There are many viable systems of logic, and from a theory of legal logic we should expect more than that it is merely possible to express legal reasoning by means of it. For that last purpose a stripped down version of propositional logic suffices, as we have seen above. This brings me to the second argument line, to the effect that a logic that is meant to deal with legal reasoning should use a conceptual framework that resembles as much as possible that of the legal domain. The temptation to use a simpler logic should be resisted, because the simplicity of the logic is bought at the cost of more difficult and unnatural formalization of domain theories. Moreover, the translation of informal arguments into the language of the logic asks for more 'creativity' of the translator. It is tempting to use this creativity to ensure that intuitively valid arguments come out valid on the translation, and that intuitively invalid arguments come out invalid. But then the logic has lost much of its use, because the verdict on the validity of the informal argument lies with the translator, and not with the logic.

So, what should we expect from legal logic? Not a general theory for legal problem solving, but tools that facilitate the logical evaluation of *informal* legal arguments and that seek, for this purpose to adopt as much as possible the conceptual framework of real legal reasoning. The study of legal logic should start with the law, and not with formal logic [7]. The central question should not be how we can use logical tools for the evaluation of legal arguments [cf. 10], but how we can cast the forms of valid legal reasoning into a logical system. We should take the law as the starting point for our research on legal logic, and not already existing systems of non-legal logic.

Acknowledgement

The author would like to thank Henry Prakken for useful comments on a draft of this paper. He does not expect Prakken to agree with all of its contents, however.

References

[1] Dworkin, R. (1996). *Freedom's law. The moral reading of the American Constitution.* Harvard University Press, Cambridge.

[2] Hage, J.C., R. Leenes, and A. Lodder (1994). Hard cases; a procedural approach. *Artificial Intelligence and Law*, vol. 2, pp. 113-167.

[3] Hage, J.C. (1996). A Model of Legal Reasoning and a Logic to Match. *Artificial Intelligence and Law* **4**, nos. 3-4 (1996), pp. 199-273. Also in H. Prakken and G. Sartor (eds.), *Logical Models of Legal Argumentation*, Kluwer Academic Publishers, Dordrecht, pp. 43-117.

[4] Hage, J.C. (1997). *Reasoning with rules*, Kluwer Academic Publishers, Dordrecht.

[5] Hage J.C. (2000). Dialectical Models in Artificial Intelligence and Law. *Artificial Intelligence and Law* **8**, (2000), p. 137-172.

[6] Lodder A. (1999). *DiaLaw. On Legal Justification and Dialogical Models of Argumentation.* Kluwer, Dordrecht.

[7] McCarty, L.T. (1997) Some Arguments about Legal Arguments. *Proceedings of the Sixth International Conference on Artificial Intelligence and Law*, ACM, New York, 1997, pp. 215-224.

[8] Peczenik, A. and J.C. Hage (2000). Legal Knowledge about What?, *Ratio Juris* **13**, no. 3, p. 326-345.

[9] Prakken, H. and G. Sartor (1996). A Dialectical Model of Assessing Conflicting Arguments in Legal Reasoning. *Artificial Intelligence and Law*, **4** no. 3/4. pp. 331-368. Also in H. Prakken and G. Sartor (eds.), *Logical Models of Legal Argumentation.* Kluwer Academic Publishers, Dordrecht 1997.

[10] Prakken, H. (1997). *Logical tools for modeling legal argument, A Study of Defeasible Reasoning in Law*, Kluwer, Dordrecht.

[11] Prakken, H. (2000), An exercise in formalizing teleological case-based reasoning (extended abstract). J. Breuker e.a (eds.) *Proceedings of the Thirteenth Jurix Conference.* IOS Press, Amsterdam, p. 49-58.

[12] Verheij, Bart (1996). *Rules, Reasons, Arguments. Formal studies of argumentation and defeat.* Thesis Maastricht University.

[13] Verheij, H.B., J.C. Hage and H.J. van den Herik (1998). An integrated view of rules and principles. *Artificial Intelligence and Law* **6**, no. 1, p. 3-26.

[14] Verheij, Bart (1999). Logic, Context, and Valid Inference. Or: Can there be a Logic of Law? In H.J. van den Herik (ed.), *Proceedings of the Twelfth Jurix Conference*, GNI, Nijmegen, p. 109-121.

[15] R.P. Loui, Ampliative Inference, Computation and Dialectic, in R. Cummins and J. Pollock (eds.), *Philosophy and AI. Essays at the interface.* MIT Press, Cambridge 1991.

[16] R.P Loui, How a formal theory of rationality can be normative. *Journal of Philosophy* **90** (1993), p. 137-143.

Contrary to Duty Obligations
A Study in Legal Ontology

Jaap Hage
Department of Metajuridica
Faculty of Law
Universiteit Maastricht
The Netherlands
jaap.hage@metajur.unimaas.nl

Abstract. In this paper the problems in deontic logic around contrary to duty obligations are used to conduct a study in basic normative ontology. Three causes of the problems around contrary to duty obligations are identified, that is 1) the attempt to analyze obligations in terms of what is ideally the case, 2) the application of deontic inheritance to the presuppositions of obligations, and 3) the failure to distinguish between what will be called 'inclusive' and 'exclusive ought-to-do'. These three causes are all attributed to insufficient distinctions on the ontological level.

1 The Relevance of Deontic Logic for Legal Ontology

A central issue in legal ontology is the study of normative positions. Such normative positions include being under an obligation, having a right, being entitled, etc.[1] The study of these positions and their mutual relations is a study of basic (legal) ontology, and includes the study of the relations between what ought to be done, what is permitted, and what is obligatory. In short, the central topics of deontic logic are part of the study of normative positions, which is in turn part of legal ontology.

In this paper I hope to make a contribution to the development of legal ontology by focusing on an issue that has plagued the development of deontic logic for quite a while. I refer to the issue of contrary-to-duty obligations (CTDO's). Since Chisholm [4] criticized the Standard System of Deontic Logic (SDL) for not being able to deal with duties which arise as a consequence of a norm violation, the issue of CTDO's has not disappeared from the stage of deontic logic.

My main thesis in this paper is that the complications that arise in connection with CTDO's have little to do with CTDO's themselves, but are consequences of deficient theories of the nature of obligations. Before starting my argument, I want to warn the reader that she should not expect a proper paper on deontic logic, let alone the umpteenth attempt to 'solve' the CTDO-paradoxes. My focus will be on analysis, not on the development of a logical system.

[1] See e.g. [1, 2, 3].

Jaap Hage, 'Contrary to Duty Obligations – A Study in Legal Ontology' in Bart Verheij, Arno R. Lodder, Ronald P. Loui and Antoinette J. Muntjewerff (eds.), *Legal Knowledge and Information Systems. Jurix 2001: The Fourteenth Annual Conference*. Amsterdam: IOS Press, 2001, pp. 89-102.

2 Ought-to-do and Ought-to-be

Prescriptive and prohibitory norms have as one of their main functions to guide human behavior. They indicate what people or organizations should or should not do. There seem to be two different ways in which this purpose can be achieved. A norm can indicate what kind of action is to be performed or refrained from, and for which actors this holds. Such norms are called ought-to-do (or Tun-sollen) norms.

A norm can also indicate how the world should look like, which states of affairs ought (not) to be the case. These norms are called ought-to-be (Sein-sollen) norms. Ought-to-be norms sometimes seem to occur in legal practice. In a sense they are problematic, however, because they do not specify what ought to be done, and which actors are to do what ought to be done.

It seems to me that ought-to-be norms can be given two different interpretations, which should be distinguished very carefully. On the one interpretation, ought-to-be norms specify how the world would ideally be. On this interpretation, ought-to-be norms themselves do not prescribe or prohibit behavior, because there is no logical relation between what is ideally the case and what ought to be done. Only if ought-to-be norms are complemented with the prescription to strive for the ideal, they guide behavior. But then the 'real' norm is the ought-to-do norm that prescribes to strive for the ideal. The ought-to-be norm merely provides content to this prescription.

On the other interpretation, ought-to-be norms prescribe to see to it that the obligatory state of affairs is achieved or maintained, depending on whether the ideal state in question already obtains. Briefly stated, the obligation is to see to it that the obligatory state of affairs obtains. On this interpretation, the ought-to-be norm is 'really' an ought-to-do norm in disguise. It is an incomplete ought-to-do norm, because it leaves the actor unspecified. This deficiency can be remedied, however, by saying that the actors are those who are responsible for seeing to it that the obligatory state of affairs is achieved or maintained.

If this analysis is correct, ought-to-be norms as such only seem to exist. In reality they are either no norms (in the sense of behavior guiding entities) at all, but the formulations of ideals, or they are ought-to-do norms with unspecified actors. On this analysis there would only be ought-to-do norms, and deontic logic should therefore be a logic of ought-to-do norms.

2.1 Attempts to Reduce Ought-to-do to Ought-to-be

It may seem, however, that there are real ought-to-be norms nevertheless. In this connection one might think of norms of the form 'It ought to be that X does (or: refrains from doing) A'. Moreover, one might even argue that ought-to-do norms are nothing else than such ought-to-be norms. 'X ought to do A' would on this view be analyzed as 'It ought to be the case that X does A'.

Such an analysis would in my opinion be defective. The sentence 'X ought to do A' means amongst others that X is responsible for doing A. This responsibility is lost on the analysis that it ought merely be the case that X does A. If it ought to be the case that X does A, it may very well also be the case that not X, but Y is responsible for X's doing A. In other words, if 'X ought to do A' is analyzed as 'It ought to be the case that X does A', something of the meaning of the original sentence is lost.

One might attempt to rescue the ought-to-be analysis by distinguishing between:

a It ought to be the case that X does A; and

b It ought to be the case that Y sees to it that X does A.

The former sentence might then be read as expressing that X is the responsible person for his own doing A, while the second sentence would be read as expressing that Y is responsible for X's doing A. This 'rescue' does not work, because either the second sentence leaves unspecified whether Y is responsible for his seeing to it that X does A, or it is not possible anymore to express that ideally Y sees to it that x does A, but that Y is not responsible for doing so.

Moreover, there is another objection against the ought-to-be analysis. Let us assume that sentences of the form 'It ought to be the case that ....' specify an ideal situation. On this assumption, the sentence 'It ought to be the case that X does A' means that in the ideal situation X does A. It may, however, be the case that X has promised to do A, while the world would be very slightly better if X would not do A. In this case, I feel that we can say that both X ought to do A, and that ideally X would not do A. Otherwise the obligation to keep one's promises would not exist if somebody promises to do what will lead to a sub-ideal outcome (the value of promise-keeping included). This is an understandable moral position (a kind of utilitarianism), but it should not be made the correct position on purely logical grounds.

This counter-intuitive result can be avoided by not assuming that 'It ought to be the case that ...' indicates an ideal situation. However, if this assumption is not made, it is unclear how the phrase in question should be interpreted. The temptation is big to interpret 'It ought to be the case that X does A' as meaning the same as 'X ought to A', but then an ought-to-be is reduced to an ought-to-do, rather than the other way round.

In my opinion it is best to interpret ought-to-be sentences as specifying ideal situations, and on this interpretation ought-to-be and ought-to-do cannot be reduced to each other.

2.2 *Standard Deontic Logic as a Logic of Ideals*

SDL is an extension of propositional logic. Its language allows the formation of deontic sentences by pre-fixing a deontic operator, typically O, F, or P, to a sentence. Since the deontic operators operate on sentences, the resulting logic is a logic of the ought-to-be type. A sentence of the form O(P) would typically be read as 'It is obligatory that P', or 'It ought to be the case that P'.

SDL is best characterized by its semantics. A sentence of the form O(P) is interpreted as true iff the sentence P is true in all 'ideal' worlds. F(P) is true iff P is false in all ideal worlds, while P(p) is true iff P is true in at least one ideal world.

The 'official semantics' for SDL is formulated more precisely, by defining an accessibility relation R over the set of possible worlds. For each possible world w there is a non-empty set of possible worlds that stand in this relation to (are accessible from) w. The sentence is true in w iff the sentence is true in all the worlds that stand in the relation R to w. Although this official semantics is more precise, I also gave the intuitive reading, because it is, as we will see, more revealing about the nature of SDL.

The semantics of SDL validates a rule of inference to the effect that the logical consequences of what is obligatory are obligatory too. That this rule is validated is immediately clear if one realizes what is obligatory in a world is the case in its ideal alternatives. In these alternatives the facts that are logically implied by the facts that obtain must also obtain. Therefore the logical consequences of what is obligatory in a world w is the case in all ideal alternatives of w, which means that they are obligatory in w too. For instance, if O(P&Q) is true in w, P&Q is true in all its ideal alternatives. Therefore P is true in all its alternatives, which means that O(P) is true in w.

A special case of this general rule is the rule that allows arguments of the form *deontic detachment*:

> Obviously, if both $p \rightarrow q$ and p are true in all ideal worlds, q must be true in all ideal worlds too.

Given its semantics, SDL is a suitable logic for ideals. It specifies what logically follows from facts that ideally obtain. The facts that follow from what is ideal are ideal themselves. Apparently the characterization of the worlds that are accessible from a world w as ideal worlds relative to w is aptly chosen.

2.3 The Chisholm Paradox

We have seen that ought-to-be sentences can both be interpreted as sentences about what is ideally the case, and as ought-to-do sentences in disguise. An interesting question is whether SDL is also a suitable logic for this latter interpretation of ought-to-be sentences. Is SDL a suitable logic if O(P) is interpreted as 'The person who is responsible for situation P ought to see to it that P is the case'?

Briefly stated, the answer to this question is an unambiguous 'No'. SDL is not suitable for the ought-to-do interpretation of ought-to-be sentences. The first indication that this is so can be found if the rule for deontic detachment is inspected. If somebody ought to see to it that Q if P, and if he also ought to see to it that P, this does not logically imply that he ought to see to it that Q.

An example might make this clearer. Suppose that John ought to see to it that he helps his neighbors and also that if he helps them, he tells them so. Do these obligations together imply that John ought to see to it that he tells his neighbors that he will help them? Obviously not. John ought only tell his neighbors that he will help them if he will actually help them. The mere obligation to help them is not sufficient.[2] And yet this inference, a special case of deontic detachment, is validated by SDL. SDL leads to counterintuitive results if interpreted as an ought-to-do logic in disguise, because deontic detachment is not suitable for reasoning with ought-to-do obligations.

Chisholm [4] has employed this insight by showing how SDL leads to paradoxical results if interpreted as an ought-to-do logic in disguise. Chisholm's case ran as follows:

---

[2]The attentive reader will have noticed that I moved from ought-to-see-to-it terminology to ought-to-do terminology. This is on purpose. I think that in the present context the ought-to-see-to-it terminology is forced and only motivated by a misguided desire to stick as much as possible to ought-to-be like terminology.

- A certain man ought to go to assist his neighbors.
- He ought to tell them he is coming if he goes.
- If he does not go then he ought not to tell them he is coming.
- He does not go.

According to the usual model theoretic semantics of SDL this can be translated in terms of ideals as follows[3]:

- In the ideal situation a certain man goes to the assistance of his neighbors.
- In the ideal situation, if he does go he tells them he is coming.
- If he does not go then in the ideal situation he does not tell them he is coming.
- He does not go.

From the first two premises follows (by deontic detachment) that in the ideal situation, our man tells his neighbors he is coming. From the last two premises follows (by Modus Ponens) that in the ideal situation he does not tell that he is coming. In other words, framed as a theory about what is ideally the case, this set of premises is inconsistent. And yet, interpreted as a theory of what ought to be done, the premises are consistent.

The point of this paradox is that if ought-sentences are interpreted as sentences about what is the case in an ideal situation, they cannot be used to express what ought to be done in sub-ideal situations. Since there can obviously be obligations about what to do in sub-ideal situations (in particular CTDO's) SDL is unsuitable to deal with an important category of obligations. This point can even be generalized. If ought-sentences are interpreted as saying what is the case in all worlds that belong to a particular subset of possible worlds, whether these worlds are ideal or not, the resulting logic cannot be used to express CTDO's.

This is far from surprising, because SDL is a logic for ought-to-be interpreted as ideals, and not for ought-to-be interpreted as ought-to-do in disguise. The Chisholm paradox is a good way to point this out, but the validity of deontic detachment in SDL also sufficiently demonstrates that SDL should not be used as a logic for what ought to be done. If deontic logic is taken to be a logic for ought-to-do (and not for what is ideally the case), SDL or variants of it that allow deontic detachment should not be used for deontic logic. This conclusion is based on general considerations concerning ought-to-be 'obligations' and ought-to-do obligations, and not merely on difficulties in SDL to deal with CTDO's. Attempts to contest the conclusion by pointing out sophisticated logical theories that can 'deal with' CTDO's in a SDL-like logic are not sufficient, unless they are accompanied by a philosophical theory that explains how ought-to-do obligations can be reduced to ought-to be's. As yet I have never seen such a philosophical theory.[4]

3 Deontic Inheritance

Some may think that I am too rash in limiting the validity of deontic detachment to a logic for ideals. Deontic detachment, it may be argued, is a special case of deontic inheritance, the

[3]There are all kinds of intricacies involved in the formalisation of this example, which are beyond the scope of this paper..

[4]The absence of satisfactory philosophical theories about the (non-)relation between ought-to-do and ought-to-be explains why this paper hardly pays any attention to the numerous attempts to deal with CTDO's within the boundaries of SDL.

validity of which is a desirable characteristic in deontic logic.

Informally stated, deontic inheritance is the phenomenon that if a state of affairs or an action is obligatory, its implications are also obligatory. For instance, if cars ought to be both locked and well-parked, it follows that cars ought to be locked. Or, if John ought to repay all his debts, it follows that John ought to repay his debt to Alice.

Both examples provide in my opinion illustrations of well-used deontic inheritance. But precisely what do they illustrate? The first example is probably best interpreted as dealing with deontic inheritance in a logic of ideals. If it ought to be the case that cars are both locked and well-parked, this means that in the ideal case, cars are both locked and well-parked. From this it follows, unproblematically as far as I can see, that in the ideal case cars are locked. This is precisely the kind of deontic inheritance that SDL allows, and in connection with what is ideally the case, this is also as it should be.

The second example leads to some complications. It may well be that if some type of action 'implies' some other type of action, the obligation to perform the first kind of action 'implies' the obligation to perform the second kind of action. The question, however, is what it means that an action implies another action. Actions are not propositions or sentences, and the implication can therefore not be logical entailment. The implication must here be some other kind of relation. Let us call this relation 'involvement', and let us hypothesize that if an action involves some other action, this latter action inherits the obligatory nature of the former action.

The question that still needs to be answered is when one action involves another action. A thorough investigation of this issue lies outside the scope of this paper, but in connection with CTDO's, one particular kind of involvement seems especially interesting. There is a kind of action that is closely related to propositions, namely seeing to it that some state of affairs obtains.[5] This close relation can be exploited by characterizing the involvement between two actions of the type 'seeing to it that ...' in terms of the entailment relation between the states of affairs that ought to be seen to. Some problems with CTDO's which were raised in connection with SDL then turn up again in connection with the logic for ought-to-do.

3.1 Some Linguistic Conventions

To avoid cumbersome sentences in discussing actions of the see-to-it type, I introduce some formalism. The two-place predicateOd is used to express ought-to-do obligations. The first parameter denotes the actor, the second the action type that is to be performed. For instance, Od(john, pay_debts) would mean that John ought to pay his debts.

A second convention is that if P is a sentence, *p denotes the state of affairs expressed by this sentence. If, for instance, the sentence Closed(window) expresses that the window is closed, *closed(window) denotes the state of affairs that the window is closed.

The function-expression stit/1 is used to transform states of affairs into action types. Stit stands for 'see to it that'. For instance, Od(john, stit(*closed_window)) would mean that John ought to see to it that the window is closed. This is an ought-to-do sentence, which should be distinguished from the sentence that it ought to be the case that John sees to it that the

[5]The notion of 'seeing to it that ...' has been developed in agency theory. A brief overview of this literature can be found in [5].

window is closed. In contrast to the latter, the former sentence expresses John's responsibility for seeing to it that the window is closed, and does not express that in the ideal case, John sees to it that the window is closed.

The one-place function expression ¬ is used to transform an action type into the action type which is refraining from the first action type. For instance, ¬cycle denotes the action type refrain from cycling.[6] In this connection I will assume that Od(actor, ¬action) entails ~Od(actor, action).

Finally the two-place predicate Involves is used to express that performing the action type denoted by its first parameter involves performing the action type denoted by its second parameter. For instance, the sentence

Involves(fulfill_duties, pay_debts)

expresses that fulfilling one's duties involves paying one's debts.

3.2 Deontic Inheritance for Ought-to-do

Having the linguistic tools in place, we can look at the logical characterization of action types that involve each other. An attractive looking hypothesis is that if some sentence entails another sentence, seeing to it that the state of affairs expressed by the first sentence obtains involves seeing to it that the state of affairs expressed by the second sentence obtains. In our primitive formalism: if P entails Q, stit(*p) involves stit(*q). This hypothesis would have the desired consequence that seeing to it that the cars are locked and well-parked, involves seeing to it that the cars are locked:

Involves(stit(*locked(cars) & well_parked(cars)), stit(*locked(cars)))

Or, in general[7]:

$$N(P \rightarrow Q) \rightarrow \forall x(\text{Involves}(\text{stit}(*p), \text{stit}(*q)))$$

This can be combined with the theory that if some action type involves another action type, the obligation to perform the first type of action 'entails' the obligation to perform the second type of action[8]:

$$\text{Involves}(a, b) \rightarrow (\text{Od}(x, a) \rightarrow \text{Od}(x, b))$$

[6] The operator '~' is used for negation.

[7] The combination of the necessity-operator N in combination with the material conditional is used to express entailment.

[8] In my opinion this entailment is better represented as a rule, but to avoid additional complications I ignore that here.

3.3 The Paradox of the Good Samaritan

The construction proposed above to translate logical relations between sentences to involvement-relations between action types has the consequence that some paradoxes related to CTDO's re-appear. I will illustrate this by discussing the paradox of the Good Samaritan [6]. The biblical case of the Good Samaritan runs as follows: A Jew is robbed and the Samaritan ought to help the Jew who was robbed. This case might be formalized as:

O(Helps(samaritan, robbed_jew))
N(Helps(samaritan, robbed_jew) → Robbed(jew))

These two sentences allow under (a somewhat extended version of) SDL the derivation of

O(Robbed(jew))

In other words, it is possible to derive from the sentence that it is obligatory that the Samaritan helps the robbed Jew, that the Jew ought to be robbed. A crucial assumption in this connection is that the sentence that the Samaritan helps the robbed Jew entails[9] the sentence that the Jew was robbed and that this entailment makes that the obligatoriness of the helping is inherited by the being robbed.

One way to solve this paradox is to make a scope distinction and leave the proposition that somebody was robbed outside the scope of the deontic operator[10]:

$\exists x$(Robbed(x)) & Od(samaritan, help(x))

Notice, however, that in this formalization the deontic predicate occurs within the scope of the existential quantifier and that the resulting sentence is not of the ought-to-be type anymore (even disregarding the replacement of the O-operator by the Od-predicate). Apparently an adequate analysis of this type of case requires a deontic logic that is not of the ought-to-be type.

The question that is now to be addressed is whether the problem that occurs in an ought-to-be setting re-appears in an ought-to-do setting with stit action types. The following formalization nicely illustrates the point that I want to make:

Od(samaritan, stit(*helps(samaritan, robbed_jew)))
N(Helps(samaritan, robbed_jew) → Robbed(jew))

Under the hypothesis formulated in the previous section, the entailment of Robbed(jew) by Helps(samaritan, robbed_jew)would, through deontic inheritance, allow the derivation of Od(stit(samaritan, robbed_jew)). The problem that occurred in connection with SDL seems to

[9]Later in this section I will raise doubts concerning this 'entailment'.

[10]The scope distinction proposed here was inspired by a similar distinction proposed by Smullyan [7] in connection with alethic modal logic. A strongly related approach was proposed by Castañeda [8]. He distinguished between actions (practitions) and factual circumstances implied by those actions. For instance, the action of helping the robbed Jew implies the factual circumstance that the Jew was robbed. According to Castañeda, the obligation has a deontic focus which is only directed on the helping, and not on the fact that the Jew was robbed.

re-appear under the present version of ought-to-do- logic. Apparently the transition from ought-to-be to ought-to-do logic is not sufficient, and a deeper solution is required.

This deeper solution is in my opinion that the relation between the state of affairs that the Samaritan helps the robbed Jew and the state of affairs that the Jew was robbed must be analyzed more thoroughly. The first state of affairs does not entail the second state of affairs, but *presupposes* it. That is a different relation than that between the state of affairs that the cars are both locked and well-parked on the one hand and that the cars are locked on the other hand. This latter relation would in my opinion be one of *entailment* proper.[11] The first state of affairs so to speak 'comprises' the second one. In such a case, deontic inheritance seems unobjectionable. An obligation to bring about a particular state of affairs extends to what this state of affairs comprises. If one state of affairs presupposes another one, however, deontic inheritance seems in general not to be acceptable. The obligation to bring about a particular state of affairs does not extend to this state of affairs' presuppositions.

Therefore I propose to limit the notion of entailment that allows deontic inheritance, in order to exclude presupposition. This rescues the hypothesis of the previous section that in connection with stit action types, deontic inheritance can be based on entailment relations between sentences. The rescue goes at the cost, however, of having an entailment relation that is in need of further elucidation.

It turns out that the paradox of the Good Samaritan can easily be avoided by means of a scope distinction in connection with an analysis in ought-to-do terminology. The paradox threatens to re-occur if the action types in the case are analyzed as stit-type actions. This re-occurrence can in turn be avoided by limiting deontic inheritance to entailment relations between sentences that do not include presupposition.[12]

4 Doing Something in a Particular Way

A distinction that is superficially related to that between a state of affairs or action and its presuppositions is that between performing an action in a particular way and performing it as such. The latter distinction plays a role in, amongst others, the case of the cycling children.

The case of the cycling children [10] is more difficult to handle than that of the Good Samaritan, because it involves proper entailment between action types. The case runs as follows: In London, children, including Alice, ought not cycle on the streets. But if they cycle, they should do so on the left hand side of the road. Suppose that Alice happens to cycle. She should therefore cycle on the left. Cycling on the left involves cycling, and therefore, it seems, if Alice cycles, she ought to cycle, which is in contradiction with the prohibition to cycle.

I will confine my discussion of this case to an analysis in terms of non-stit action types.[13] Given this starting point, the case can be formalized as:

[11] In the appendix to this paper, I attempt to analyze the distinction between presupposition and entailment.

[12] The solutions of the Good Samaritan paradox can, with minor adaptations, also be used for the paradox of the Knower [9], which also results from treating presupposition as entailment.

[13] If the case is formalised in terms of stit-actions, it strongly resembles the stit-analysis of the case of the Good Samaritan and should be treated analogously.

Od(alice, ¬cycle)
Cycles(alice) → Od(alice, cycle_left))
Involves(cycle_left, cycle)
Cycles(alice)

These sentences allow the derivation of

Od(alice, cycle)

which is inconsistent with the first premise.

The problem with this case is the step from 'Alice ought to cycle on the left' to 'Alice ought to cycle'. It seems that not always when some action involves another action, the obligation to perform the first action extends to the second action.

To solve this problem, we must pay attention to an ambiguity in the sentence 'Alice ought to cycle on the left'. Suppose that Alice is not a child, but a soldier who has received the command to cycle on the left hand side of the road to some building. In this case Alice's obligation is twofold. Not only should she cycle to the building, but she should do so on the left hand side of the road. In this case there is no problem to derive the obligation to cycle from the obligation to cycle on the left.

The original case is different, because there the obligation to cycle on the left is an obligation to do the cycling on the left. This obligation does not imply the obligation to cycle. Apparently the obligation to do something in a particular way can regard both the main action and the way it is performed, or only the way in which the main action is to be performed.

Let me introduce two new conventions to explicate this distinction. The first convention is that the term denoting an action type can be extended to indicate the way in which the main action is to be performed. This extension is done by indicating the modus operandi between square brackets, as follows: cycle[on_the_left]

The second convention is the introduction of an additional predicate for ought-to-do Od_m, which expresses that the obligation is not directed at the main action, but only at the mode in which the main action is to be performed:

Od_m(alice, cycle[on_the_left])

Given these conventions, the sentence

Od(actor, action[mode])

entails the sentence

Od_m(actor, action[mode])

but not the other way round. The rule that if some action type involves another action type, the obligation to perform the first action type extends to the second action type, only holds for the original Od, and not for the relation Od_m.

The original cycle-case should then be formalized as follows:

Od(alice, ¬cycle)
Od_m(alice, cycle[on_the_left])
Involves(cycle[on_the_left], cycle)
Cycles(alice)

On this formalization it is not possible anymore to derive

Od(alice, cycle)

which is as it should be.

The second cycle-case (where Alice is a soldier) should be formalized as:

Od(alice, ¬cycle)
Od(alice, cycle[on_the_left])
Involves(cycle[on_the_left], cycle)

Barring defeasibility this set is inconsistent, because by means of deontic inheritance it is possible to derive

Od(alice, cycle)

The approach to the case of the cycling children proposed here is also available for other cases that seem problematic because of the distinction between doing *something* in a particular way, and doing something *in a particular way*. These other cases include that of the Gentle Murder [11].

5 Ontological Conclusions

It becomes time to look back and draw some conclusions. The first conclusion is that there is no single problem with CTDO's.

The first problem, that arises in connection with the Chisholm-case, is the consequence of treating sentences that express what ought to be done as if they were saying what would be the case in an ideal world. The Chisholm-case brings out clearly that such an analysis of ought-to-do makes it impossible to express what ought to be done in a non-ideal world. However, this is not a problem of CTDO's, but the problem of a wrong analysis of ought-to-do sentences.

The second problem has to do with the role of presuppositions. This problem is exemplified by the case of the Good Samaritan. It arises through deontic inheritance. If the truth of a sentence has certain presuppositions, these presuppositions will be true in all possible worlds in which this sentence is true. In combination with a logic that treats obligations as states of affairs that ought to be the case, this leads to the problem that if a state of affairs ought to be the case, its presuppositions also ought to be the case.

The philosophical solution to this problem is that deontic inheritance should not be combined with presuppositions. If an action type ought to be performed, this ought does not extend to the presuppositions of this action.[14] An ought-to-do of an action type only extends to

[14]Most often these presuppositions will not even be actions, but states of affairs, and the ought-to-do of the action type cannot extend to the presuppositions for that very reason. This explains the attractiveness of Castañeda's distinction between practitions and factual circumstances.

other action types which the obligatory action type involves. An action type does not involve its presuppositions.

Technically this solution can be translated into formalization in two ways. One is the non-occurrence of the presupposition as, or within, a parameter of the ought-to-do-predicate, as is shown by the following analysis of the case of the Good Samaritan:

$$\exists x(\text{Robbed}(x) \rightarrow \text{Od}(\text{samaritan}, \text{help}(x)))$$

This solution is only available if the deontic expressions are not treated as operators on sentences, as is done in SDL.

The second way is not to treat presupposition as a kind of entailment. This solution does not work within SDL, because the semantics of SDL cannot distinguish between presuppositions and entailment.[15] It is available in the ought-to-do approach proposed above, however, because this approach makes use of a dedicated predicate 'involves' that can be defined as to exclude presuppositions, as is shown in the appendix.

Notice that this second problem has again nothing to do with CTDO's. Philosophically it is the problem how to deal with presuppositions, and technically it is a problem of scope or the definition of involvement. CTDO's merely provide a suitable occasion to highlight this problem that already existed independently.

The third problem arises because of an ambiguity in sentences of the form 'X ought to do A in way W'. The obligation on X may concern both doing A and doing it in way W, or it may only concern doing A in way W, without committing X to doing A. This problem underlies the cases of the cycling children and the gentle murder.

On a superficial analysis, this problem can be seen as a case of presuppositions, where doing a in way W presupposes doing A. A more transparent solution is to distinguish between two versions of ought-to-do, that reflect the ambiguity of these sentences. There is an inclusive ought-to-do that concerns both the action type and the way in which it is performed, and an exclusive ought-to-do, which only concerns the way an action type is performed.

Deontic inheritance based on the involvement of action types is only allowed in the case of the inclusive ought-to-do. Cycling on the left involves cycling, but the obligation to cycle on the left only implies the obligation to cycle if the first obligation is inclusive.

Notice that also in this third case, CTDO's merely function as an occasion to bring out a problem that in itself has nothing to do with CTDO's. Actually, I think that there is no intrinsic problem with CTDO's at all. I see no good reason why obligations that arise as a consequence of a violation of another obligation should be any different from other obligations. Their only special characteristic seems to be that they are useful to highlight deficiencies in logical theories that exist independently of them. For this characteristic we should be grateful, because it helps us to improve our logical theories.

Which improvements should we make as a consequence of these seeming problems? First and foremost we should sharply distinguish between sentences that express what is ideally the case and sentences that express what ought to be done. In my opinion it is principally impossible to express what ought to be done in terms of what would ideally be the case, or

[15] On the analysis given in the appendix, both entailed and presupposed states of affairs obtain in all possible worlds in which the entailing or presupposing state of affairs obtains. This suffices for deontic inheritance to work in SDL.

– in general – what would be the case in a particular set of worlds. The fundamental point is that there is an irreducible difference between what ought to be done and what is the case. Therefore, in my opinion, logics that analyze what ought to be done in terms of what is the case in any world, ideal or sub-ideal, are bound to fail. If this failure is not brought to light by CTDO's, there will turn up some other problem.

The second improvement that should be made is that a clear theory should be developed about the legitimacy of deontic inheritance. It seems to me to be beyond doubt that deontic inheritance is acceptable in a large number of case. It seems also beyond doubt that there are cases, such as those which involve presuppositions, in which deontic inheritance is not acceptable.

As yet, I know of no good theory that explains when deontic inheritance is acceptable, and when not. As a first hypothesis I would say that 'deontic' inheritance is acceptable in a logic of what is ideally the case, in the sense that if something is ideally the case, its logical consequences (excluding presuppositions) are also ideally the case. Deontic inheritance is acceptable in a logic for ought-to-do in the case of action types that involve each other. This merely shifts the problem, however, to the question when one action type involves another action type.

The third improvement is to distinguish between an inclusive and an exclusive ought-to-do, and to connect this distinction to the allowance of deontic inheritance. In section 4 I have indicated how this might be done.

Appendix: Entailment and Presupposition

A familiar theory of presupposition runs that if the truth of sentence A presupposes the truth of sentence B, the falsity of A also presupposes the truth of B [12, p. 167f.]. For instance, both 'The king of France is bold' and 'The king of France is not bold' presuppose the truth of the sentence 'France has a king'. Let me use this theory to give an analysis that distinguishes between entailment and presupposition.

I will treat both presupposition and entailment as relations between states of affairs and will exploit the convention about the relation between states of affairs and the sentences expressing them exposed in section 3.1. Given these assumptions, the difference between entailment and presupposition can be characterized as follows[16]:

Presupposition

Presupposes(*a, *b) is true, iff $N(A \rightarrow B)$ & $N(\sim A \rightarrow B)$ & $\sim N(B)$ is true.

Entailment

Entails (*a, *b) is true, iff $(N(A \rightarrow B) \,\&\, \sim N(\sim A \rightarrow B)) \vee N(B)$ is true.

Intuitively this boils down to that a state of affairs *a presupposes some other state of affairs *b if *b does not obtain in all possible worlds, but does obtain in all possible worlds in which either *a or *∼a obtains.[17] State of affairs *a entails state of affairs *b if either *b obtains in all possible worlds, or if it obtains in all possible worlds in which *a obtains, but not in all

[16]Here the N-operator should be interpreted as 'in all possible worlds it is the case that ...'

[17]This presupposes a semantics (interpretation function on sentences) according to which *∼s does not by definition obtain in all possible worlds in which *s does not obtain.

possible worlds in which $*\sim a$ obtains. Clearly, it is not possible that a state of affairs both entails and presupposes some other state of affairs

Given the above definitions of entailment and presupposition, it is possible to define an involves-relation between action types that excludes presupposition:

Involvement

Involves(action_1, action_2) is true, iff N($\forall x$(Entails(*performs(x, action_1), *performs(x, action_2))) is true.

Given this definition of involvement, cycling on the left involves cycling, but helping a robbed person does not involve anything about robbing.

References

[1] Hohfeld, W.N. Fundamental Legal Conceptions as Applied in Judicial Reasoning, 23 *Yale Law Journal*, 16 (1913).
[2] Lindahl, L. *Position and Change; A Study in Law and Logic*. Reidel, Dordrecht 1977.
[3] Allen, L.E. and C.S. Saxon. A-Hohfeld: A Language for Robust Structural Representation of Knowledge in the Legal Domain to Build Interpretation-Assistance Expert Systems. J-J. Ch. Meyer and R.J. Wieringa (eds.), *Deontic Logic in Computer Science. Normative System Specification*. John Wiley & Sons, London e.a. 1993, p. 205-224.
[4] Chisholm, R.M. Contrary-to-duty Imperatives and Deontic Logic, *Analysis* 24 (1963), p. 33-36.
[5] Bartha, P. Moral Preference, Contrary-to-Duty Obligation and Defeasible Oughts. P. McNamara and H. Prakken (eds.), *Norms, Logics, and Information Systems*, IOS Press, Amsterdam e.a.(1999), p. 93-108.
[6] Lewis, D. Semantic analyses for dyadic deontic logic. S.Stendlund (ed.), *Logical Theory and Semantic Analysis*, Reidel, Dordrecht 1974, p. 1-14.
[7] Smullyan, A.F. Modality and description. *The Journal of Symbolic Logic* vol. 13 (1948) nr. 1, p. 113-127.
[8] Castañeda, H.N., The Paradoxes of Deontic Logic: The Simplest Solution to All of Them in One Fell Swoop. R. Hilpinen (ed.), *New Studies in Deontic Logic*, Reidel Dordrecht 1981, p. 37-86.
[9] Åqvist, L.. Good Samaritans, Contrary-to-Duty Imperatives, and Epistemic Obligations. *Noûs* 1 (1967), p. 361-379.
[10] Prakken, H. and M. Sergot, Contrary-to-duty obligations and defeasible deontic reasoning, *Studia Logica* 57(1) (1996), p. 91-115.
[11] Forrester, J.W. Gentle murder, or the adverbial Samaritan. *Journal of Philosophy* 19 (1984), p. 193-197.
[12] Levinson S.C. *Pragmatics*. Cambridge University Press 1983.

Some Operators for Refinement of Normative Systems

Juliano S.A. Maranhão
Faculty of Law
University of São Paulo
Brazil
jsam@uol.com.br

Abstract. Refinement is an operation of theory change where new or old beliefs (norms) are restricted by some specific condition, instead of being fully accepted or rejected. We present constructions, based on AGM partial meet contraction and revision, for operators of external, internal and global refinement and show that they satisfy reasonable AGM-like postulates. Then we apply these operators to a hard case and show that global refinement has advantages to cope with the problem of gaps in normative systems.

1 Introduction

The identification of the relevant conditions to the enforcement of legal rules is a problem, which, according to H.L.A. Hart, lies in the very core of legal reasoning:

"in the case of legal rules, the criteria of relevance and closeness of resemblance depend on many complex factors running through the legal system and on the aims or purpose which may be attributed to the rule."..."to characterize these would be to characterize whatever is specific or peculiar in legal reasoning."(9, p.127).

An attempt to solve this problem would be to define as *relevant* those conditions which are explicitly mentioned by a norm in the normative system as a condition of application of a normative solution (obligatory, forbidden, permitted). This would be, according to Alchourrón and Bulygin (1, p.154), a description of the *thesis of relevance* of the normative system. But in legal cases there may be circumstances in which the normative solution provided by the legal system violates the (moral or political) purposes of the regulation. Or at least there may be circumstances in which the opposite normative solution to that indicated by the system seems to further these purposes better. Clearly, these circumstances are, in some sense, *relevant*, even though they were unforeseen by the lawgiver. According to Alchourrón and Bulygin, they would belong to a description of the *hypothesis of relevance* of the normative system, which always express a value judgement about its axiological adequacy (1, p.156-157). If a condition which *ought to* be relevant according to the hypothesis of relevance is not present in the descriptive thesis of relevance of the normative system, they speak of an *axiological gap*. An axiological gap should then be distinguished from a *normative gap* which is present

Juliano S. A. Maranhão, 'Some Operators for Refinement of Normative Systems' in Bart Verheij, Arno R. Lodder, Ronald P. Loui and Antoinette J. Muntjewerff (eds.), *Legal Knowledge and Information Systems. Jurix 2001: The Fourteenth Annual Conference*. Amsterdam: IOS Press, 2001, pp. 103-115.

when the lawgiver does not provide any normative solution to a relevant case (according to the thesis of relevance).

For example, in a regulation constituted by the single norm "it is forbidden to smoke in this room", the thesis of relevance describes the condition of "being inside the room" as relevant. But one may argue that according to the purpose of the rule, which is, say, "non disturbance", smoking in the room should be permitted, if the smoker is next to an open window. This last condition is in the hypothesis of relevance and since the proposed solution conflicts with the non-smoking rule, it constitutes an axiological gap.

In a recent paper (13), Rodriguez claims that the hypothesis of relevance and eventual axiological gaps should not be immediately identified with prescriptive (axiological) discourse, as they may be understood as conveying information about a second normative system which is actually a reconstruction, by the legal interpreter, of the so-called *mens legislatoris*. This descriptive account gives expression to a well-known argument employed in claims for axiological gaps, according to which, the legislator would have provided a different solution had he known the unpredictable circumstance. So the new solution, which is supposed to fill the gap, is provided as a description, in the name of the (rational and fair) legislator, of a qualified normative system.

It is then clear that, in such reconstructions, the interpreter, in a concealed way, *changes* the original normative system, providing new normative solutions to hold in "unforeseen" cases and, accordingly, introducing new conditions to support old normative solutions. Let us call *refinement* this dynamic process of change by qualification of norms (or beliefs). So an important step in pursue of Hart's *desideratum* to characterize reasoning about relevant normative conditions consists in investigating the rationality of refinement. In the case of an axiological gap, the interpreter should solve the conflict between the old and the proposed solution remaining as faithful as possible to the lawgiver's will. Thus, it is desirable that the resulting refined system be *consistent* and that the modification of the original system be *minimal*. How should we then define refinement operations in order to satisfy these demands?

Minimal and consistent belief change is the object of concern of Belief Revision. But standard models in this field, such as the AGM model (3), and even recent non-prioritized approaches (8), are not suited to the present purposes, since in these models conflicting information (norm), be it new or old, is *fully* rejected and not restricted by some condition as in refinement. But refinement operators can be developed out of the AGM model. In (11), an operator of belief change called *external refinement* was proposed to model processes where a condition is introduced to restrict the new (input) information, in case it conflicts with one of the original beliefs. In the present work, some new operators of refinement are introduced. In the operation called *internal refinement*, the agent, when confronted with conflicting new information, introduces a condition to one of his original beliefs. In the operation called *global refinement* both new and old beliefs are restricted by corresponding conditions. These operators are then applied to a (hard) antitrust case and it is shown that global refinement has advantages to cope with normative gaps in refined normative systems.

2 The AGM Partial Meet Contraction and Revision Operators

In the AGM model (3), beliefs of an agent are represented by a logically closed set K of formulas in propositional language $\mathcal{L}$. That is, given an inference relation $\vdash$ betweeen sets of formulas and formulas in $\mathcal{L}$, a Tarskian consequence operator on sets of formulas Cn is defined as $Cn(\Gamma) = \{\alpha \in \mathcal{L} : \Gamma \vdash \alpha\}$. Cn is assumed to satisfy self-deductibility, monotonicity and idempotence. A set $\Gamma \subseteq \mathcal{L}$ is logically closed iff $\Gamma = Cn(\Gamma)$. We also call logically closed sets theories. The expansion of a theory K by α is represented by $K + \alpha = Cn(K \cup \{\alpha\})$.

The AGM model is governed by the following postulates for theory contraction, which are suppose to capture the underlying intuitions for rationally giving up beliefs (the contraction of K by α is denoted by $K \div \alpha$):

K÷1) *ct-closure*: $K \div \alpha$ is a theory
K÷2) *ct-success*: if $\nvdash \alpha$ then $\alpha \notin K \div \alpha$
K÷3) *ct-inclusion*: $K \div \alpha \subseteq K$
K÷4) *ct-vacuity*: if $\alpha \notin K$ then $K \div \alpha = K$
K÷5) *ct-recovery*: $K \subseteq (K \div \alpha) + \alpha$
K÷6) *ct-extensionality*: if $\vdash \alpha \leftrightarrow \beta$ then $K \div \alpha = K \div \beta$

To accept information which contradicts previous beliefs demands revision (the revision of K by α is denoted by $K * \alpha$), which should satisfy the following postulates:

K∗1) *r-closure*: $K * \alpha$ is a theory
K∗2) *r-success*: $\alpha \in K * \alpha$
K∗3) *r-inclusion*: $K * \alpha \subseteq K + \alpha$
K∗4) *r-vacuity*: if $K \nvdash \alpha$ then $K + \alpha \subseteq K * \alpha$
K∗5) *r-consistency*: if $\nvdash \neg\alpha$ then $K * \alpha \neq \mathcal{L}$
K∗6) *r-extensionality*: if $\vdash \alpha \leftrightarrow \beta$ then $K * \alpha = K * \beta$

While Gärdenfors (7) suggested the above postulates for belief change, Alchourrón and Makinson (2) provided explicit definitions of contraction functions modelling such processes.

Definition 1. *Le Γ be a set of formulas and α a formula. The remainder set $\Gamma \perp \alpha$ of Γ is the set of subsets Δ of Γ such that:*
(i) $\Delta \nvdash \alpha$
(ii) there is no Δ' such that $\Delta \subset \Delta' \subseteq \Gamma$ and $\Delta' \nvdash \alpha$

As a tool for choosing elements from the remainder set, AGM introduce a selection function f.

Definition 2. *Let Δ be a set of formulas. A selection function for Δ is a function f such that for all sentences α:*
(a) If $\Delta \perp \alpha \neq \emptyset$, then $f(\Delta \perp \alpha)$ is a non-empty subset of $\Delta \perp \alpha$.
(b) If $\Delta \perp \alpha = \emptyset$, then $f(\Delta \perp \alpha) = \{\Delta\}$.

The *partial meet contraction* of a theory K by α is then given by the intersection of the elements chosen by the selection function, i.e. $K \div_f \alpha = \bigcap f(\Delta \perp \alpha)$.

A revision of a belief set K by α, is then the contraction of K by $\neg\alpha$ composed with its expansion by α: $K * \alpha = (K \div \neg\alpha) + \alpha$. This is the so-called *Levi identity*.

One of the main results of the AGM classical paper (3) was the proof that the Gärdenfors postulates are axiomatic characterizations of Alchourrón and Makinson's constructions, that is, let K be a theory:

Theorem 1. *An operator* $\div$ *on* K *is a* partial meet contraction *iff it satisfies K÷1-6.*

Theorem 2. *An operator* $*$ *on* K *is a* partial meet revision *iff it satisfies K∗1-6.*

3 The Conditionalization Function

As the main tool to the construction of external, internal and global refinement we introduce the conditionalization function c. Intuitively, the conditionalization function does the work of finding the proper condition to a considered new (original) information in the process of external (internal) refinement. As we are not interested here in the reasons by which agents choose this or that condition, any formula may be chosen.

Definition 3. *A conditionalization function is a function* c *on the set and into the set of formulas* $\mathcal{L}$, *such that* $c(\alpha) = \beta \to \alpha$.

Proposition 3. *The conditionalization function satisfies* implication*:* $\vdash \alpha \to c(\alpha)$.

The following restraints on the conditionalization function will prove to be useful for the construction of the different operators of refinement:

Definition 4. *A conditionalization function is non-tautological iff, for any formula* α, *if* $\nvdash \alpha$ *then* $\nvdash c(\alpha)$.

Definition 5. *A conditionalization function is* maximal *iff, for any* α, $\vdash c(\alpha) \leftrightarrow \alpha$.

Definition 6. *A conditionalization function is* e-maximal *iff, for any* α*: if* $K \nvdash \neg\alpha$ *then* $\vdash c(\alpha) \leftrightarrow \alpha$.

Definition 7. *A conditionalization function is* i-maximal *iff, for any* α*: if* $K \nvdash \alpha$ *then* $\vdash c(\alpha) \leftrightarrow \alpha$.

Definition 8. *A conditionalization function is* extensional *iff, for any* α*: if* $\vdash \alpha \leftrightarrow \beta$ *then* $\vdash c(\alpha) \leftrightarrow c(\beta)$.

Definition 9. *A conditionalization function is* negation invariant *iff, for any* α *and any* β, $c(\alpha) = \beta \to \alpha$ *iff* $c(\neg\alpha) = \beta \to \neg\alpha$.

4 External Refinement

External refinement is the theory change which is obtained through the acceptance, under a certain condition, of a new conflicting information. Here a condition is stipulated for the information which is coming into the belief set.

External refinement of a theory K by α, an operation which will be denoted by $K \Subset \alpha$ is simply a partial meet revision of K by a refined formula $\beta \to \alpha$. Given this picture, some basic conditions become plausible.

K⋐1) *e-closure:* $K \Subset \alpha$ is a theory
K⋐2) *e-inclusion:* $K \Subset \alpha \subseteq K + \alpha$
K⋐3) *e-success*: $\beta \to \alpha \in K \Subset \alpha$

K⋐4) *e-consistency*: if $\nvdash \neg\alpha$ then $K \Subset \alpha \neq \mathcal{L}$
K⋐5) *e-vacuity*: if $K \nvdash \neg\alpha$, then $K \Subset \alpha = K + \alpha$
K⋐6) *e-extensionality*: if $\vdash \alpha \leftrightarrow \beta$, then $K \Subset \alpha = K \Subset \beta$

In the refinement of K by α, the agent is going to accept into our belief set K a formula which is weaker than α, so it is reasonable to expect that the resulting theory will be smaller than the expansion of K by α. Success, in the AGM sense, that $\alpha \in K \Subset \alpha$, will obviously not hold. Indeed the very idea of external refinement is to avoid r-success, thus being much more cautious with the accepted information. However, the conditioned input will always be accepted, so that we obtain a kind of success where the input information is accepted if the condition also holds. For vacuity, if faced with new information which does not conflict with original beliefs, the agent may fully accept it, having no reason for modification. The operation should not be dependent on the logical form of the input, so extensionality should hold.

Using the same strategy as the one employed by Fermé and Hansson (5), the construction of external refinement is straightforward.

Definition 10. *Let K be a theory, $*$ a partial meet revision operator and c a conditionalization function. The external refinement based on c and $*$ is the operation such that, for any α, $K \Subset \alpha = K * c(\alpha)$.*

Theorem 4. *Let $\Subset$ be an operator of external refinement based on a partial meet revision operator $*$ and on a* e-maximal *and* extensional *conditionalization function c. Then $\Subset$ satisfies K⋐1-6.*

In addition to these, the following interesting property is satisfied by this construction. For a theory K and $c(\alpha) = \beta \rightarrow \alpha$:

relative vacuity: if $\neg\alpha \in K$ and $\beta \notin K$, then $K \Subset \alpha = K + (\beta \rightarrow \alpha)$.

Suppose that the new information contradicts our belief set. So we are going to refine it in order to avoid inconsistency. Suppose now that the stipulated condition under which the new information holds is not the case in our original belief state. Then, the contradiction will not arise if we only add the refined input into the belief set. That is the meaning of relative vacuity

External refinement is a generalization of partial meet revision, since partial meet revision can be defined as refining by use of a maximal conditionalization function.

Definition 11. *Let $\Subset$ be an operator of external refinement, c a maximal conditionalization function and K a theory. Then the operator $*$ of partial meet revision of K by α is the operation such that for every α, $K * \alpha =_{df} K \Subset \alpha$.*

It is easy to see that the operator $*$ thus defined satisfies the r-postulates $K*$1-6. As the reader may notice, external refinement is non-prioritized, that is, that α or $\neg\alpha$ belongs to $K \Subset \alpha$ is open and depends on the choice on the remainder set.

5 Internal Refinement

Internal refinement parallels a process of contraction where some belief will be weakened and others abandoned. The example below shows how internal refinement is intended to work, and its advantages over the AGM model:

Suppose Ciclano believes that water boils at 100^oC (α). Some day he cooks beans at his home in La Paz and notices that water boiled at a temperature below 100^oC ($\neg\alpha$). As he has noticed that pressure conditions are relevant, that is, not being on sea level ($\neg\beta$) is a *refuting condition* for α, his mistake was to believe that *whatever the case may be* water boils at 100^oC, i.e. both in $\beta \rightarrow \alpha$ and $\neg\beta \rightarrow \alpha$. Ciclano may be right about his belief that "on the sea level water boils at 100^oC" ($\beta \rightarrow \alpha$). Nothing in his water boiling experience showed the contrary, but it did show that in presence of the refuting condition water boils at a temperature below 100^oC. So the only mistake was to believe that "if one is not on the sea level then water boils at 100^oC" ($\neg\beta \rightarrow \alpha$). Hence, it would be a misinterpretation of the experiment to perform an AGM revision and to believe in $\neg\alpha$ whatever the case may be, since it would then follow that "on the sea level water boils at a temperature below 100^oC". As there are no grounds for this last statement, the most rational epistemic attitude seems to be a contraction by $\neg\beta \rightarrow \alpha$. We then expect Ciclano's absolute belief in α to be abandoned and the conditional $\beta \rightarrow \alpha$ to be preserved.

In the above example, it is suggested that employing a contraction by $\neg\beta \rightarrow \alpha$ on a theory K that contains α will preserve $\beta \rightarrow \alpha$. This suggestion is warranted by the following lemma:

Lemma 5. *Let $\div$ be an operator of partial meet contraction and K a theory. If $\alpha \in K$, then $\beta \rightarrow \alpha \in K \div (\neg\beta \rightarrow \alpha)$.*

Using the above lemma, a suitable construction for internal refinement using partial meet contraction and the conditionalization function is straightforward:

Definition 12. *Let K be a theory, $\div$ a partial meet contraction operator and c a conditionalization function. The* internal refinement *based on c and $\div$ is the operation such that, for any α, $K \Supset \alpha = K \div c(\alpha)$.*

Let us examine the properties satisfied by the proposed construction of internal refinement.

Theorem 6. *Let K be a theory, $\Supset$ an operator of internal refinement on K and c a conditionalization function. Then $\Supset$ satisfies:*

K⋑1) i-closure: *$K \Supset \alpha$ is a theory*
K⋑2) i-inclusion: $K \Supset \alpha \subseteq K$
K⋑3) i-recovery: $K \subseteq (K \Supset \alpha) + c(\alpha)$

Further plausible properties are satisfied if we introduce restraints on the conditionalization function.

Theorem 7. *If the conditionalization function c is,*

non-tautological, *then $\Supset$ satisfies K⋑4)* i-success: *if $\nvdash \alpha$ then $c(\alpha) \notin K \Supset \alpha$*
i-maximal, *then $\Supset$ satisfies K⋑5)* i-vacuity: *if $\alpha \notin K$ then $K \subseteq K \Supset \alpha$.*
extensional, *then $\Supset$ satisfies K⋑6)* i-extensionality:
if $\vdash \alpha \leftrightarrow \gamma$ then $K \Supset \alpha = K \Supset \gamma$.

From now on, we are going to refer to internal refinement as the operation based on non-tautological, i-maximal and extensional conditionalization function c. It is then a particular case of partial meet contraction.

Theorem 8. *Every internal refinement operator is an operator of partial meet contraction on theories, but the reciprocal does not hold.*

Corollary 9. *Let $\Supset$ be an internal refinement operator and c an arbitrary conditionalization function such that $c(\alpha) = \neg\beta \rightarrow \alpha$. Then $\Supset$ satisfies* i-preservation*: if $\alpha \in K$, then $\beta \rightarrow \alpha \in K \Supset \alpha$.*

The adequacy of this construction is given by its satisfaction of the Gärdenfors postulates for contraction in addition to its satisfaction of i-success and i-preservation, which captures the idea of rejecting the old belief when the refuting condition is present and accepting it when it is absent.

6 Global Refinement

Global refinement is a composition of internal and external refinement, where the agent will both refine an original belief and accept that under the refuting condition the contrary holds.

Suppose Beltrano is in a room at a hospital and believes, due to a "*do not smoke*" sign fixed at the front door, that it is forbidden to smoke inside ($\neg\alpha$). A person sitting next to an open window starts smoking and he calls the nurse, who, surprisingly, tells him that smoking there is allowed (α). Instead of believing that she is joking (rejecting α) or the sign is outdated (rejecting $\neg\alpha$), he takes both seriously and reinterprets the regulation considering the fact that the smoker is next to an open window (β) as an exceptional condition. So he comes to believe that smoking is permitted if one is next to an open window ($\beta \rightarrow \alpha$), *otherwise* smoking is forbidden ($\neg\beta \rightarrow \neg\alpha$).

Given this picture, we suggest the following rules to govern the global refinement of our beliefs with respect to a new information α, where β is the condition for acceptance of α and for refuting $\neg\alpha$.

K⊚1) *g-closure*: $K \circledcirc \alpha$ is a theory
K⊚2) *g-inclusion*: $K \circledcirc \alpha \subseteq K + \alpha$
K⊚3) *g-consistency*: if $\nvdash \neg\alpha$ then $K \circledcirc \alpha \neq \mathcal{L}$
K⊚4) *g-success*: $\beta \rightarrow \alpha \in K \circledcirc \alpha$
K⊚5) *g-vacuity*: if $K \nvdash \neg\alpha$ then $K + \alpha \subseteq K \circledcirc \alpha$
K⊚6) *g-extensionality*: if $\vdash \alpha \leftrightarrow \beta$ then $K \circledcirc \alpha = K \circledcirc \beta$
K⊚7) *g-preservation*: $\neg\alpha \in K$, then $\neg\beta \rightarrow \neg\alpha \in K \circledcirc \alpha$

Such rules capture the intuitions underlying our discussion of refinement: the result of global refinement should be a consistent theory (g-closure and g-consistency). If it is globally refined by a belief, then this belief will hold under a certain condition, while its negation will hold under the oposite condition if originally believed unconditionally (g-success and g-preservation). As for the introduction of a weakened information some beliefs must be abandoned, the refined theory is always a subset of the expansion of the original theory by the full information (g-inclusion). If the new information does not conflict with any original beliefs then there is no problem in accepting it (g-vacuity). Refining by equivalent information should yield the same globally refined theory (g-extensionality).

The construction of the global refinement operator is based on internal refinement and the conditionalization function:

Definition 13. *Let K be a theory, $\Supset$ an operator of internal refinement and c a conditionalization function. Then the operation of global refinement of K by α is such that, for any α, $K \circledcirc \alpha = (K \Supset \neg\alpha) + c(\alpha)$.*

Theorem 10. *Let $\circledcirc$ be an operator of global refinement on a theory K, α any formula, and c an arbitrary conditionalization function such that $c(\alpha) = \beta \rightarrow \alpha$. Then $\circledcirc$ satisfies K$\circledcirc$1-4. If c is extensional and e-maximal, then $\circledcirc$ satisfies K$\circledcirc$5-6. If c is also negation invariant, then $\circledcirc$ satisfies K$\circledcirc$7.*

7 A hard case

Let us examine the application of refinement operators to a hard antitrust case. Section 2 of the *Sherman Act* forbids any act which constitutes an "attempt to monopolize". A later statute, the *Clayton Act*, forbids, in its Section 7, acquisitions which may "substantially lessen competition" or "tend to create a monopoly". The purpose (rationale) of this norm is to protect competition within the market, which, by its turn, serves further goals like productive market efficiency and welfare of consumers. The table below sums up the antitrust merger regulation by Sherman and Clayton Acts:

ShermanAct(1)/ClaytonAct(7)

Relevant Cases	Normative Solutions
1. market power	Forbidden to merge
2. not market power	Permitted to merge

Suppose there is a market with only two active players which are merging and that the acquired firm is going bankrupt, thus being forced to leave the market if not acquired. May or may not such acquisition be carried out according to Section 7 of the *Clayton Act*?

In a literal interpretation of the statutes we have, closing the regulation under classical consequence, the following solutions with respect to failing firms.

Literal statutory interpretation

Relevant Cases	Normative Solution
1. failing and market power	Forbidden to merge
2. not failing and market power	Forbidden to merge
3. failing and not market power	Permitted to merge
4. not failing and not market power	Permitted to merge

The table shows that if the merger enhances market power, then it is forbidden and it does not matter whether the acquired firm is failing or not. But economic theory shows that if the firm is failing, its acquisition does not harm competition and benefits market's productive efficiency, maintaining productive assets which otherwise would be lost. Then, the interpreter faces a conflict between the action which is necessary to satisfy the statute (to omit the acquisition) and the action which seems to satisfy antitrust purposes (to acquire the failing firm).

A fresh solution intending to allow such acquisition would introduce an inconsistency in the antitrust system.

This problem, which shows a conflict between antitrust valid rules and its policy, was indeed solved by the courts. The innovative decision was enacted in *International Shoe Co. versus FTC (280 U.S. 291,302-303 (1930))*, when the Supreme Court held that acquisition of a failing company does not violate Section 7 of the *Clayton Act* (4, p.338), what means that "if the acquired firm is failing, an acquisition which tends to crate a monopoly is permitted". This interpretation motivated the *Celler-Kefauver Amendments* in 1950 making explicit the qualification in the text of the legal statute. Latter, following the Supreme Court interpretation in *Citizen Publishing Co. versus United States (394 U.S., 131, 138-139(1969))*, new relevant properties (conditions) were added by courts like "the ability of the failing firm to reorganize successfully" and "the presence of a viable alternative purchaser with less anticompetitive risk", which are now exceptions to the failing defense. These later changes were recognized by the *1992 Merger Guidelines* to the enforcement of antitrust law (4, p.338).

Antitrust jurists are supposed to interpret such authoritative decision and present theories about the proper solutions provided by the reconstructed normative system with reference to mergers in all relevant cases (including the hypothesis of failing firms). Such a comprehensive analysis will form the theoretical basis for new court decisions and amendments of the original statute. In order to model such reconstructions, we should then evaluate the systems resulting from external, internal and global refinement.

As a first approximation to the application of refinement operators to law, the standard deontic system SDL (cf.(6)) will be employed, leaving aside problems for the representation of conditionals or action in deontic logic. Let p stand for "market power", m for "merge" and f for "failing". The modal operator O represents obligation (Op means that p is obligatory, $O\neg p$ that p is forbidden and $\neg O\neg p$ that p is permitted). The capital letter S will represent the set of norms (formulas) contained in the literal interpretation of the Sherman and Clayton acts. It is assumed that theories about the statute are logically closed $S = Cn(S)$. The norm which is going to be challenged by refinement is that according to which "whenever the merger creates market power then it is forbidden", i.e. $p \rightarrow O\neg m \in S$.

If external refinement is applied, where f is the refuting condition, we obtain both that $(p \rightarrow O\neg m) \notin S \Subset \neg(p \rightarrow O\neg m)$ and $(f \rightarrow \neg(p \rightarrow O\neg m)) \in S \Subset \neg(p \rightarrow O\neg m)$. From e-closure it follows that $(f \rightarrow (p \wedge \neg O \neg m)) \in S \Subset \neg(p \rightarrow O\neg m)$ and hence $((f \wedge p) \rightarrow \neg O\neg m) \in S \Subset \neg(p \rightarrow O\neg m)$ and also $((f \wedge \neg p) \rightarrow \neg O\neg m) \in S \Subset \neg(p \rightarrow O\neg m)$. There is no indication about the normative solution if $\neg f \wedge p$ is the case. As the proposition $\neg p \rightarrow \neg O\neg m$ is not conflicting with the input and thus was not challenged by the new solution, it follows $(\neg p \rightarrow \neg O\neg m) \in S \Subset \neg(p \rightarrow O\neg m)$ [1]. Hence we have both $((f \wedge \neg p) \rightarrow \neg O\neg m) \in S \Subset \neg(p \rightarrow O\neg m)$ and $((\neg f \wedge \neg p) \rightarrow \neg O\neg m) \in S \Subset \neg(p \rightarrow O\neg m)$. The table below summarizes the reconstructed regulation.

---

[1] This follows from the upper bound property of AGM revision on which external refinement is based. According to this property, if a formula α does not by itself contradict the input (β), then there is at least one maximal subset Γ of the revised theory such that $\alpha \in \Gamma$ and $\Gamma \nvdash \beta$. So its easy to maintain α in the refined set assigning preference to those sets in the remainder which contain α.

Reconstruction A: external refinement.

Relevant Cases	Normative Solution
1. failing and market power	Permitted to merge
2. not failing and market power	(gap)
3. failing and not market power	Permitted merge
4. not failing and not market power	Permitted merge

Now, employing internal refinement, a sort of refined derogation is obtained, where instead of simply excluding the interpreted norm $p \to O\neg m$, only one of its consequences, namely the axiologically inadequate $f \to (p \to O\neg m)$ is extracted. By w-success we have $f \to (p \to O\neg m) \notin S \Supset (p \to O\neg m)$ and by w-preservation it follows $\neg f \to (p \to O\neg m) \in S \Supset (p \to O\neg m)$. The following reconstruction of the normative system would hold by application of internal refinement:

Reconstruction B: internal refinement

Relevant Cases	Normative Solution
1. failing and market power	(gap)
2. not failing and market power	Forbidden to merge
3. failing and not market power	Permitted merge
4. not failing and not market power	Permitted merge

In his later approach to deontic logic (first fully developed in (14)), von Wright argues that satisfiability (logical possibility to satisfy the norms) is the main standard of rationality to judge norm-giving-activity, what also applies to interpretive reconstruction of statutes. As the reconstructions of antitrust law by external and internal refinement provide consistent normative systems and an amendment based on either of them would create statutes free of contradictions, the resulting refined systems are rational.

However, externally or internally refined antitrust systems contain normative gaps and law professors, judges or lawyers would not hesitate to call the resulting regulation defective. For this reason it was argued in (12) that von Wright's standards of rationality should be improved by a standard of completeness, which would label irrational any law-giving act or interpretive reconstruction resulting in a system with at least one gap. According to the proposed standard, the lawgiver or the interpreter must define the deontic status of the action in all 2^n possible cases which are generated by the n conditions considered relevant. Now, using both satisfiability and completeness as rational standards, the proposed reconstructions by external and internal refinement would be irrational.

Let us then examine the application of the global refinement operator. By g-preservation and g-success we have both $\neg f \to (p \to O\neg m) \in S \circledcirc (p \to O\neg m)$ and $f \to \neg(p \to O\neg m) \in S \circledcirc \neg(p \to O\neg m)$. Hence, by g-closure, it follows $((\neg f \wedge p) \to O\neg m) \in S \circledcirc (p \to O\neg m)$ and $((f \wedge p) \to \neg O\neg m) \in S \circledcirc \neg(p \to O\neg m)$. The table below illustrates the result:

Reconstruction C: global refinement.

Relevant Cases	Normative Solution
1. failing and market power	Permitted to merge
2. not failing and market power	Forbidden to merge
3. failing and not market power	Permitted to merge
4. not failing and not market power	Permitted to merge

Thus, as global refinement preserve completeness, it has advantages over internal and external refinement as a model for the reconstruction of normative systems performed by legal dogmatic in order to justify exceptional normative solutions.

Ulrich Klug argued in (10, p.128) that it is reasonable to admit the contested validity of reasoning *a contrario sensu* when the condition for the normative solution has the strong sense of an exception. Accordingly, if an unpredicted property is to be considered relevant, then its presence should yield a different result than that in which it is absent. Note that in Reconstruction A, filling the gap in case 2 with the same normative solution as in case 1 would yield the irrelevance of the failing firm condition, and even the irrelevance of the presence or absence of market power. Mergers would be permitted whatever the circumstances might be. In Reconstruction B, by its turn, repeating the normative solution of case 2 in case 1 would amount to a redundant modification, in the sense that the resulting theory would be the same as that of literal statutory interpretation. The reconstruction provided by global refinement legitimates reasoning *a contrario*, since if the merger enhances market power, then the condition that the acquired firm is failing is both sufficient and necessary for its approval. It may be argued that such conditions are rarely adequate, since new unpredicted conditions may come along. But such a reconstruction may be acceptable as a provisory regulation, being sufficient to cope with legal cases until challenged by another refuting condition. Then the globally refined theory may be subject to further refinement of this sort.

Acknowledgements

I must thank Jorg Hansen for his criticism and suggestions on earlier versions, which motivated several modifications. I am grateful for the grant I receive from Fundação de Apoio à Pesquisa do Estado de São Paulo-FAPESP (99/02292-0).

References

[1] Alchourrón, C. and Bulygin, E. *Introducción a la metodologia de las ciencias juridicas y sociales*, Astrea, 1975. Originally published as *Normative Systems* by Springer Verlag in 1971.

[2] Alchourrón, C. and Makinson, D. Hierarchies of regulation and their logic. In Hilpinen (ed), *New Studies in Deontic Logic*, 1981, pp.125-148.

[3] Alchourrón, C., Gärdenfors, P. and Makinson, D. On the logic of theory change. *Journal of Symbolic Logic*, 50(2):510-530, 1985.

[4] American Bar Association. Section of Antitrust Law, *Antitrust Law Developments*, 4th ed., 1997.

[5] Fermé, E. and Hansson, S. O. Selective Revision. *Studia Logica*, 63, v.3, pp.331-342, 1999.

[6] Follesdal, D. and Hilpinen, R. Deontic Logic: and introduction, in Hilpinen (ed.). Deontic Logic, Introductory and Systematic Readings, Dordrecht, Reidel, 1971.

[7] Gärdenfors, P. Rules for rational change of belief. In Philosophical Essays dedicated to L.Aqvist, pp. 88-111, 1981.

[8] Hansson, S. O. (ed.). *Theoria: special issue on non-prioritized belief revision*, v.63, 1-2, 1997.
[9] Hart, H. L. The Concept of Law, 2nd ed., Clarendon Press, Oxford, 1994.
[10] Klug, Ulrich. *Juristische Logik*, Berlin, 1966.
[11] Maranhão, J. Refinement: a tool to deal with inconsistencies. *Proceedings of the Eight International Conference on Artificial Inteligence and Law - ICAIL-2001*, New York:ACM Press.
[12] Maranhão, J. Von Wright's skeptical turn on the logic of norms and the problem of gaps in normative systems. To appear in *Archiv für Rechts- und Sozialphilosophie (ARSP)*, 2002.
[13] Rodriguez, Jorge Luiz. Axiological gaps and Normative Relevance. *Archiv für Rechts- und Sozialphilosophie (ARSP)*, 2000.
[14] von Wright, Georg Henrik. Norms, Truth and Logic, in *Practical Reason*, Cornell, 1983.

Appendix with Proofs:

Lemma 5. Suppose that $\alpha \in K$. By ct-success we have $\neg\beta \rightarrow \alpha \notin K \div \neg\beta \rightarrow \alpha$. Thus, by ct-closure, $\alpha \notin K \div \neg\beta \rightarrow \alpha$. By ct-recovery, $K \div \neg\beta \rightarrow \alpha \cup \{\neg\beta \rightarrow \alpha\} \vdash \alpha$ and thus $K \div \neg\beta \rightarrow \alpha \cup \{\beta\} \vdash \alpha$, since $\beta \vdash \neg\beta \rightarrow \alpha$. By deduction, we have that $K \div \neg\beta \rightarrow \alpha \vdash \beta \rightarrow \alpha$ and hence by ct-closure, $\beta \rightarrow \alpha \in K \div \neg\beta \rightarrow \alpha$.

Theorem 6. *i-closure* and *i-inclusion* follows immediately from ct-closure and ct-inclusion; for *i-recovery*, consider that, by ct-recovery, it holds that $K \subseteq (K \div c(\alpha)) + c(\alpha)$. Thus $K \subseteq (K \Supset \alpha) + c(\alpha)$.

Theorem 7. For the proof of *i-success*, suppose that $\nvdash \alpha$. If c is non-tautological then $\nvdash c(\alpha)$. Hence by ct-success $c(\alpha) \notin K \div c(\alpha) = K \Supset \alpha$; to prove *i-vacuity*, suppose that $K \nvdash \alpha$. If c is i-maximal, then $\vdash c(\alpha) \leftrightarrow \alpha$. It follows then from ct-extensionality and ct-vacuity that $K \div \alpha = K \div c(\alpha) = K \Supset \alpha = K$; for *i-extensionality*, suppose that $\vdash \alpha \leftrightarrow \gamma$. If c is extensional, we have $\vdash c(\alpha) \leftrightarrow c(\gamma)$ and by ct-extensionality, we obtain $K \Subset \alpha = K \div c(\alpha) = K \div c(\gamma) = K \Subset \gamma$.

Theorem 8. It is obvious that $\Supset$ satisfies ct-closure, ct-inclusion, ct-vacuity and also ct-extensionality as it satisfies the corresponding i-properties. For ct-success suppose that $\nvdash \alpha$. If c is non-tautological, then $\nvdash c(\alpha)$. By *i- success* it follows that $c(\alpha) \notin K \Supset \alpha$. Since c satisfies implication and $\Supset$ satisfies *i-closure* we have $\alpha \notin K \Supset \alpha$. Now we turn to ct-recovery. From *i-recovery* it follows that $K \subseteq (K \Supset \alpha) + c(\alpha)$, and as c satisfies implication, we have $K \subseteq (K \Supset \alpha) + \alpha$. Thus every internal refinement is a partial meet contraction. To prove that the reciprocal is false, consider the following partial meet contraction and observe that i-success does not hold: $Cn\{p, \neg q \rightarrow p\} \div p$.

Theorem 9. *g-closure* and *g-success* are immediate by construction. To prove *g-inclusion* we have that by i-inclusion $K \Supset \neg\alpha \subseteq K$ and, as c satisfies implication, we obtain $K \circledcirc \alpha = (K \Supset \neg\alpha) + c(\alpha) \subseteq K + \alpha$. For *g-consistency*, suppose that $\nvdash \neg\alpha$. Then it follows from i-success that $\neg\alpha \notin K \Supset \neg\alpha$ and by i-closure that $K \Supset \neg\alpha \nvdash \neg\alpha$. Hence, by implication of c, $K \Supset \neg\alpha \nvdash \neg c(\alpha)$. By classical logic we have that $K \Supset \neg\alpha \cup \{c(\alpha)\} \nvdash \neg c(\alpha)$ and thus $K \circledcirc \alpha \nvdash \neg(\beta \rightarrow \alpha)$, which means that $K \circledcirc \alpha \neq \mathcal{L}$. To prove *g-vacuity*, suppose that $K \nvdash \neg\alpha$, then by i-vacuity $K \Supset \neg\alpha = K$. If c is e-maximal, then it holds that $\vdash c(\alpha) \leftrightarrow \alpha$ and hence $K \circledcirc \alpha = (K \Supset \neg\alpha) + c(\alpha) = K + c(\alpha) = K + \alpha$. For the proof of *g-extensionality* $\vdash \alpha \leftrightarrow \gamma$ implies $\vdash c(\neg\alpha) \leftrightarrow c(\neg\gamma)$. Thus, $K \Supset \neg\alpha = K \Supset \neg\gamma$ and hence $K \circledcirc \alpha = K \circledcirc \gamma$. For *g-preservation*, note that if c is negation invariant, then for $c(\alpha) = \beta \rightarrow \alpha$ we have $c(\neg\alpha) = \beta \rightarrow \neg\alpha$ and thus by i-preservation we have that $(\neg\beta \rightarrow \neg\alpha) \in K \Supset \neg\alpha$. Hence $(\neg\beta \rightarrow \neg\alpha) \in (K \Supset \neg\alpha + c(\alpha)) = K \circledcirc \alpha$.

eADR
A Simple Tool to Structure the Information Exchange between Parties in Online Alternative Dispute Resolution

Arno R. Lodder Paul E.M. Huygen
Computer/Law Institute
Vrije Universiteit Amsterdam
The Netherlands
{lodder, p.e.m.huygen}@rechten.vu.nl

Abstract. This paper deals with a simple tool that we have developed to support the parties in online dispute resolution (ODR). The tool helps the participants to bring forward the statements of the dispute in a structured and concise way. After each added statement the online tool shows the structured layout of the statements. As an example, the tool has been applied on a domain name dispute.

For AI & Law, the development of applications like these is important for at least two reasons. First, a large group of AI & Law people realize that practical application of theoretical AI & Law research is a necessity for our field to survive. In the described tool insights obtained from theoretical argumentation research are applied. Second, ODR is a quite successful and essential part of e-commerce. By exploring the field of ODR, which - from an AI & Law perspective - undeniably has a lot of interesting elements, AI & Law might contribute to the success of ODR.

1 Introduction

Judges and/or juries decide cases in lawsuits. An alternative to litigation is alternative dispute resolution (ADR). ADR is meant to save money and time, and to resolve conflicts without too much technical legal discussion being necessary. Normally, three types of ADR are distinguished (see, e.g. [12]): negotiation, mediation, and arbitration. In case of negotiation parties negotiate in order to resolve a conflict or to work out a compromise, without a third party being involved. In case of mediation an independent third party, the mediator, moderates the discussion between the parties. However, the mediator does not have the power to impose a solution upon the parties. The influence of the third person is most prominent in case of arbitration. Like in litigation, the arbiter decides the case. Although a decision by an arbiter can be binding, it can also be non-binding, depending on the arbitration rules agreed upon.

With the rise of e-commerce, a new phenomenon has originated: e-disputes. In order to solve these online disputes, companies started to offer online dispute resolution services,

Arno R. Lodder and Paul E.M. Huygen, 'eADR – A Simple Tool to Structure the Information Exchange between Parties in Online Alternative Dispute Resolution' in Bart Verheij, Arno R. Lodder, Ronald P. Loui and Antoinette J. Muntjewerff (eds.), *Legal Knowledge and Information Systems. Jurix 2001: The Fourteenth Annual Conference*. Amsterdam: IOS Press, 2001, pp. 117-129.

like negotiation, mediation and arbitration, commonly known under the general term Online Dispute Resolution (ODR) or *e*ADR. The number of ODR-sites grows each month, in September 2001 already 50 sites were online. Among the most popular ODR-sites at the moment are those that solve domain name disputes. Assume that we register the domain name jurix.org or jurix.net (both domain names were still free September 2001). It is well imaginable that after this registration a dispute starts between us and the Dutch/Belgian association for knowledge-based systems. These type of disputes are currently solved online in a special arbitration procedure.

In this paper a tool has been developed, that facilitates parties in online ODR, by structuring the information they put forward during the procedure. The tool does not replace ODR, but it is meant to be incorporated into existing ODR-procedures. Although the tool is generic, the focus in this paper is on domain name disputes. For reasons of clarity, we like to express that the tool is not an automated reasoning tool. Although even legal knowledge-based systems can best be used as decision support systems and not as systems executing decisions automatically, the present tool is by definition only supporting: it helps to structure the argumentation.

The remainder of the paper is structured as follows. First, section 2 provides a short introduction into the field of ODR including examples of online initiatives of all three types of ODR (negotiation, mediation, and arbitration). In section 3 the characteristics of domain name disputes are described, including a short sample case. In section 4 a simple model has been defined, that helps to structure the information that is exchanged by parties in ODR in general, and domain name disputes in particular. Section 5 describes the main features of the implementation of the model.

2 The Target Domain: Online ADR or ODR

Over the last few years, a lot of ADR-sites appeared on the Internet. Although governments can be quite slow in picking up new developments, the significance to solve e-disputes in an appropriate way is also recognized by them. For instance, in the recent Directive on Electronic Commerce (2000/31/EC, *PbEG L* 178/1) the European Union has stressed that online ADR should be stimulated [8].

At the beginning of 2000 there were only a few ODR-sites, at this moment there are over 50 of them. There is a wide variety in the services offered. Some sites are dedicated to a particular type of conflict (financial, insurance, family matters), to specific parties (businesses, consumers) or to a specific ADR-type (negotiation, mediation or arbitration). Other sites accept all disputes from no matter what party, and offer the whole range of ADR-procedures. For the three types of ADR, online initiatives are briefly discussed.[1]

First, online negotiation is prominently present on the internet. With negotiation software parties can present their interests, proposals and desired outcomes. The tools vary from very simple, blind-bidding systems[2] to more advanced support.[3] Argumentation does not always

[1] A service that is not discussed is online expert evaluation. In that case an expert tests the strength of your case (the opposing party is not involved here).

[2] <http://www.cybersettle.com/>.

[3] <http://www.onlineresolution.com/index-on.cfm>, <http://www.smartsettle.com/>.

play a role in negotiation. Parties make proposals and compare them with those of the other party. Proposals are not necessarily backed by arguments. Nevertheless, sometimes agreement may be reached sooner if supporting statements can be adduced for proposals.

Blind-bidding is a special branch of online negotiation that is also referred to as settlement. Blind-bidding sites are amongst the most successful ODR-sites. Cybersettle,[4] the first site that offered blind-bidding, claims that 475 insurance companies use their system, and that they are responsible for over $30 million of settlements. Several other sites offer this type of automated negotiation.[5] All sites have slightly different algorithms to settle the case, but the basic principle is the same. The demanding party enters the sum he wants, and the opponent indicates how much he is willing to offer. No party sees what the opponent enters. If the amounts are within a certain range, the dispute is settled. If not, the parties can start mediation, arbitration or litigation (or give negotiation another try). At most sites, the number of bidding rounds is restricted, but some sites offer an 'infinite' number of bidding rounds.

Second, a branch still in its infancy but developing fast, is online mediation. A successful mediation project was carried out in 1999 on the eBay site [4]. eBay is an online auction site, where consumers can offer products. In two weeks time 225 complaints were filed. In 108 cases mediation was actually started, 50 cases were mediated successfully. Just like in the eBay project, some online mediation consists of exchanging e-mails via a mediator.[6] Other sites use web-based environments in which parties can negotiate with the help of the mediator, sometimes called e-rooms.[7] An e-room contains various folders. Because each issue is dealt with in a different folder, it helps the parties to focus. The e-room also has a folder containing a blind-bidding tool. Several other sites offering online mediation.[8]

Third, in 1996 the Virtual Magistrate Project was one of the first online arbiters. The researchers aimed at online business-consumer (B2C) disputes. At the end of the project in 1998, only one case had been brought in.[9] One of the first commercial online ADR-initiatives started in 1999. The iCourthouse[10] is a special type of non-binding arbitration, where juries decide cases. While normally all members of the jury are present in the courtroom, in the iCourthouse a jury, that may consist of over 50 people look at a case online and give their opinion. The decision of the jury is non-binding.

The world-wide web not only makes it possible to solve disputes, but it also induces new conflicts. For instance, parties involved in e-commerce transactions may start disputes about payment, delivery, etc. Disputes that have a genuine international character benefit especially from online ADR. Since the physical location of parties does not matter online, parties might be located in different countries or even continents. An example is online arbitration on domain name disputes.

[4]Rumors says they are (almost) bankrupt.

[5]See for example <http://www.123settle.com>, <http://www.allsettle.com>, <http://www.clicknsettle.com>, <http://www.settleonline.com>, and <http://www.ussettle.com>.

[6]<http://www.consensus.uk.com/e-mediator.html>.

[7]Cf. Colin Rule's company: <http://www.onlineresolution.com/index-om.cfm>.

[8]See, <http://www.internetneutral.com/>, <http://www.mediate-net.org/>, <http://www.webassured.com/>, <http://www.webmediate.com>.

[9]<http://www.thestandard.com/article/display/0,1151,1443,00.html>. The failure to obtain cases was one of the reasons mediation was used in the eBay-project.

[10]<http://www.i-courthouse.com/>.

3 Domain Name Disputes

The Internet Corporation for Assigned Names and Numbers (ICANN)[11] coordinates the registration of top-level domain names (e.g, .com, .net, .biz, and .names). Whoever is registering a domain name has to agree that in case of complaints he submits to a mandatory administrative proceeding before one of the providers approved by the ICANN. For instance, our registration of jurix.org. and jurix.net as mentioned in the introduction is only possible if we agree that in case of complaints (e.g., by Jurix) we submit to arbitration. In November 1999 the first provider was approved: the World Intellectual Property Organization (WIPO).[12] There are three other providers: the National Arbitration Forum (NAF), eResolution and CPR.[13]

The parties in the dispute about registered domain names are referred to as the complainant and the respondent. The arbiter deciding the issue is called the panel (3 persons) or panelist (1 person). The complainant has to assert and prove three issues:

a *Identity* - the registered domain name is identical or confusingly similar to a trademark or service mark in which the complainant has rights; and
b *Illegitimacy* - the owner of the domain name has no rights or legitimate interests in respect of the domain name; and
c *Bad faith* - the domain name has been registered and is being used in bad faith.

The procedure is special, because even prior to the proceeding it is clear what the issues are. How is information during the proceedings exchanged? At the beginning of 2001 on the sites of NAF and CPR both the complainant and the respondent could download MS-Word documents that after being completed could be either e-mailed or faxed. In addition to that, WIPO and eResolution also had web-based forms for both the complainant and the respondent.

Both the parties and the panel would benefit if the information entered by the parties is structured. In the WIPO forms for example, just one single field is used for all three above issues, whereas eResolution structures the information by using one field for each issue. The approach of eResolution is preferable to that of WIPO. With the models of the next section, the information can be further structured.

As an example of a domain name case we discuss the DavidGilmour.com case of December 15, 2000. The complainant in the dispute is David Gilmour, (former) member of Pink Floyd, and the respondent is Mr. Cenicolla of Logic Minds, who owns the domain name davidgilmour.com.[14]

The complainant adduced basically the following information to support the 'Identity' issue: The name David Gilmour represents the goodwill in the musical works and other projects with which he has been involved since the 1970s. Although the name is not registered as trademark, two companies bear his name. Moreover, the registered domain name is identical to the artist's name. In support of the 'Illegitimacy' issue, it was adduced that the respondent has

[11] <http://www.icann.org/>.

[12] <http://www.arbiter.wipo.int/domains/>.

[13] See <http://www.arbforum.com/domains/>, <http://www.eresolution.ca/services/dnd/arb.htm>, and <http://www.cpradr.org/ICANN_Menu.htm>. For an overview of these and maybe additional providers, see <http://www.icann.org/udrp/approved-providers.htm>.

[14] <http://www.arbiter.wipo.int/domains/decisions/html/d2000-1459.html>.

no involvement with Gilmour or his company and that there is no evidence that respondent is known under the domain name. Finally, the 'Bad faith' issue was supported by the following: The domain name has been registered by an organization that has a number of other domain names of celebrities registered. The domain name davidgilmour.com is only used as link to the Logicminds home page, which is a site that offers domain names for sale. On this Logicminds site there is advertisement for the sale of the domain name davidgilmour.com.

The respondent, Mr. Cenicolla, claims to have registered the domain davidgilmour.com to communicate with fans of David Gilmour (but he has not used it for that purpose yet). He also claims to have the intention to obtain a license for Gilmour merchandise (but he actually has not asked one yet) and he states that including any Gilmour merchandise on davidgilmour.com would promote Gilmour's work. Finally, he asserts that the domain name davidgilmour.com was only offered for sale by mistake and has been removed from the 'for sale'-list.

Mr. Cenicolla has a weak case, if any. It probably comes as no surprise that the panelist decided in favor of David Gilmour. For the details of the case, check the URL of footnote 14. In section 5.1 it is shown how the information in this case can be structured using the model that is described next.

4 A Simple Model for Structuring the Information Exchange

One of the purposes of dialog systems is, to structure the argumentation of the players [7]. In most systems, logical concepts characterize the moves of the players. Formal notions of arguments, defeat, rules, preferences, etc., are not necessary for the tasks of information ordering and displaying the basic structure of the argumentation. Moreover, for the sake of easy usability, these concepts can better be left out. Previous models that aimed at presenting argumentation in a simple way, like DiaLaw [6], Zeno [3] and Room 5 [9], are still too complex to be really useful for online application. The purpose of the present model is to structure the information of the parties in online ADR. Although structuring the statements in an argument is a simple task, it is very helpful to provide insight into the structure of the argument. Our model is not meant to replace existing ADR procedures, but to be incorporated into them.

The dialog system can be used by a single player, to test the acceptability of his statements critically, and to adduce as many supporting statements as he believes necessary to convince an imaginary opponent. However, the idea underlying the model is, that a party hands over the result of a single player game to the opponent. In case of online arbitration, the arbiter can use the model to gather the information necessary for deciding the case. But, the model can also be used by the parties in case of online negotiation. A human mediator can use the model to structure the online mediation process. At this moment the model is not aimed at representing n-party (n>2) discussions,[15] but because most (online) disputes are between two parties the model represents mere 2 party disputes.

[15]On this topic see for example JIME's document discussion interface, which is an example of the Digital Document Discourse Environment (D^3E), at <http://d3e.open.ac.uk/>.

4.1 Defining The Model

The central elements are the parties, the statements and the games' board. They are defined as follows.

THE PARTIES

There are two parties, the Complainant and the Respondent.

STATEMENTS

A statement is an expression in natural language.
Each statement deals with only one topic.
An issue is a statement.
Supporting statements support an issue.
Attacking statements attack a statement.

THE GAMES' BOARD

The games' board is empty at the first turn. The games' board consists of all statements added by the parties according to the rules. The parties move alternately, exchanging after each turn the games' board.

The Complainant and Respondent can introduce statements according to the rules that are discussed below. Statements are not required to be cast in a prescribed format, but they can be put forward in natural language. The only requirement is that a statement addresses a single topic. There are three types of statements. Besides statements that formulate issues, there are statements that support issues and statements that attack other statements. The games' board is a metaphor, used to describe the collection of statements added by the parties.

In most existing dialog systems, parties can perform four types of moves: claim, accept, question and withdraw. However, by only allowing parties to claim statements, the information of the parties in online arbitration can be structured sufficiently with two simple rules.

RULE 1 - ISSUES AND SUPPORTING STATEMENTS

First step: Introduce an issue
Second step: Adduce one or more statements supporting the issue (supporting statements).

RULE 2 - ATTACKING STATEMENTS

In reaction to any statement of the opponent, one or more statements can be put forward (attacking statements).

The first rule is about the introduction of issues and supporting statements, the second rule about the reaction to statements. Using these rules three models have been defined, the basic model, the 2-turn-issue model, and the n-turn model. Only the n-turn model is discussed here.

THE N-TURN MODEL

First turn: Complainant executes rule 1 as often as necessary.
Consecutive turns: The parties execute rule 2, and execute rule 1 as often as necessary.

In the first turn, the Complainant executes rule 1. He starts with identifying issues (first step). Subsequently he adduces statements supporting the issues (second step). Note that a statement deals with only one topic, reason why he can enter one or more supporting statements. Finally, the Complainant applies the two steps of rule 1 again if there are more issues to be identified. If the Complainant is finished, he hands over the games' board.

In consecutive turns the parties can react to all statements they do not agree with. Note that an issue is a statement, so the parties can also react to issues. At each turn the parties can introduce new issues. It might be that providers of ODR want to restrict the introduction of issues. Therefore, and in line with civil proceedings, the not discussed 2-turn issue model restricts the introduction of issues to the first two turns.

The following picture (figure 1) shows the games' board. In the picture, IC/IR denotes *Issue of the Complainant/Respondent*, SupSC/SupSR denotes *Supporting Statements of the Complainant/Respondent*, and AtSC/AtSR denotes *Attacking Statements of the Complainant/-Respondent*. The symbols i, j, k, l, m, n, o, and p are natural numbers, where $i, j > 0$ and $k, l, m, n, o, p \geq 0$.

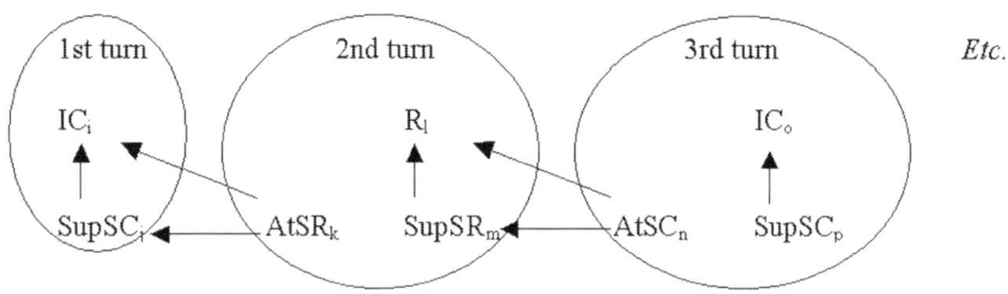

Figure 1: Games' board of the n-turn model

The Complainant has introduced at least one Issue and one Supporting Statement ($i, j > 0$) in the first turn. In the second turn, the Respondent did not react (k=0), or has entered one or more statements (k>0) attacking either the issue or the supporting statement. He can also introduce new issues (l>0), and introduce statements supporting them (m>0). The third turn and consecutive turns are the same as the second turn.

4.2 Comments and Possible Extensions

The computer does not check the content of the statements, so parties may enter irrelevant statements. This cannot be avoided in an open environment. Note, however, that it is in the best interest of the parties to at least not enter irrelevant or obstructive statements intentionally. In case of negotiation and mediation this could hinder that consensus will be reached, and in case of mediation and arbitration it could annoy the mediator or arbiter, respectively.

Since the models should become part of an existing ODR-procedure, it is not defined at what moment the dispute ends. This is to be decided by the rules of the proceedings, e.g., the domain dispute resolution rules. Possible stop criteria are time constraints or a maximum number of turns. Another stop criterion could be that the dispute ends if a party has not added any statements, so if the games' board is handed over without any additional statements.

Based on desires of ODR-sites, the model can be adapted. For instance, on request of an arbiter (or sites offering mediation or negotiation) the following rule about the status of the statements could be implemented.

> **SILENCE IMPLIES CONSENT**
> An issue is agreed upon if neither one of its supporting statements has been attacked, nor the issue itself has been attacked. A statement is agreed upon if it has not been not attacked.

Another additional rule might extend the type of moves. As already indicated, for structuring the information of the parties in online arbitration the move of type *claim* seems to suffice. In case of mediation, the mediator may want to use moves to withdraw and to accept in the following way.

> **WITHDRAW AND ACCEPT**
> A party who introduced an issue may at any time withdraw the issue.
> His opponent may at any time accept the issue.

In particular for negotiation it might be necessary to also include the move *question*.

> **QUESTION**
> A party can question a statement of his opponent, if the statement is not an issue.
> If a statement has been questioned, it becomes an issue.

These are just a few examples of additional rules. Other changes could be made of course. However, the present model already helps to structure the information of the parties in ODR.

5 Towards an Implementation

Currently the model of the previous section is being implemented with the following design considerations:

- Platform independence. The program ought to be used without the need to install special tools except a state-of-the-art Internet browser;
- Graphical user interface for easy use;
- Benefits of Internet. More specific, allow remote players (and possibly a remote arbiter) to settle their dispute over the Internet;
- Open source software, that is easy to comprehend and is not bound to a single supplier.

The Java programming language meets most of the above mentioned requirements. Java 'applets' can be downloaded and run automatically by Internet browsers, independent of the operating system of the user's computer. Apart from the browser, the user does not need to install anything on her computer to run the program. Obviously, Java has been designed to take full advantage of the facilities of Internet. For example, it enables interaction between programs that run on separate locations, all over the world. A graphical user interface can be easily developed with Java. The only drawback of using Java may be, that the standards are not defined and maintained by an independent committee, but by the company who developed Java, i.e. Sun Microsystems, Inc. However, in our view and for our purposes, Java can be considered as equivalent to open source, given the free accessibility of the Java tools, the wide acceptance of Java and the platform independent implementation via Internet browsers.

In order to facilitate comprehensibility and accessibility of the program code (by other people than the author), the program has been made using the 'Literate Programming' concept. Literate programming is a programming method, developed by Knuth [5]. The idea is, to approach computer programs from the perspective of a report or prose. The focus is on description (and documentation) of the approach in human-readable form. This is in contrast to the normal approach of focusing on the code. As a result, program code and documentation are intimately intertwined in a single document.

There exist several tools for literate programming.[16] We have chosen the tool Nuweb [1]. Nuweb has the advantages over similar packages that it is extremely simple to use. To run the program, to examine the program code (as a HTML document) or to download the code of the program (Java sources as well as Nuweb document), the reader is invited to visit the following URL: <www.rechten.vu.nl/~CLI/odr>.

The central data structure used for the implementation is a *Statement*, which is defined as the following tuple:

S = {i, p, t, o, s, c}, where

- i is the identifier,
- p is the parent, that is the identifier of the statement to which this statement (S) responds,
- t is the type of the statement (i.e. issue, support or attack),
- o is the owner of the statement (i.e. the complainant or the respondent),
- s is a short phrase of the statement,
- c is the content, the full text of the statement.

The identifiers of the statements are integer numbers for bookkeeping purposes. With the i and p identifiers, the statements can be structured as a tree or a relational database. However, in the current implementation the statement set has been structured as a linked list. The advantages of the combination of a short phrase and a full text statement are, that the short statements can be used to present the argument in a comprehensive form in the graphical user interface, whereas the user retains the ability to underpin the statement with a full text, in which she can refer to other sources of information. Because the user is forced to condense the statement text into a short phrase, she is encouraged to address only one issue per statement.

In the current application, the complainant and the respondent both run their own component (Java applet). The person whose turn it is, adds statements to the set of statements. When she is finished, the complete set of statements is sent to the component of the other party over the Internet.

[16] See the Literate programming web site: <www.literateprogramming.com>.

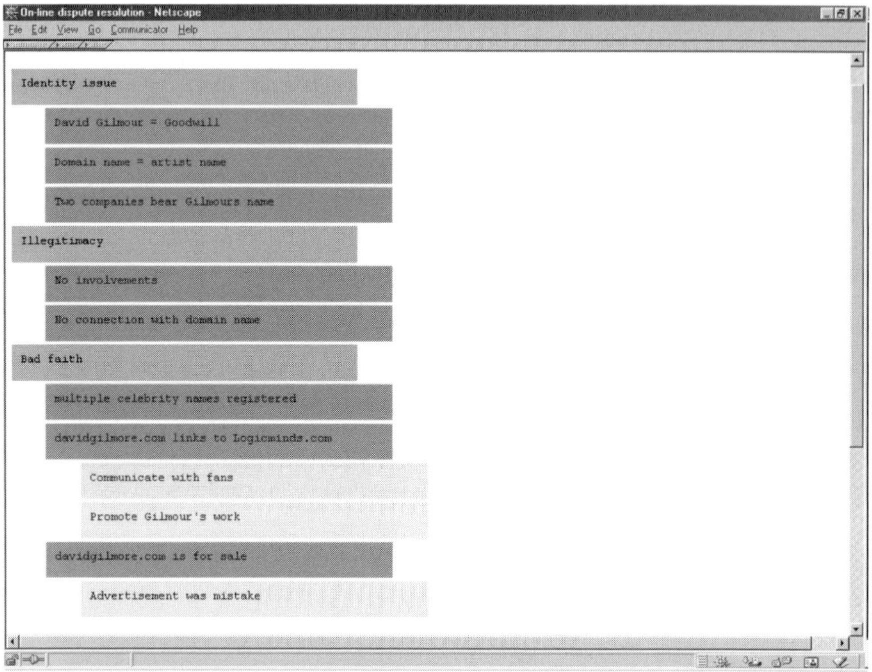

Figure 2: The ODR Applet

5.1 The User Interface

Figure 2 is a screen-shot of the *odr* applet, running in a Netscape browser. It represents the case discussed in section 3. Each statement occupies a line and the indentation indicates the structure of the statements in the argument. The color indicates whether a statement is an issue, a supporting or an attacking statement. When the user clicks on a statement with the mouse, she can read the full text of the statement, and she can attach another statement to it, if she is entitled to do so.

Note that the above screen-shot is a reconstruction to show the working of the model. Because the program has not been applied by the parties during the process, the following analysis of the Gilmour case may be inaccurate on points. The first step of David Gilmour, the complainant, is to identify an issue (rule 1). Normally, a complainant is free to assert any issue. Since in a domain case three particular issues have to be asserted (see section 3), Gilmour starts with identifying the Identity issue. Subsequently, Gilmour has to adduce one or more statements supporting the issue (second step). In this case he asserts three supporting statements, shown in the indented fields under the Identity issue. Since there are two issues left, rule 1 is executed two times more. The second time the Illegitimacy issue is identified and two supporting statements are adduced. The third and last time, the Bad faith issue is identified and three supporting statements are adduced. There are no additional issues left, so by handing over the games' board in which the information is structured as in the first

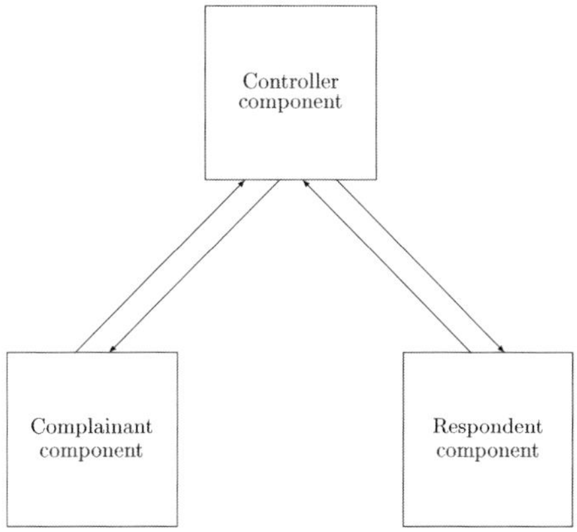

Figure 3: ODR tool modeled as a set of communicating components

column, the complainant's turn ends.

The respondent, Mr. Cenicolla, can attack all statements of his opponent he does not agree with (rule 2). However, in the current case, he does not attack the Identity and the Illegitimacy issue, nor does he attack the statements supporting these issues. The respondent only attacks the second supporting statement of the Bad faith issue with two statements, and the third supporting statement of the Bad faith issue with one statement.

In the current case, the games' board has not been handed over after the second turn, so the program stops here. Obviously, the ODR-providers can indicate how many times the games' board may be handed over and within what time constraints it must be handed over.

By structuring the Gilmour case, several things are clear at a glance. First, the respondent did not attack any of the statements with respect to the first two issues. So, for the first two issues the arbiter solely has to concentrate on the statements adduced by the complainant. Regarding the third issue the arbiter also has to take into account the statements of the respondent. Even in a relatively simple case like this one, the arbiter would benefit from the structured presentation of the arguments in the dispute, that our tool provides. In more complex cases, the structured presentation would turn out to be even more profitable.

5.2 Network-based Interactions

In order to make optimal use of the advantages that Internet can offer, the system has been set up as a set of three components (figure 3), the controlling component, running at a central site and components for the complainant and the respondent.

The latter components are in fact Java applets. The communication between the components proceeds as follows:

1 The complainant component starts up, registers with the controller and obtains a unique case number.

2 The complainant sends the case number to the respondent.

3 The complainant enters her issues and supporting statements on the graphical user interface of the complainant component.
4 When the complainant is finished, the complainant component sends the set of statements to the controller component.
5 The respondent component starts up, registers with the controller component and passes the unique case number.
6 The controller component sends the statements from the complainant to the respondent component. The respondent component displays the statement on its graphical user interface.
7 The respondent enters her attacking statements. Depending on the model used, the respondent may add issues and statements supporting her issues.
8 When the respondent is finished, the respondent component sends the set of statements to the controlling component.
9 In the simplest single-turn model, the controller component processes the statements and generates a report in PDF-format that can be downloaded by the parties. In the other models, the statements will be repeatedly sent to the parties, and the report is generated when both parties are finished.

The implementation as a set of components has the following advantages:

- Users can run the components as applet on their computers without need to download or install anything. Since Java applets are 'untrusted code', they are generally not allowed to use resources like disk space or printers on the computer on which they run. The component concept precludes the need to use such resources on the computers of the complainant or the respondent.
- Applications can be developed, in which the controller component resides on a computer owned by an organization that can play an arbiter role. In this case, the controller component stores the statements, and makes them available for the arbiter.

6 Concluding Remarks and Future Research

ODR is a new phenomenon that is likely to become a popular way to resolve disputes. From an AI & Law (in particular an argumentation) perspective, we aimed to improve the structure of the information exchanged between parties in ODR. For that purpose a model has been defined, and an implementation of the model described. To illustrate how the information is structured, we analyzed an ODR arbitration case on a domain name dispute.

The model consists of a simple set of rules, and the parties are allowed only to assert one of three types of statements: issues, supporting statements, and attacking statements. The model is not meant to replace existing ODR-procedures, but to be included in the forms used by the ODR providers. Although the model is generic, the focus in this paper was primarily on online arbitration. Suggestions have been made on how the models could become more valuable for mediation (by allowing the parties also to accept and withdraw statements) and negotiation (by adding questioning of statements).

A first and modest step has been taken towards a fully fledged ODR tool. The tool proposed should be improved and supplemented. For a proper evaluation of the present tool a comparison with other tools is indispensable. An example of a tool that helps in building so-called reasoning maps that are comparable to this paper's playing board is Reason!Able.[17] Regrettably, due to time and space limits comparison with Reason!Able and other tools is not possible, but should be left for future research.

The evaluation of the present tool should concentrate on possible extensions of the model (e.g. by adding positions), and in particular design issues. Another interesting extension of the current model, though really complicating the matter, is adapting the tool for an n-party dispute.

Clearly, a lot of really interesting research still has to be done in the field of support tools for ODR.

References

[1] Preston Briggs, *Nuweb, A simple literate programming tool*, Rice University, Houston, TX, 1993, see also <ftp://ftp.cs.rice.edu/public/preston>.

[2] T.F. Gordon (1995). *The Pleadings Game - An artificial Intelligence Model of Procedural Justice*. Kluwer, Dordrecht.

[3] T.F. Gordon & N. Karacapilidis (1997), The Zeno Argumentation Framework, *Proceedings of the sixth International Conference on Artificial Intelligence and Law*, New York: ACM, pp. 10-18.

[4] E. Katsh, J. Rifkin & A. Gaitenby (2000), E-Commerce, E-Disputes, and E-Dispute Resolution: In the Shadow of "eBay Law", *Ohio State Journal on Dispute Resolution*, Vol. 15:3, p. 705-734.

[5] Donald E. Knuth. *Literate Programming*. CSLI Lecture Notes Number 27. Stanford University Center for the Study of Language and Information, Stanford, CA, USA, 1992.

[6] A.R. Lodder & A. Herczog (1995), DiaLaw - A dialogical framework for modeling legal reasoning, *Proceedings of the fifth International Conference on Artificial Intelligence and Law*, New York: ACM, pp. 146-155.

[7] A.R. Lodder (1999), *DiaLaw – on legal justification and dialogical models of argumentation*, Dordrecht: Kluwer Academic Publishers.

[8] A.R. Lodder & H.W.K. Kaspersen (eds.), *eDirectives: Guide to European Union Law on E-commerce*, The Hage-London-Boston: Kluwer Law International, to appear.

[9] R.P. Loui, J. Norman, J. Altepeter, D. Pinkard, D. Craven, J. Lindsay & M. Foltz (1997), Progress on Room 5, A Testbed for Public Interactive Semi-Formal Legal Argumentation, *Proceedings of the sixth International Conference on Artificial Intelligence and Law*, New York: ACM, pp. 207-214.

[10] H. Prakken & G. Sartor (1997), Reasoning with precedents in a dialogue game, *Proceedings of the sixth International Conference on Artificial Intelligence and Law*, ACM, New York, pp. 1-9.

[11] B. Verheij (1999), Automated Argument Assistance for Lawyers, *Proceedings of the Seventh International Conference on Artificial Intelligence and Law*, ACM, New York, pp. 43-62.

[12] M. Wang (2000), 'Are Alternative Dispute Resolution Methods Superior to Litigation in Resolving Disputes in International Commerce', *Arbitration International*, vol. 16, no. 2, p. 189-211.

[17] See <www.goreason.com>.

Reconstructing Causal Reasoning about Evidence: a Case Study

Henry Prakken Silja Renooij*
Institute of Information and Computing Sciences
Utrecht University
The Netherlands
{henry, silja}@cs.uu.nl

Abstract. When procedural-support systems are to be useful in practice, they should provide support for causal reasoning about evidence. Such support should be both rationally well-founded and natural to the users of such systems. This article studies two possible foundations for such support, logics for defeasible argumentation and logical models of causal-abductive reasoning. A court decision about a car accident is reconstructed in the two formalisms, and the results are compared on both their rationality and their naturalness. It is concluded that more research is needed to combine the strong points of the two approaches.

1 Introduction

This article addresses the reconstruction of causal reasoning about evidence in procedural-support systems. Procedural-support systems are AI & Law programs that lack domain knowledge and thus cannot solve problems, but that instead help the participants in a dispute to structure their reasoning and discussion, thereby promoting orderly and effective disputes. For instance, they support humans in building arguments for and against their claims, such as the ArguMed system of Verheij [16]. Or they keep track of what has been claimed, conceded and disputed and which arguments for and against claims have been provided, such as the Pleadings Game [2] and ZENO [4] systems. Sometimes they also check whether the parties' input to the system respects the disputational protocol, such as the Pleadings Game and DiaLaw [7]. After a decade of theoretical research on such systems (see also e.g. Loui et al. [8], Lodder [7], Bench-Capon et al. [1], Hage [5], Prakken [11]) their practical application becomes within reach, for instance, in online dispute resolution [6] and in case management; cf. e.g. the CaseMap system (www.casesoft.com).

Although much theoretical insight has been gained, one issue has so far largely been ignored, namely, the support of reasoning about evidence, especially about causation (with the

*The second author was partly supported by the Netherlands Computer Science Research Foundation with financial support from the Netherlands Organisation for Scientific Research (NWO). The authors thank Annette ten Teije for her useful comments on an earlier version of this paper.

Henry Prakken and Silja Renooij, 'Reconstructing Causal Reasoning about Evidence: a Case Study' in Bart Verheij, Arno R. Lodder, Ronald P. Loui and Antoinette J. Muntjwerff (eds.), *Legal Knowledge and Information Systems. Jurix 2001: The Fourteenth Annual Conference*. Amsterdam: IOS Press, 2001, pp. 131-142 exception of the MarshalPlan system of Schum and Tillers [14]). Yet this kind of reasoning is an important element of many legal cases, so procedural-support systems should ideally facilitate its reconstruction. The question then arises which reasoning formalisms provide suitable foundations for such support.

In this paper we investigate the suitability of two candidates, logics for defeasible argumentation and logical models of abductive-causal reasoning (see Prakken and Vreeswijk [13] and Lucas [9] for overviews of these two areas). We do so by reconstructing the reasoning in a Dutch court decision about a car accident with the two formalisms, and comparing the results. To the best of our knowledge, this is the first time that a formal model of abductive-causal reasoning is applied to legal reasoning.

An important requirement for procedural-support systems is that they should employ concepts that are natural to the intended users; see e.g. Gordon and Karaçapilidis [3], Prakken [12]. For instance, users should not be forced to use complicated formal syntax, and the system should structure the users' reasoning in terms that are natural and familiar to them rather than with difficult mathematical or logical computations. Accordingly, the problem statement of this paper can be rephrased as follows: to which extent can the reasoning in the studied case be reconstructed in the two formalisms in a way that is both rationally acceptable and reasonably close to the actual text of the decision?

The two formalisms have been chosen since there are grounds to believe that they have the potential to support such reconstructions. Argumentation systems model reasoning in terms of intuitive concepts, such as argument, counterargument, attack, defeat and dispute; moreover, arguments need not be complex logical derivations but can also be, for instance, linked or tagged pieces of natural language. Models of abduction can be based on simple and natural causal models, which, moreover, can easily be depicted in a graphical way.

The rest of this paper is structured as follows. In Section 2 the case to be reconstructed is presented, after which in Section 3 the two formalisms will be presented. Then in Section 4 an abductive-logical reconstruction and in Section 5 an argument-based reconstruction of the case is given. The results are compared and discussed in Section 6.

2 The Case

The case to be reconstructed concerns a one-car accident which took place while the driver and a passenger were returning late at night from a birthday party. The passenger sued the driver for the damages he suffered, claiming that driver had caused the accident by losing control over the car while there was no sign of another car or obstacle. Driver argued in defence that not she but plaintiff had caused the accident, by suddenly pulling the handbrake. We reconstruct the case as it took place in the court of appeal, as reported in the Dutch Supreme-Court decision HR 23 October 1992, NJ 1992, 813. The case is a civil case, which means that the judge must decide it on the basis of the facts adduced by the parties, and that s/he must accept undisputed factual claims. If a factual claim is disputed, the judge allocates the burden of proof and, after evidence is provided, decides whether this evidence indeed proves the claim to-be-proven.

The report of the police officers who arrived at the scene just after the accident makes the following undisputed observations. The accident occured beyond an S-curve. Tire marks caused by locked tires (skidmarks) were found just beyond the curve, and tire marks caused by a sliding vehicle (yaw marks) were found 25 meters further down the road. The police officers heard the driver saying three times that passenger had pulled the handbrake, and they observed that the handbrake was in pulled position. A second, technical police report, also undisputed, adds to this that at or near the accident site there was no sign of any obstacles or other unusual circumstances. Both police reports give a detailed analysis of the tire marks. There also is an undisputed expert witness report, stating that with the type of car that accidented, pulling the handbrake while driving can cause the wheels to lock. A final undisputed fact (of which the text of the decision reveals no source) is that the passenger had drunk alcohol.

Now, following the text of the decision as closely as possible, the court's decision can be summarised as follows. The court starts with a summary of plaintiff's and defendant's main arguments (first paragraph), then assesses a secondary argument of plaintiff (second paragraph), and finally (in the remaining paragraphs) assesses plaintiff's main argument. (Our summary leaves implicit the reasoning step from 'The report says that P' to P. This simplification is warranted since the police and expert reports were undisputed.)

> Plaintiff says that driver lost control over vehicle, thereby causing the accident. Defendant says that passenger pulled the handbrake beyond the S-curve, which caused the wheels to lock, which in turn caused skidding, leading to the accident.
>
> Given the nature and location of the skidmarks (starting after the curve and straight for 12 meters) and yaw marks (located 25m beyond the curve), the evidence insufficiently supports plaintiff's suggestion that driver had been speeding in the S-curve. Rather, this evidence suggests that driver had slowed down in the S-curve.
>
> The court regards another cause for the accident not unlikely, given:
>
> - driver's testimony that "passenger pulled the handbrake".
> - the handbrake was in pulled position after the accident.
> - the expert testimony that pulling the handbrake can cause the wheels to lock.
> - the location, nature and shape of the tire marks.
>
> In addition, the court attaches some value to:
>
> - the fact that driver and passenger were returning from a birthday party late in the night;
> - the fact that passenger had drunk, so that it is not inconceivable that he interfered with the driving.
>
> In this case, the sole fact that the car crashed is insufficient to conclude that defendant is responsible for causing the accident, since alternative causes cannot be sufficiently excluded.

$$\frac{C \Rightarrow E \quad E}{C}$$

Figure 1: The basic scheme of abduction

The reader will observe that this text does not allow a straightforward logical reconstruction. For instance, in the second paragraph the court evaluates a secondary argument of plaintiff, which cannot be found in the rest of the court's decision, and which is not mentioned in the court's final conclusion. Also, the phrase "In addition, the court attaches some value to" is very vague.

3 The Formalisms

3.1 Abductive Logical Models

We now describe abductive logical models, which were mainly developed for doing diagnosis. Abduction is often described as reasoning from effects to causes, as in 'if fire then smoke; smoke, so fire' (see Figure 1). Taken by itself this scheme is, of course, nothing but the well-known fallacy of affirming the consequent. However, in a setting where alternative abductive explanations are generated and compared, it can still be rational to accept an abductive conclusion, namely, if no better explanation is available. Clearly, such reasoning is defeasible, since additional facts might give rise to new explanations.

Abductive-logical models simulate the abductive inference scheme of Figure 1 with a particular use of classical-logical inference. Basically, given a set T of causal rules and a set F of observed facts, they produce one or more *explanations* H of sets of possible causes ("hypotheses") for these observations in terms of the causal rules. More precisely, an explanation is a set H such that

- $H \cup T \vdash f$ for every $f \in F$; and
- $H \cup T$ is consistent.

The causal rules in T are often assumed to be of the following form:

$$c_1 \wedge \ldots \wedge c_n \rightarrow e$$

were $c_1, \ldots, c_n$ are literals, standing for causes that in conjunction produce the effect e, which also is a literal. Causal rules can be chained, since effects can in turn be causes of other effects.

In legal cases the task typically is to find the most likely cause of one or more particular observations (the 'explanandum'). For instance, in our case the task is to find the most likely cause of the car crash, since the one who caused the accident is responsible for the resulting damages. However, usually there will also be additional observations, viz. the evidence; for instance, in our case we have evidence of tire marks, of the position of the handbrake after the accident, etcetera. Alternative explanations should be compared on the extent to which they explain or contradict these additional observations. Accordingly, we define an *abductive causal problem* for present purposes as a tuple $\langle T, C, O, F, A \rangle$ where

- T is a causal theory;
- C is a set of possible causes;
- O is a set of possible observations;
- $F \subseteq O$ is a set of facts to be explained (the explanandum);
- $A \subseteq O$ is a set of additional evidence, disjoint from F.

A *solution* to such a problem is a set $H \subseteq C$ such that H explains F.

Abductive-logical models have been augmented with several other features, but for present purposes this is all we need.

Many metrics have been proposed for comparing alternative solutions. Here are some obvious criteria (which all three order sets in terms of set inclusion):

- the smaller H, the better;
- the larger the set of explained additional evidence, the better;
- the smaller the set of contradicted additional evidence, the better.

It should be noted that we have deviated from most logical models of abduction in that they usually require solutions to explain all additional evidence A as well as the explanandum F, and that they do not allow explanations to contradict the additional evidence. We think that such a definition for solutions is too strong for legal practice and that the additional evidence A should only be used to assess the quality of solutions.

3.2 Logics for Defeasible Argumentation

Argument-based logics formalise nonmonotonic reasoning as the construction and comparison of arguments for and against certain conclusions. The input of an argumentation system is a set of arguments and a relation of strength between arguments, and the output is an assignment of a status to arguments. Typically this status is defined in terms of three classes: the 'winning' or *justified* arguments, the 'losing' or *overruled* arguments, and the 'ties', i.e., the *defensible* arguments, which are involved in an irresolvable conflict. In some systems, the strength relations between arguments are themselves derived within the system.

As for attacks on arguments, a common distinction in the literature is that between *rebutting* and *undercutting* attacks. Rebuttals are arguments with opposing conclusions, while undercutters deny that an argument's premises support its conclusion. A third kind of attack has also been distinguished (but is often reduced to one of the other kinds), *assumption* attacks, which deny an explicit assumption made in an argument.

Most argument-based systems have so far been applied to 'rule-' or 'logic-based' reasoning, but their general setup leaves room for defining any notion of an argument, including inductive, abductive and analogical arguments. In reasoning about evidence especially inductive and abductive reasoning is important. In this paper we concentrate on abductive reasoning.

4 Abductive-Logical Reconstruction

We now turn to an abductive-logical reconstruction of the case. We first give its causal structure, obtained from the information provided by all available sources, in Figure 2. The signs associated with the arcs in the figure indicate whether the proposition at the head of an arc supports (+) or contradicts (−) the proposition stated at the tail of the arc. The darkly shaded nodes represent the evidence that was observed to be true, while the only lightly shaded node represents a piece of evidence that was observed to be false. Note that although the figure resembles a Qualitative Probabilistic Network [17] it has no relation to the QPN formalism whatsoever.

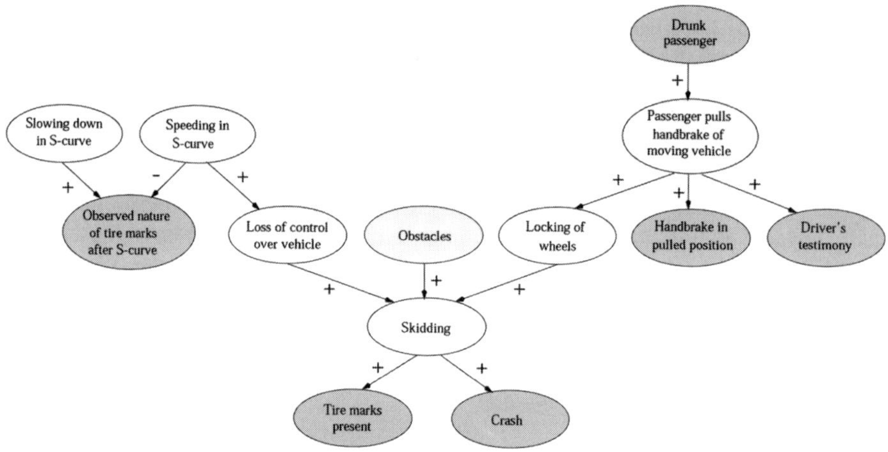

Figure 2: Causal structure for the case.

We now list the causal theory and observations. Since the outcome of the case depends on who caused the accident, the task is to find the best explanation for the observation *accident*. So, our 'explanandum' F contains just *accident*, and the evidence A contains the following facts:

(1) $\neg$ *obstacles*
(2) *tire marks present*
(3) *observed nature of tire marks*
(4) *handbrake in pulled position after accident*
(5) *driver said "passenger pulled handbrake"*
(6) *passenger was drunk*

For simplicity we have not distinguished between the skidmarks and yaw marks. Note also that the content of the expert witness report is not part of the evidence, since in fact this report states a causal rule, namely, rule r_5 below.

The causal theory T is directly derived from the links in Figure 2.

r_1: *skidding* $\Rightarrow$ *accident*
r_2: *skidding* $\Rightarrow$ *tire marks present*
r_3: *obstacles* $\Rightarrow$ *skidding*
r_4: *loss of control* $\Rightarrow$ *skidding*
r_5: *wheels locked* $\Rightarrow$ *skidding*
r_6: *speeding in curve* $\Rightarrow$ *loss of control*
r_7: *speeding in curve* $\Rightarrow \neg$ *observed nature of tire marks*
r_8: *slowing down in curve* $\Rightarrow$ *observed nature of tire marks*
r_9: *passenger drunk* $\Rightarrow$ *passenger pulls handbrake*
r_{10}: *passenger pulls handbrake* $\Rightarrow$ *wheels locked*
r_{11}: *passenger pulls handbrake* $\Rightarrow$ *handbrake in pulled position after accident*
r_{12}: *passenger pulls handbrake* $\Rightarrow$ *driver said "passenger pulled handbrake"*

Now C, the possible causes, consists of all antecedents of any of these causal rules, while O, the possible observations, includes all consequents of any such rule plus (1) and (6).

Next we list the formal counterparts of the solutions offered by plaintiff (π) and defendant (δ). For plaintiff we choose to combine his main and secondary argument as summarised by the judge.

$H_\pi = \{(7)$ *speeding in curve*, (8) *loss of control*$\}$
H_π additionally explains (2)
H_π contradicts (3)

$H_\delta = \{(9)$ *passenger pulled handbrake*$\}$
H_δ additionally explains (2,4,5)
H_δ contradicts nothing

Using any of the three criteria mentioned at the end of Section 3.1, we see that defendant's solution is clearly better: we have that $H_\pi \not\subset H_\delta$, while H_δ explains more and contradicts less evidence. So along these criteria the court's relative assessment of the two solutions is more than warranted (since plaintiff had the burden of proving that defendant caused the accident, it sufficed for the court to say that plaintiff's solution is not more likely).

This abductive reconstruction of the court's decision seems reasonably close to the actual wording of the decision (subject to the caveats made in Section 2). However, an aspect of the decision that is not captured is the court's use of passenger's observed drunkenness as an extra factor favouring defendant: although (6) could be added to H_δ, this would not improve its quality according to the metrics proposed above.

5 Argument-Based Reconstruction

We next give an argument-based reconstruction of the case. It will be presented semiformally, since for present purposes the style of formalisation is more important than the precise details. The reconstruction follows a 'modus-ponens' approach (very usual in nonmonotonic logic), in which, roughly, arguments are constructed with standard-logical reasoning and 'modus-ponens-like' reasoning with default conditionals. In particular, we exclude the construction of abductive arguments, i.e., arguments based on the scheme of Figure 1 above. This is for the simple reason that the notion of an abductive argument has not yet been defined for argument-based systems. For the rest, we will display arguments as trees of inference steps. The causal and evidential rules 'warranting' the various inference steps will be left implicit.

Given the choice for a modus-ponens approach, one question immediately arises: must causal knowledge be represented as $cause \Rightarrow effect$ rules or as $effect \Rightarrow cause$ rules? In terms of Pearl [10], do we want to represent causal knowledge as *causal rules* or as *evidential rules?*

The causal model of Figure 2 suggests that we need both kinds of rules, since we both need to do *explanation*, i.e., derive causes from effects, and *prediction*, i.e. derive effects from causes. For instance, we must be able to explain the evidence *driver's testimony* and *handbrake in pulled position* with the hypothesis *passenger pulled handbrake*, but then we must be able to predict *wheels locked* from this hypothesis. In our modus-ponens approach this requires the two rules

r: *driver said "passenger pulled handbrake" & handbrake in pulled position* $\Rightarrow_E$ *passenger pulled handbrake*
r': *passenger pulled handbrake* $\Rightarrow_C$ *wheels locked*

The first is an evidential rule and the second a causal rule.

More generally, in a modus-ponens approach causal knowledge should be represented as follows: each time we want to do a prediction, we must write a causal rule, while each time we want to do an explanation, we must write an evidential rule.

However, caution is required here: Pearl [10] shows that if the modus-ponens approach is applied to a mixture of causal and evidential rules, not all modus ponens inference steps may be made. Consider the following case

$$\frac{P_C \quad P \Rightarrow_E Q}{Q}$$

where $P \Rightarrow_E Q$ is an evidential rule and the subscript in P_C indicates that P has been derived from a causal rule. In this case modus ponens (which here is an abduction in disguise!) is invalid, since we have already concluded that P was caused by something else. Add, for instance, to the above two rules r and r' the following evidential rule

r'': *wheels locked* $\Rightarrow_E$ *excessive braking*

If we chain r and r' resulting in a causal prediction of *wheels locked*, then we should not subsequently use *wheels locked* to derive its alternative cause *excessive braking* with r'', since we already know its cause.

Our formalisation (Figures 3 – 7) respects this requirement. For instance, plaintiff's argument chains the evidential rule $0 \wedge 1 \Rightarrow 7$ with the causal rule $7 \Rightarrow 8$ and the 'responsibility' rule $8 \wedge 7 \Rightarrow 14$. Further, defendant's argument chains the evidential rule $4 \wedge 5 \Rightarrow 9$ with the causal rules $9 \Rightarrow 10$, $10 \Rightarrow 11$ (which actually is the content of the expert report), $11 \Rightarrow 0$ and with the responsibility rule $0 \wedge 9 \Rightarrow 15$. So, none of the arguments chains a causal with an evidential rule.

As for the attack relations, note that plaintiff's and defendant's arguments rebut each other, while the court's two counterarguments J_1 and J_2 undercut and rebut, respectively,

$$\frac{\dfrac{\dfrac{(0)\ accident \qquad (1)\ \neg obstacles}{(7)\ speeding\ in\ curve}}{(8)\ loss\ of\ control} \qquad (7)\ speeding\ in\ curve}{(14)\ driver\ caused\ accident}$$

Figure 3: Plaintiff's (= passenger's) argument P (including P^{sub})

$$\frac{\dfrac{\dfrac{\dfrac{\dfrac{(4)\ handb\ in\ pulled\ pos \qquad (5)\ driver\ said\ \text{“}pass\ pulled''}{(9)\ pass\ pulled\ handbrake}}{(10)\ wheels\ locked}}{(11)\ skidding}}{(0)\ accident} \qquad (9)\ pass\ pulled\ handb}{(15)\ passenger\ caused\ accident}$$

Figure 4: Defendant's (= is driver's) counterargument D

$$\frac{(3)\ observed\ nature\ of\ tire\ marks}{\{0,1\}\ don't\ support\ 7} \qquad \frac{(3)\ observed\ nature\ of\ tire\ marks}{(12)\ slowing\ down\ in\ curve}$$

Figure 5: Judge's counterarguments J_1 and J_2

$$\frac{(3)\ observed\ nature\ of\ tire\ marks}{J_2\ not\ weaker\ than\ P^{sub}}$$

Figure 6: Judge's first priority argument J_{p_1}

$$\frac{(5) \quad (4) \quad (13)\ expert\ report \quad (2) \quad (3) \quad (6)\ passenger\ was\ drunk}{D\ not\ weaker\ than\ P}$$

Figure 7: Judge's second priority argument J_{p_2}

plaintiff's subargument P^{sub}, which concludes (7) from (0) and (1). As for argument assessment, the court's first priority argument prefers J_2 over P^{sub} while its second priority argument says that plaintiff's argument P is not stronger than defendant's counterargument D. It should be obvious that, given these priority arguments, no reasonable argument-based system will regard plaintiff's argument as justified.

This argument-based reconstruction also seems reasonably close to the actual text of the decision. Strong points are that the court's assessment of the evidence can be formally expressed as arguments, and that the contributions of the three parties to the dispute are distinguished as separate arguments, rather than being mixed in one global analysis. On the other hand, the argument-based reconstruction seems rather ad hoc in its treatment of causation. For instance, whether a cause-effect relationship is stated as a causal or an evidential rule depends on how the rule is used in the reasoning process rather than on an analysis of the concepts underlying causal reasoning. Also, the court's assessment of the conflicting arguments can merely be expressed, not be justified, as done by the abductive-logical reconstruction.

6 Discussion

Of course, from a single example no definite conclusions can be drawn. The present results can be no more than clues for further research. With this in mind, the following can be said. Recall that the aim was to compare the two formalisms on their rational well-foundedness and on their naturalness for users of procedural-support systems.

As for rational well-foundedness, we think that the abductive-logical analysis of our case does better than the argument-based formalisation. The former is based on clear and intuitive concepts of causal reasoning. Furthermore, it not only *expresses* the court's decision, but also provides criteria for assessing its rational quality (although the question as to the proper criteria is still far from solved; see e.g. Thagard and Shelley [15]). Finally, the abductive reconstruction is reasonably close to the actual wording of the decision, which compares alternative explanations of the accident.

On the other hand, as for naturalness, the 'deep' causal analysis forced by the abductive-logical model cannot really be found in the court's decision, so that the 'shallow' argument-based reconstruction seems closer to the text of the decision and therefore more natural. (Here, of course, the issue arises whether a procedural-support system should merely offer support for *structuring* the user's reasoning or also for *improving* it.) In sum, both approaches have their strong and weak points, and there is no clear 'winner'.

However, it is easy to imagine hypothetical variants of our case where limitations of the abductive-logical approach become apparent. While in this approach the causal theory and the observations are beyond debate, in legal cases anything can be disputed. Consider a hypothetical variant of the case in which the adversaries disagree about whether pulling the hand brake while driving can cause skidding. In fact, this is a dispute about the 'backing' or justification of a causal rule, where the expert witness testimony can be used to argue for its backing, but where counterarguments (such as questioning the witness' expertise) are allowed. With abductive-logical models, a choice between conflicting views on causation has to be made when designing the causal theory. An argument-based system, by contrast, can easily deal with conflicting arguments on causation. On the other hand, as yet no argument-based account of abductive reasoning and its relation with other kinds of reasoning is available.

Concluding, this article has provided some preliminary evidence that abductive-logical models have the potential to be useful in legal procedural-support systems. However, to realise this potential, more theoretical research is needed on embedding abductive-logical models in dialectical models of argumentation and dispute. Also, empirical research is needed on whether the various formalisms and concepts are indeed close to the thinking of the potential users of procedural-support systems. For instance, do lawyers really think in terms of causal structures? Are they familiar with the distinctions causal vs. evidential rules and prediction vs. explanation? And do lawyers naturally think in terms of argument, attack and defeat, or perhaps in terms of other concepts? Finally, the criteria on which the two formalisms where compared in this paper, rational well-foundedness and naturalness, only provide necessary but not sufficient conditions for usefulness in procedural-support systems. Such usefulness must still be investigated in future research.

References

[1] Bench-Capon, T., Geldard, T. and Leng, P. [2000]. A method for the computational modelling of dialectical argument with dialogue games, *Artificial Intelligence and Law* **8**: 233–254.

[2] Gordon, T. [1994]. The Pleadings Game: an exercise in computational dialectics, *Artificial Intelligence and Law* **2**: 239–292.

[3] Gordon, T. and Karaçapilidis, N. [1997]. The Zeno argumentation framework, *Proceedings of the Sixth International Conference on Artificial Intelligence and Law*, ACM Press, New York, pp. 10–18.

[4] Gordon, T., Karaçapilidis, N., Voss, H. and Zauke, A. [1997]. Computer-mediated cooperative spatial planning, *in* H. Timmermans (ed.), *Decision Support Systems in Urban Planning*, E & FN SPON Publishers, London, pp. 299–309.

[5] Hage, J. [2000]. Dialectical models in artificial intelligence and law, *Artificial Intelligence and Law* **8**: 137–172.

[6] Katsh, E. and Rifkin, J. [2001]. *Online Dispute Resolution: Resolving Conflicts in Cyberspace*, Jossey-Bass.

[7] Lodder, A. [1999]. *DiaLaw. On Legal Justification and Dialogical Models of Argumentation*, Law and Philosophy Library, Kluwer Academic Publishers, Dordrecht/Boston/London.

[8] Loui, R., Norman, J., Alpeter, J., Pinkard, D., Craven, D., Linsday, J. and Foltz, M. [1997]. Progress on Room 5: A testbed for public interactive semi-formal legal argumentation, *Proceedings of the Sixth International Conference on Artificial Intelligence and Law*, ACM Press, New York, pp. 207–214.

[9] Lucas, P. [1997]. Symbolic diagnosis and its formalisation, *The Knowledge Engineering Review* **12**: 109–146.

[10] Pearl, J. [1988]. Embracing causality in default reasoning, *Artificial Intelligence* **35**: 259–271.

[11] Prakken, H. [2001a]. Modelling reasoning about evidence in legal procedure, *Proceedings of the Eighth International Conference on Artificial Intelligence and Law*, ACM Press, New York, pp. 119–128.

[12] Prakken, H. [2001b]. Relating protocols for dynamic dispute with logics for defeasible argumentation, *Synthese* **127**: 187–219.

[13] Prakken, H. and Vreeswijk, G. [2001]. Logics for defeasible argumentation, *in* D. Gabbay and F. Günthner (eds), *Handbook of Philosophical Logic*, Vol. 4, Kluwer Academic Publishers, Dordrecht/Boston/London. Second edition, to appear.

[14] Schum, D. and Tillers, P. [1991]. Marshaling evidence for adversary litigation, *Cardozo Law Review* **13**: 657–704.

[15] Thagard, P. and Shelley, C. [1996]. Abductive reasoning: Logic, visual thinking, and coherence, *in* M. D. Chiara, K. Doets, D. Mundici and J. van Benthem (eds), *Logic and Scientific Methods. Volume One of the Tenth International Congress of Logic, Methodology and Philosophy of Science, Florence, August 1995*, Kluwer Academic Publishers, Dordrecht/Boston/London, pp. 413–427.

[16] Verheij, B. [1999]. Automated argument assistance for lawyers, *Proceedings of the Seventh International Conference on Artificial Intelligence and Law*, ACM Press, New York, pp. 43–52.
[17] Wellman, M. [1990]. Fundamental concepts of qualitative probabilistic networks, *Artificial Intelligence* **44**: 257–303.

Previous Publications by JURIX

Conference Proceedings

- *Legal knowledge and information systems: The Thirteenth Annual Conference*
  JURIX 2000 (Twente)
  Breuker, J.A., Leenes, R., Winkels, R. (eds.)
  ISBN 1 58603 144 9 (IOS Press)
  ISBN 4 274 90416 4 C3000 (Ohmsha)
- *Legal knowledge based systems: The Twelfth Conference*
  JURIX 1999 (Leuven)
  Herik, H. Jaap van den, Marie-Francine Moens, Jon Bing, Bea van Buggenhout, John Zeleznikow, Carolus Grütters (eds.)
  ISBN 90 71478 64 5
- *Legal knowledge based systems: The Eleventh Conference*
  JURIX 1998 (Groningen)
  Hage, J.C., T.J.M. Bench-Capon, A.W. Koers, C.N.J. de Vey Mestdagh, C.A.F.M. Grütters (eds.)
  ISBN 90 71478 58 0
- *Legal knowledge based systems: The Tenth Conference*
  JURIX 1997 (Amsterdam)
  Oskamp A., R.V. De Mulder, C. van Noortwijk, C.A.F.M. Grütters, K. Ashley, T. Gordon (eds.)
  ISBN 90 71478 54 8
- *Legal knowledge based systems: Foundations of Legal Knowledge Systems*
  JURIX 1996 (9th conference Tilburg)
  Kralingen R.W., H.J. van den Herik, J.E.J. Prins, M. Sergot, J. Zeleznikow (eds.)
  ISBN 90 361 9657 4
- *Legal knowledge based systems: Telecommunications and AI & and Law*
  JURIX 1995 (8th conference Maastricht)
  Hage J.C., T.J.M. Bench-Capon, M.J. Cohen, H.J. van den Herik (eds.)
  ISBN 90 5458 252 9
- *Legal knowledge based systems: The relation with Legal Theory*
  JURIX 1994 (7th conference Amsterdam)
  Prakken H., A.J. Muntjewerff, A. Soeteman (eds.)
  ISBN 90 5458 190 5

- *Legal knowledge based systems: Intelligent Tools for Drafting Legislation, Computer-Supported Comparison of Law*
  JURIX 1993 (6th conference Enschede)
  Svensson J.S., J.G.J. Wassink, B. van Buggenhout (eds.)
  ISBN 90 5458 089 5
- *Legal knowledge based systems: Information Technology and Law*
  JURIX 1992 (5th conference The Hague)
  Grütters C.A.F.M., J.A. Breuker, H.J. van den Herik, A.H.J. Schmidt, C.N.J de Vey Mestdagh (eds.)
  ISBN 90 5458 0341 3
- *Legal knowledge based systems: Model-based legal reasoning*
  JURIX 1991 (4th conference Rotterdam)
  Breuker J.A., R.V. de Mulder, J.C. Hage (eds.)
  ISBN 90 6040 989 2
- *Legal knowledge based systems: Aims for research and development*
  JURIX 1990 (3rd conference Leiden)
  Noortwijk C. van, A.H.J. Schmidt, R.G.F. Winkels (eds.)
  ISBN 90 6040 948 5
- *Legal knowledge based systems: An overview of criteria for validation and practical use (Exploring the quality of applications resulting from research programs in the Netherlands)*
  JURIX 1989 (2nd conference Utrecht)
  Kracht D., C.N.J. de Vey Mestdagh, J.S. Svensson (eds.)
  ISBN 90 6040 917 5
- *RI-paradigmata: Toekomst van Nederlands onderzoek in de rechtsinformatica (Paradigms in legal informatics: Exploring the future of Dutch research programmes in legal informatics)*
  JURIX 1988 (1st conference Amsterdam)
  (In Dutch with summaries in English)
  Berg P. van den, C.A.F.M. Grütters, O.W.M. Kamstra, T. van Willigenburg (eds.)
  ISBN 90 6040 886 1

Reports

- *Informatietechnologie en Recht*
  (Rapport van de tijdelijke adviescommissie Informatietechnologie en Recht met betrekking tot de opzet van onderzoek op het gebied van informatietechnologie en recht)
  1991 (In Dutch)
  Franken H., J.C. Arnbak, J.M.A. Berkvens, B.K. Brussaard, A.W. Koers,
  I.Th.M. Snellen, A.H.J. Schmidt (red.)
  ISBN 90 6040 966 3
- *Information Technology and the Law*
  1991 (English version)
  Franken H., J.C. Arnbak, J.M.A. Berkvens, B.K. Brussaard, A.W. Koers,
  I.Th.M. Snellen, A.H.J. Schmidt (eds.)
  ISBN 90 6040 987 6

Contact Information on JURIX

Those who are interested in the activities of JURIX may contact

Ronald Leenes	Vice-President and Secretary of JURIX
Address:	University of Twente Faculty of Public Administration and Public Policy P.O. Box 217 NL-7500 AE Enschede The Netherlands
Phone:	+31 53 489 4231 +31 53 489 3270 (Secretariat)
Fax:	+31 53 489 4734
E-mail:	r.e.leenes@bsk.utwente.nl
Jurix Website:	http://www.jurix.nl

Author Index